The Curriculum Compendium

Other Titles from Bloomsbury Education

The Headteacher's Handbook: The essential guide to leading a primary school
    by Rae Snape
Education: A Manifesto for Change by Richard Gerver
Time to Shake Up the Primary Curriculum: A step-by-step guide to creating a global, diverse and inclusive school by Sarah Wordlaw
The Wellbeing Curriculum: Embedding children's wellbeing in primary schools
    by Andrew Cowley

The Curriculum Compendium

Inspirational case studies to transform your school curriculum

edited by
Rae Snape

BLOOMSBURY EDUCATION
LONDON OXFORD NEW YORK NEW DELHI SYDNEY

BLOOMSBURY EDUCATION
Bloomsbury Publishing Plc
50 Bedford Square, London, WC1B 3DP, UK
29 Earlsfort Terrace, Dublin 2, Ireland

BLOOMSBURY, BLOOMSBURY EDUCATION and the Diana logo are trademarks of
Bloomsbury Publishing Plc

First published in Great Britain, 2024 by Bloomsbury Publishing Plc

Text copyright © Rae Snape, 2024

All contributions and their illustrations are copyright of the contributor named

Material from Department for Education documents used in this publication
are approved under an Open Government Licence:
www.nationalarchives.gov.uk/doc/open-government-licence/version/3

Rae Snape has asserted her right under the Copyright, Designs and Patents Act,
1988, to be identified as Author of this work

Bloomsbury Publishing Plc does not have any control over, or responsibility for, any
third-party websites referred to or in this book. All internet addresses given in this
book were correct at the time of going to press. The author and publisher regret any
inconvenience caused if addresses have changed or sites have ceased to exist,
but can accept no responsibility for any such changes

All rights reserved. No part of this publication may be reproduced or transmitted
in any form or by any means, electronic or mechanical, including photocopying,
recording, or any information storage or retrieval system, without prior
permission in writing from the publishers

A catalogue record for this book is available from the British Library

ISBN: PB: 978-1-8019-9090-5; ePDF: 978-1-8019-9093-6; ePub: 978-1-8019-9092-9

2 4 6 8 10 9 7 5 3 1 (paperback)

Typeset by Newgen KnowledgeWorks Pvt. Ltd., Chennai, India
Printed and bound in the UK by CPI Group (UK) Ltd., Croydon, CR0 4YY

To find out more about our authors and books visit www.bloomsbury.com
and sign up for our newsletters

This book is dedicated to all the wonderful people in my family who have been, currently are, or may be, teachers in the future: Deirdre, Derek, Sarah, Naomi, Barbara, John, Guy, Charlie and Jupiter. Much love to you all.

This book is also dedicated to the thousands of teachers, assistant teachers, essential support staff, site managers, headteachers, teacher educators and volunteers who help to make our schools such caring, vibrant and inspiring places to be. Your work changes lives! Especial thanks to all my fabulous colleagues, children and community at Milton Road Primary School. You make the days joyful, magical and memorable!

Many thanks to wonderful Mary Myatt for encouraging me to put this book together and to my incredibly patient and brilliant editor, Emily Evans!

Enormous thanks to each of the wonderful contributors who so kindly and generously shared their amazing knowledge and wisdom with me. You each bring so much thought, passion, creativity and innovation to the education system. Your work is inspiring and fills me with hope and optimism for the future! Thank you.

Contents

Foreword by Emma Turner xi
Introduction xiii
How to use this book xix

A unique compelling narrative 1
  By Rae Snape

Part 1 Leadership and management – vision and ethos

Introduction 7

1. **The world beneath our feet** 12
   By David Aston, Dr Jen McGaley, Sally Todd, Caroline Wendling and Lucy Wheeler

2. **Making learning memorable** 20
   By Ben Erskine

3. **Releasing the imagination and celebrating the art of the possible** 30
   By Dr James Biddulph

4. **A curriculum matched to context** 37
   By Kyrstie Stubbs

5. **Da Vinci life-skills curriculum and assessment** 44
   By Rosina Dorelli and Zachary Reznichek

Editor's reflection on Part 1 52

Part 2 Leadership and management – operational excellence

Introduction 53

    6. A curriculum of PRIDE 59
    By Christopher Harrison

    7. A curriculum that sparkles 71
    By Craig Chaplin and Philippa Rollins

    8. Intentional inclusion = conscious curricula 78
    By Nicole Ponsford

    9. Shaking up the curriculum 84
    By Sarah Wordlaw

    10. Change at pace 91
    By Tom Turnham

Editor's reflection on Part 2 95

Part 3 Quality of education

Introduction 97

    11. Curriculum continuity from KS1–5 – history as a case study 101
    By Alex Fairlamb

    12. From digital consumers to content creators 109
    By Allen Tsui

    13. Opening doors to ambitious English 116
    By Bob Cox

    14. Curriculum planning in PE – what children need vs what teachers want 122
    By Ian Roberts and Heather MacNeil

15. Arts-rich ambition 130
   By Nancy Wayman

Editor's reflection on Part 3 136

Part 4 Behaviour and attitudes to learning

Introduction 139

16. Outdoor learning 144
   By Christian Kitley

17. Going beyond the National Curriculum with an explorer curriculum 150
   By Joe Hallgarten and Jo Franklin

18. Learning adventure curriculum 160
   By Jonathan Le Fevre

19. Battling the powers that be to champion Ed Tech 167
   By Matt Jessop

20. Finding natural wonder 172
   By Ruthie Collins

Editor's reflection on Part 4 179

Part 5 Behaviour and respect

Introduction 181

21. Mental health and wellbeing in the curriculum 186
   By Andrew Cowley

22. Curriculum K – putting health at the heart of education 194
   By Ben Levinson and Kayleigh Cowx

23. Teaching mental resilience 202
   By Lucy Bailey

24. Who says children must sit to learn? Can we move *and* learn? 208
   By Paula Manser

25. A learning framework to put wellbeing at the heart of school 215
   By Rachel Musson

Editor's reflection on Part 5 222

Part 6 Personal development

Introduction 225

26. The metacognitive curriculum 231
   By Anoara Mughal

27. I am a problem solver… How about you? 239
   By Dr Anita Devi

28. The joy of not knowing – a curriculum for lifelong learners 245
   By Dr Marcelo Staricoff

29. Big picture learning – the student is the curriculum 254
   By Professor Scott Boldt

30. Evolving education 260
   By Lucy Stephens

Editor's reflection on Part 6 269

Final thoughts 273
Contributor biographies 275
Editor biography 283
References 285
Index 291

Foreword

Designing a curriculum for a school could be seen as akin to a simple mapping of a journey from A to B; a concise listing of the turns, waypoints and directions to be followed in order to end up at a pre-determined end point. However, as with any journey, there is the practicality of knowing where you need to end up and then the delight and joy of planning by which mode of transport, past which landmarks, and with which travelling companions you will travel.

When we attempt to neatly box things off within curriculum design, when we focus solely on the technical or the minutiae of the 'know' or the 'do', we can so easily lose sight of the need for carefully curated sense-making alongside deliberately crafted moments of awe and inspiration.

Curriculum design is both the planning of a journey and the telling of a story. It is the taking by the hand of the young cognitive adventurer and pointing out the landmarks of each subject discipline, marvelling at their grandeur and intricacies and unravelling their mysteries through carefully narrated content. And there is no one way in which to do this best. This book is a testament to that.

Through a broad and thought-provoking set of curriculum case studies, expertly curated by Rae, we are walked through the design journey of multiple schools in multiple settings. We explore the need for careful sequencing of content so that children can connect and make sense of their curriculum, and we are introduced to the innovative and personal lenses through which each setting has chosen to design the children's curriculum. Because each one *is* the children's curriculum. Each school within the case studies is serving a unique group of young learners and each has crafted their curriculum content and approach with associated thoughtfulness, uniqueness and clarity.

Throughout these case studies, academic excellence is at the heart of design. But, just as there is no 'average' child or 'average' school, these case studies outline that there is no single way to design an effective curriculum to achieve this. Each case study outlines what is in their curricular approach and details 'how' this is achieved, alongside a deeply embedded and shared understanding of the associated 'why' it has been designed in this way. This book provides a rich vein of thought-provoking and deeply researched approaches to effective curriculum design. It is a refreshing reminder that innovation and creativity are not the antonyms of meticulous attention to design detail and careful curation of content.

What unites these case studies is their thoughtfulness in the design process. They encompass the needs and delights of their children's communities and lived experiences, the respect for subjects' academic disciplines, and the need to remember that children's time at school is not only preparation for future phases in their lives but also a time to explore and enjoy their school experience.

There is wisdom, detail and sheer joy in abundance throughout these case studies. They serve as evidence that our profession is wise, generous and devoted to ensuring that our children's curriculum journeys are more than just a route from A to B – they are designed in such a way as to make them highly skilled and informed young citizens of our world, equipped with the knowledge and proficiencies to continue their learning adventures.

Emma Turner
Primary school improvement partner, curriculum advisor, author and speaker.

Introduction

Where it all began: The history of the National Curriculum

I would have been about my son Charlie's age, 23, when I had my first memorable encounter with the National Curriculum. The year was 1989 and I was standing in the morning room, watching my mum come in from school laden with a bundle of white A4 folders. My mum was also in education. She worked as a primary teacher, although her actual job title was a Section 11 teacher. Section 11 was the start of EAL provision in schools, going back to 1966 when a local government act made funds available to meet the education needs of people arriving from Commonwealth countries. I remember the moment clearly. As Mum piled folder upon folder onto the morning room table I enquired as to what this was all about, but her only response was to say with a sigh, 'This is not all of them; there's another lot in the car!'.

This collection of folders was the National Curriculum, a collection of 12 programmes of study. These were set out in sturdy binders, one for each subject, detailing the aims and objectives of what should be taught at each Key Stage and the attainment standards to be reached at the end.

As educators we are all very familiar with the idea of a National Curriculum, the legal framework of subjects and standards for what has to be taught in schools, which was first introduced as part of the Education Reform Act 1988 and, at the time, applied to schools in England and Wales.

The origins of the National Curriculum can be traced back to Prime Minister James Callaghan, to a speech he made in 1976 called the 'Great Debate'. What is interesting about the Great Debate, which took place nearly three decades ago, is that the concerns of business leaders that he talked about remain perennial and ubiquitous to this day. The Great Debate was a seminal moment because it stimulated a national, system-changing discussion on the purpose of education.

> *I am concerned on my journeys to find complaints from industry that new recruits from the schools sometimes do not have the basic tools to do the job that is required. The goals of our education... are to equip children to the best of their ability*

for a lively, constructive place in society and also to fit them to do a job of work. Not one or the other.

(Callaghan, 1976, 'Towards a national debate')

In his speech Callaghan paraphrased Richard Henry Tawney, an English economic historian: 'What a wise parent would wish for their children, so the state must wish for all its children' (Callaghan, 1976). Jim Callaghan was in power for only three years and did not have enough time to put his National Curriculum plan into action; however, the idea was picked up by Margaret Thatcher's government and it was her education secretary Kenneth Baker who introduced the National Curriculum from 1987.

The National Curriculum of 1987 had four broad purposes:

- an entitlement for pupils to a broad and balanced curriculum;
- setting standards for pupil attainment and to support school accountability;
- improving continuity and coherence within the curriculum;
- aiding public understanding of the work of schools.

Over the years, there have been various changes to the National Curriculum: the 12 folders slimmed down to a single tome, the Jim Rose Curriculum of 2008, which was unfortunately shelved before it even got started, and the National Curriculum 2014, with programmes of study going online.

What is remarkable about all of these changes is the tenacity and endurance of our profession and the ability of teachers to keep going, to keep adapting and responding to whatever centrally-determined priorities are 'flavour of the month'.

Like many educators, it never ceases to amaze me as to what schools and teachers are required to teach and to simultaneously take responsibility for in an ever-burgeoning curriculum. Barely a week goes by without one of society's ills being passed down the chain for schools to resolve: extremism, exploitation, drugs, vaping, teenage pregnancy, body dysmorphia, violence, county lines, poverty, knife crime, social media, mobile phones – the list goes on – all alongside the 12 statutory subjects as part of a broad and balanced curriculum.

This broad and balanced curriculum is at the heart of expectations on schools. They must also offer a curriculum which:

- promotes the spiritual, moral, cultural, mental and physical development of pupils at the school and of society;

- prepares pupils at the school for the opportunities, responsibilities and experiences of later life.

From the National Curriculum (2014):

3.1 The National Curriculum provides pupils with an introduction to the essential knowledge they need to be educated citizens. It introduces pupils to the best that has been thought and said, and helps engender an appreciation of human creativity and achievement.

Introduction of Ofsted

Shortly before the general election in 1992, John Major was concerned about the inconsistent standards of inspection across the country, and in particular about the independence of Local Education Authority inspectors and councillors, so he created the Office for Standards in Education (Ofsted) as part of the Education (Schools) Act of 1992.

John Major wanted to introduce a more rigorous system to the Local Education Authority model, one that ensured schools were inspected every four years. And so the common inspection framework was created, thousands of inspectors were appointed and the first Ofsted inspection took place in 1993.

Over the years Ofsted has become a pressing concern in the day-to-day lives of school leaders and teachers. At the time of writing (June 2023) and following the tragic death of Ruth Perry, many school leaders are questioning the safety and validity of Ofsted to raise standards and improve lives.

The 2019 Ofsted Framework

Before September 2019, a key focus for Ofsted inspections were exam results and test data. As educators will know, this was the main metric to compare schools with each other, with schools more likely to be judged as 'Outstanding' if they could demonstrate a combination of high achievement (high test scores) with good attainment (progress). For this reason, Statutory National Attainment Tests (SATS) and other standardised national tests were, and are, often described as 'high-stakes' assessments. The fortunes of a school were at the mercy of how well a group of pupils performed through a suite of tests in a given week in May.

Over time, however, Ofsted became concerned that the focus on final exam results was leading to 'unintended consequences', with schools gaming the system through off-rolling pupils, students cramming for the tests or schools narrowing the curriculum. Following several months of research by Ofsted, the 2019 Ofsted Framework reflected a different approach which aimed to ensure that learners were receiving their entitlement to a broad and balanced curriculum that would give them a better education and a chance of success beyond the national tests.

Schools were promised that Ofsted inspectors would spend less time looking at data and more time looking at the richness of a well-rounded curriculum that schools were providing. To begin with, this sounded very positive, and spoke to what educators would want for their pupils. However, as Ofsted went round the country giving road shows that talked about schema, Jenga blocks of knowledge, deep dives, intent, implementation and impact, it soon became clear that schools would have to put in a great deal of additional work if they were going to be able to provide the amount of evidence required. This was particularly true for primary schools and even more so for small primary schools.

Through online training, Ofsted explained that the process for inspection would include asking school leaders to explain the context of their schools as well as the rationale for how the curriculum has been designed for their school – the curriculum intent, how it has been implemented to meet the needs of the learners in their settings, and the impact of all of their careful planning and sequencing. Then to triangulate and check the veracity of what senior leaders have said, inspectors would undertake 'Deep Dives'. This, schools were told, would cover a number of different elements, including:

- **Meetings with curriculum leaders:** Scrutiny of long and medium term planning, rationale for content, choices and sequencing.
- **Lesson visits:** Evaluating where a lesson sits in a sequence and leaders' and teachers' understanding of this.
- **Work scrutiny:** Observing pupils in classes, jointly with teachers and leaders where possible.
- **Teachers:** Understanding how the curriculum informs their choices about content and sequencing.
- **Pupils:** How well the children build schemas and recall knowledge, from observing lessons and questioning the children directly.
- **Connecting the evidence to reach a judgement:** Forming a view of the quality of education.

The challenges

The latest incarnation of the Ofsted School Inspection Handbook (2019) is particularly challenging, not least for the heightened focus on child protection and safeguarding processes but also for the focus on quality of education through effective curriculum design. Most readers will be aware of the terms 'Intent, Implementation and Impact' and 'Deep Dive'.

It's incredible that the Ofsted Handbook, containing 492 separate detailed bullet points, appears to equally apply to settings for four-year-old nursery children as it does for colleges with FE students.

It also seems ironic that regarding Deep Dives the Handbook states: 'We do not require schools to do additional work or to ask pupils to do work specifically for the inspection, or create unnecessary workload for teachers through our recommendations' (point 20, 2023). At the same time, class teachers are expected to produce detailed and carefully sequenced curriculum plans, as well as delivering day-to-day teaching, including adapted provision, alongside the careful pastoral support for 30 pupils. There is an expectation also that teachers will be subject specialist leaders, which is particularly challenging in primary schools as, unlike secondary teachers, we have been trained as generalists with a focus on early and primary years pedagogy and child development.

This additional role as subject leaders requires teachers to outline the vision for their subject and oversee the effective implementation of the programme of study. This includes training for other colleagues, monitoring their subject and ensuring that the lessons will be delivered with quality, consistency and fidelity to the long-term planning, as it has been documented, in *each* of the 12 subjects.

This sounds challenging enough. For small schools where teachers may lead on three, four, five or more subjects, it must be nigh on impossible!

In addition to subject leadership, schools are inspected on the extent to which they create a safe, calm and orderly environment that has a positive impact on the behaviour and attitudes of pupils. Schools must also provide for the personal development of all pupils and ensure that the leadership and management of the school leads to optimal outcomes, including safeguarding, for all pupils.

There really is a lot expected of schools in England at this time.

However, according to the Department for Education (2014):

> *3.2 The National Curriculum is just **one element** in the education of every child [author's emphasis]. There is time and space in the school day and in each week,*

term and year to range beyond the National Curriculum specifications. The National Curriculum provides an outline of core knowledge around which teachers can develop exciting and stimulating lessons to promote the development of pupils' knowledge, understanding and skills as part of the wider school curriculum.

How schools have responded to the 2019 framework

In spite of the Covid-19 pandemic interrupting normal service, schools across the country have risen brilliantly to the challenge of designing bespoke, borrowed or bought curricula for their schools. They have trained and developed staff as subject champions and leaders, they have produced reams of documentation to show how the subject has been sequenced, demonstrated how the curriculum caters for all learners, shown how progress in each subject is assessed and listed the many ways that the curriculum is enhanced through educational visits and other activities to provide cultural capital.

In addition, schools have ensured that Fundamental British Values are taught, PSHE (personal, social, health and economic education), RSE (relationships and sex education) and Citizenship lessons are delivered, radicalisation is prevented, vulnerable children are prioritised, and young people have access to careers education. Students are taught that vaping is dangerous, that too much social media is bad for mental health, that risks must be managed, that relationships must be positive and that good dental hygiene is essential!

This book, therefore, is a celebration of the many curriculum designs up and down the country that attempt to deliver on all of these societal expectations, and is an appreciation of all the schools, teachers, leaders and learners who have brilliantly risen to the challenge.

How to use this book

The aim of this book is to demonstrate some of the many creative and innovative ways schools are balancing the legal requirements of the National Curriculum with the other competing priorities, while simultaneously providing exciting and stimulating lessons.

Navigating everything that is expected from the National Curriculum, Ofsted and society at large is hugely challenging. Readers may have reached their own means of achieving this, but I hope that the examples provided will also offer some ideas and insights for other techniques, pedagogies and innovations to explore.

The Curriculum Compendium is a collection of 30 case studies of 30 curriculum designs or approaches: each different, inspiring and uniquely created for the community it serves!

The book is split into sections to reflect the four areas of the Ofsted Handbook: Quality of Education, Behaviour and Attitudes, Personal Development, and Leadership and Management. I have expanded two of the areas – Leadership and Management and Behaviour and Attitudes – to explore them in more depth.

Each case study is structured with an introduction to the contributor and their context (a school context box is provided for school-based contributors), and more information on individual contributors can be found in the Contributor Biographies at the back of the book (p. 275). The case studies aim to inspire readers with ideas to try within their own context.

Each case study covers:

- the **intent** of the school's curriculum
- the **implementation** of how their curriculum is delivered
- the **impact** it had on students, staff, parents, carers and the wider community
- how the **vision** for the curriculum **was turned into a reality**, i.e. reflections on how it was done, including processes, pitfalls, challenges, setbacks, successes and opportunities
- key **takeaways** for the reader

- useful **tool and resources**, where relevant.

Each part begins with a reflective piece based on the Ofsted theme and ends with a short summary of what the case studies have covered.

You can read *The Curriculum Compendium* from cover-to-cover, or you can just drop in to a section that particularly appeals to you. The hope is that this will be a cornucopia of helpful hints, insightful ideas and top tips to try in your own schools!

I hope you enjoy reading the 30 case studies provided in this book and find something here that will inform or inspire you as we continue to find ways to respond to the challenge of balancing our statutory responsibility of the National Curriculum and core knowledge with developing 'exciting and stimulating lessons to promote the development of pupils' knowledge, understanding and skills as part of the wider school curriculum' (National Curriculum, 2014).

If, after reading the book, you are inspired to make some additions or adaptions to the curriculum in your school, please do not hesitate to let me know via Instagram, LinkedIn or X – it would be good to carry on the conversation.

The case study for my own school, Milton Road Primary School, follows. I have been a headteacher since 2007 and this is my second headship. When I first got the headship at Milton Road in 2020, I was inspired by five words that I read on the school's website: 'Where learning is an adventure'. Those words were the inspiration behind the curriculum design in the school, which uses a compass as a motif and the motto 'We are CREW' as its ethos.

A unique compelling narrative
RAE SNAPE

School Name	Milton Road Primary School
Age group taught within school	Primary 4–11
Location of school	Cambridge, England
Any distinguishing features	<ul><li>An attractive, thoughtfully designed building with a central courtyard, an Arts Studio and a Forest School.</li><li>A supportive and talented community of pupils, parents and governors and a diligent and creative collegiate CREW.</li><li>The city centre of Cambridge, with its historic buildings, colleges, museums and art galleries is on our doorstep, just a short one-mile walk away.</li></ul>

What I find exciting about the case studies in this book is that each school's curriculum is a powerful, compelling story of the community the school serves and a description of the transformative journey the school is going on.

The idea of a 'compelling narrative', to my mind, is key when schools articulate their intent. The compelling narrative, or intent, provides colleagues, the community and children with a unifying and empowering shared mission. More recently, Ofsted have pulled back from this idea and have suggested that the intent of the curriculum design could just be the National Curriculum itself. However, I believe that a school's curriculum design and its intent is where the opportunity for creativity, innovation and autonomy lies.

Curriculum design at Milton Road Primary School

I started at Milton Road Primary School, Cambridge, in January 2020. On 4 February that year, I organised a 'community listening' event, where parents, staff and children came together to talk about their wishes and dreams for the school. It was a very successful and well-attended event where, following my introduction, the community worked together to write and draw ideas for Milton Road Primary School as their 'dream school'. In the days leading up to it and over the course of the evening, a lot of data was collected in words and pictures of what the community wanted for Milton Road. Creating a shared 'dream' for the school, is one of the initial steps in creating a Learning Community, and is one of the successful actions that Professor Ramón Flecha describes in his book *Successful Educational Actions for Inclusion and Social Cohesion in Europe* (2015).

I was grateful to two kind parents who volunteered to work with me to help synthesise the hundreds of ideas into just five key words. These were:

- identity
- connection
- adventure (learning)
- citizenship
- planet.

I was intrigued by just how closely the words from the community 'dream' aligned with Valerie Hannon's Thrive model.

As you may have spotted, the 'dream school' activity with my new community took place just a month and a half before the start of the pandemic, with the first lockdown starting on 23 March 2020. As for most schools, our priorities changed overnight: it was less about creating a dream at that point and more about how to manage a nightmare!

Another inspiration behind our curriculum design was a report that Dylan William wrote for the Schools, Students and Teachers network (SSAT), 'Redesigning Schooling – Principled Curriculum Design' (2013), where he stated that most justifications for public education can be categorised into the following four areas, paraphrased below:

Personal empowerment: To allow young people to take greater control of their own lives. In the words of Paulo Freire: 'Education is the means by

which people "deal critically and creatively with reality and discover how to participate in the transformation of their world'" (Shaull, 1970, p.34).
- **Cultural transmission:** In the words of Matthew Arnold, to pass on from one generation to the next 'the best that has been thought and known in the world' (Arnold, 1869, p.70).
- **Preparation for citizenship:** Preparing young people as citizens so that they can make informed decisions and participate in democratic society.
- **Preparation for work:** Williams says a number of reports from the Organisation for Economic Cooperation and Development (OECD) show that more educated workers are more productive and that this is linked with economic prosperity.

The four compass points of our Cambridge Connected Curriculum: CREW

The combination of all the previously discussed ideas and models, including place-based curriculum design, ultimately led to conceptualising the curriculum for Milton Road around the four points of a compass. This was to communicate that ours is a balanced, holistic and sustainable curriculum. The Connected Cambridge Curriculum uses our local area, city and world as starting points for the learning journey. The themes for each term are mapped out to connect the stories, people and places in the past and present as ways to help our young people to be successful and navigate the uncertainties of the future. Samuel Johnson said, 'When a man is tired of London, he is tired of life' (quoted in Boswell, 1791). We feel this is a good way to think about Cambridge and Greater Cambridge. There is so much on our doorstep in the urban and rural landscapes, which can be optimised to build knowledge, develop character and open windows to the rest of the world and to future possibilities.

Set around the four compass points, our Cambridge Connected Curriculum aims to offer a holistic, rounded education that balances:

- **Personal development:** positive identity, resilience, safety and health (identity/south).
- **Essential skills:** creativity, collaboration and communication (connection/east).
- **Academic rigour:** knowledge and cultural capital; lifelong learning (adventure/west).
- **Citizenship**: voice, choice and agency; empowering our pupils as changemakers (citizenship/planet/north).

Figure 1: *We are Crew logo*

The compass points also align with our school ethos, as our four core values make up the mnemonic CREW – Courage, Responsibility, Excellence and Wisdom.

The ethos of CREW is based on the work of Ron Berger, who is another amazing educational thought-leader and a source of inspiration. Finally, our curriculum is one that aims to develop the heart, head, hands and hope of our pupils and community.

> *'Fine art is that in which the hand, the head, and the heart of man go together.'*
> (Ruskin, 1859)

The aim of our curriculum is summarised in our intent:

> *'We want our children to be happy and healthy today (south), fulfilled in the future (east and west) and able to make their world an even better place (true north).'*
> (Snape, n.d.).

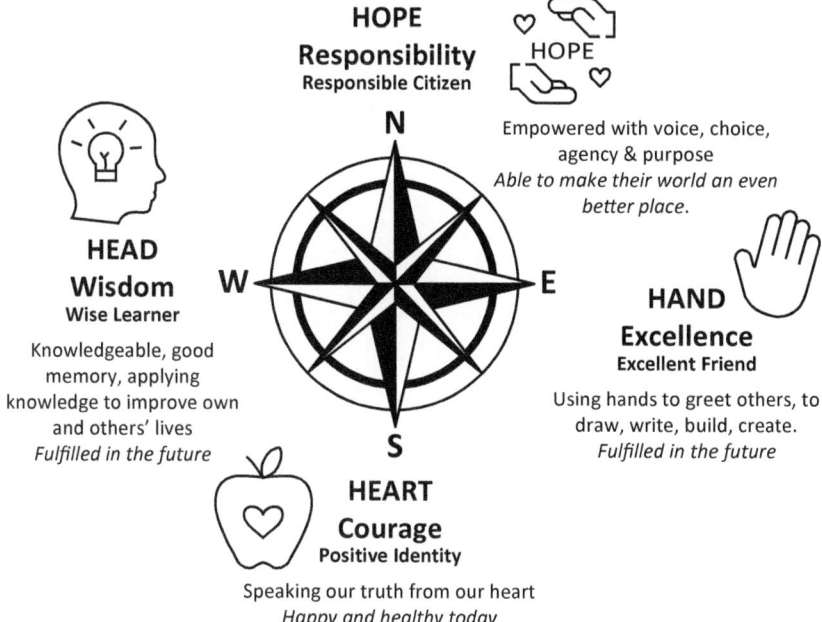

Figure 2: *The Cambridge Connected Curriculum*

I am aware that our curriculum intent could sound like an impossible dream, given the statutory responsibility we have to deliver the National Curriculum. However, the way we implement our intent through our bespoke place-based history and geography curriculum, a well-sequenced reading and writing spine, alongside a number of commercial programmes, and other initiatives, makes it realistic, manageable and pragmatic to deliver. These include Little Wandle Phonics, Maths No Problem, Hamilton Trust Science Scheme, Charanga Music, Language Angels, Access Art Primary Curriculum, EmpathyLab and Skills Builder.

Impact

Thanks to high-quality teaching in the school and an efficient and effective curriculum design, our pupils make good academic progress in reading, writing and maths and generally score highly in the SATs at the end of Year 6.

However, we know that this is only part of the story. In addition to achieving well in statutory subjects, our pupils also tend to perform well in the arts, sports and sciences. This includes music, design technology and drama, and physical education such as dancing, football, tennis, netball and gymnastics. From feedback we've received from partner secondary schools and from parents, we are told that our curriculum leads to 'all-rounders' who not only perform well in exams but are also polite, confident, creative, kind and have excellent communication skills. I always find this sort of feedback rewarding as this is exactly what we are hoping to achieve.

PART 1

Leadership and management – vision and ethos

Introduction

In September 2018, Amanda Spielman, former Chief Inspector of Schools, said:

> *The curriculum is the yardstick for what school leaders want their pupils to know and to be able to do by the time they leave school. It is, therefore, imperative that the new inspection framework has curriculum as a central focus.*
>
> (Spielman, 2018)

The word *curriculum* comes from the Latin word *currere,* which means 'to run'. It refers to a running track on which the student races to be successful, to reach their potential and to achieve their goal. This running track is the sum of everything that the child will experience and hopefully enjoy during their time in school: the knowledge, skills, values and principles that will help them to be happy and fulfilled citizens.

Leaders and teachers designing a school's curriculum should therefore think deeply about what they are trying to achieve and how the currciulum should be curated to serve in the best interest of the students and the community.

Milton Road Primary School

At Milton Road Primary School, our curriculum is based on the following design principles:

1. Children are at the heart of everything we do.
2. Our choices are shaped by years of experience and deep thinking.
3. It is place-based; a rich tapestry reflecting the wealth of resources, people, places and stories of Cambridge and beyond.
4. It is underpinned by values, including our four sustainable core values: Courage, Responsibility, Excellence and Wisdom. This is so children learn to take care of themselves, take care of each other, take care of their learning, take care of their school, community and world, and take care for the future.
5. Our curriculum is not static. Research, involving simple neuroscience, practice-informed pedagogy and a dedicated community of practitioners ensure that our curriculum keeps adapting, evolving, innovating and improving.
6. Subject-specific knowledge and vocabulary are sequenced logically. An understanding of cognitive science is applied to ensure that children remember and retain what has been taught and can make connections across subjects.
7. Essential skills such as communication, creativity, collaboration, critical thinking, computer literacy, citizenship and change-making are taught so children are prepared for careers and opportunities in the future.
8. Our currciulum is ambitious and meets the needs of all our pupils including SEND pupils.
9. The school's thoughtful and generous environment, including outdoor spaces, inspires our ethos and influences our pedagogy and curriculum implementation.

10. We work closely with parents and carers as *partners in learning* to ensure we deliver an exciting, aspirational, interesting, innovative and engaging curriculum.

Our curriculum is implemented through the objectives in the statutory National Curriculum, through programmes such as those listed above, through assemblies, through CREW time (see 'A unique compelling narrative' pp. 3–4 for more information on the meaning of CREW), cultural opportunities, educational visits and a host of other activities.

As a school, we take a relational approach to ensure that our curriculum intention is communicated as effectively as possible. A number of processes ensure that our ethos, culture and curriculum narrative become embodied through words as well as actions:

- Posters of the Five Take Care Agreements, the 'We Are CREW Not Passengers' maxim, and the Curriculum Compass and school values, are displayed throughout the school.
- At the start of the academic year there is a Meet the Teacher picnic. The teacher talks with parents about the year ahead, routines and expectations. Following that, parents and children get together for a picnic so that families can meet each other and form new connections.
- A termly map is shared with parents, which sets out the learning adventure that the children will be experiencing.
- The weekly timetable is shared with parents at the start of the week so that they can see what learning will be taking place and they can support their children with learning at home.
- Every classroom door displays the weekly planning that the children will be enjoying, along with the class reader and the book that is being used as the stimulus for the children's writing.
- Every Friday, there is a whole-school Open Family Friday, where parents are invited into school at the end of the day to come into the classroom to see their children's books.
- Children take photographs of their learning using tablets and upload them onto our learning platform, *SeeSaw*. Parents are then invited to comment on their children's work.
- As part of the curriculum, every class is encouraged to decide on and then undertake a termly act of service, charity, volunteer work or social action.

- Educational trips, visitors and special events, such as the Big Write, the Big Draw and Tiny Ted Talks, contribute to the planned curriculum.
- Towards the end of term, rather than an assembly, classes prepare and present an Expert Showcase. Children design this based on the knowledge and skills they have acquired over the term, along with their own talents, abilities and interests. Performances are given, artwork is displayed, songs are sung and speeches are written and presented.
- Termly reports and parent–teacher meetings also help to ensure that parents are fully informed of their child's learning journey: they know what the children have achieved, the progress they have made and the targets for the term ahead.
- Our school is attractive, tidy, neat and well-organised. Our expectation is that everyone has a role to play in keeping our school beautiful. A weekly whole school Tidy Friday, a litter picking crew, classroom responsibilities and indoor shoes are just some of the ways that children and colleagues contribute to this aim.

This sequence of principles is designed to ensure that the curriculum is not merely a document, but is also an ongoing communication for how we are living our school values, strengthening relationships and creating cohesion. In this way we are purposefully and proactively fostering social capital in our pupils, colleagues and community. Social capital, according to reformer L. J. Hanifan (1916) refers to:

> *The tangible substances [that] count for most in the daily lives of people: namely good will, fellowship, sympathy, and social intercourse among the individuals and families who make up a social unit.*
>
> (Quoted from Putnam, 2000, p.19.)

Hanifan urged for the importance of community involvement for successful schools, arguing that it benefits individuals as well improving the living conditions of the community. Building and securing social capital through consensus, norms, shared language, identity, optimism and mutual responsibility is an important aim for our school as it strengthens our position and role within our community.

A note on the case studies

The five case studies in this section clearly demonstrate how the vision and passion of school leaders have led to thoughtful and inspiring curriculum designs, reflecting their values such as creativity, curiosity, choice, confidence and challenge. A strong thread through these case studies is a commitment to community cohesion as well as social and cultural capital.

1 The world beneath our feet

DAVID ASTON
Headteacher – Wilburton C of E Primary School

DR JEN MCGALEY
Plant scientist – Crop Science Centre, Cambridge University

SALLY TODD
Cambridge Curiosity and Imagination (CCI) Artist

CAROLINE WENDLING
CCI Artist

LUCY WHEELER
CCI Project Manager

School Name	Wilburton C of E Primary School
Age group taught within school	4–11
Location of school	Ely, Cambridgeshire
Any distinguishing features	• Wilburton is a smaller than average semi-rural primary school in Ely, with 120 pupils on roll. • 20 per cent of the pupils are from Gypsy, Roma, Traveller and Showmen communities. • 24 per cent of the pupils on roll are SEND pupils.

Intent of the curriculum

Wilburton C of E Primary School's vision for our school is to be filled with love and learning; where children feel safe, valued and known as individuals; and are supported and challenged. This vision is encapsulated in our mission statement: for everyone to reach their full potential by learning to love and loving to learn.

We set out to achieve this vision through teaching our three core values: love, wellbeing and excellence. This project aligned closely to our six key intent statements and progressions, encapsulated within our core values:

- **Wellbeing:** to enjoy and appreciate living in the moment and to explore the awe and wonder of life itself.
- **Spirituality:** to become fully absorbed in an activity and help others to find meaning, connection and a sense of vitality.
- **Connectivity:** to maintain a calm focus for a good length of time on an activity that gives meaning and a feeling of connection to 'something bigger' beyond daily life.
- **Risk-taking:** to seek out new challenges to develop new skills, taking risks and not worrying if it doesn't work out first time round.
- **Focus:** to maintain concentration on one thing for a sustained period of time to allow enjoyment and completion of the activity.
- **Curiosity:** to be observant and ask questions to help understand things better.

Implementation

Being outdoors in nature is a key part of Wilburton's curriculum. The school sees huge benefits in using the local environment as stimulus for learning. All children take part in Forest School, using both the school grounds and their community allotment. Wilburton is a Historic England Heritage School, which has supported us to embed an understanding of local heritage and its significance across the school curriculum.

Working with Cambridge Curiosity and Imagination (CCI), Wilburton are embedding Artscaping across their curriculum through weekly art-in-nature activities designed to support good wellbeing. Artscaping has three key characteristics: to affect and be affected by arts, nature, place and space; to create a response from materials and feelings to express new ideas; and to enhance local environments in ways that bring joy. By prioritising *slowliness* and nature-connectedness, we make time for children's creativity and thinking. Important, proactive behaviours that are good for our health, our communities and our planet, are developed in parallel. See the CCI website for more information about Artscaping.

Collaborative curriculum design

This collaborative project – with artists Caroline Wendling and Sally Todd from CCI and Dr Jen McGaley from Crop Science Centre – encapsulated the very best of what Wilburton aims to do in our curriculum.

Every child spent half a day with scientist Dr Jen McGaley to learn about mycelial networks. Jen introduced the children to mycorrhizal fungi through an interactive presentation. Found in nearly all soils, these fungi form vast and complex underground networks which help plants gain water and nutrients and which can connect the roots of neighbouring plants, allowing communication and resource transfer.

The children worked in teams to find their own samples from plant roots for Jen to test in the lab, both on the school grounds, and at the community allotment. Children selected a plant and carefully cut a small root sample to put in a test tube. They labelled their work and documented details about their selected plant, including a sketch. After staining the samples Jen took pictures through a microscope, finding ample and diverse symbiotic fungi living in the roots of plants from the school grounds.

Artists Caroline and Sally used the children's findings as a starting point to imaginatively explore the trees and their root systems on the school site. They initially spent time looking at the microscope images, introducing the children to key vocabulary that supported their understanding of how fungi help plants gain water and nutrients.

Moving outside, they then started to engage children with the trees on the school site. Through 'enactment' (physically embodying the tree's shape and form) and 'deep looking', the children focused on a range of different sized trees. They created focused observational drawings using pencil, graphite pencils and soft pastels.

A number of drawing techniques enabled the children to explore relationships between the observed (the trees) and the observer (the children) and prepared the children to start to imagine the world under their feet. Together they expressed and visualised the underground invisible connections between plants. On long strips of white paper, the children gave shape, texture and colour to the mycelial networks connecting the trees and the drawings into a sort of life support. Finally, they created invisible drawings using wax, where they then painted over the drawings with homemade inks to 'reveal' their mycelial networks.

The day of Artscaping designed and delivered by the artists expanded the understanding of Jen's research into real-world images. Each day ended with a celebration event for parents to find out more, which provided the chance to look at the children's samples through the microscope and ask Jen further questions that had arisen throughout the project.

Impact

Students

Knowledge development: Children enhanced their vocabulary and clarity of thought and knowledge in terms of mycelial underground networks and broader plant-fungal interactions. The cross-curricula revisiting of this topic over a sustained period, coupled with the practical 'finding' of their samples, helped children to better understand and make links through the scaffolding of information.

Connectivity and focus: This project saw an increase in children's general ability to focus and concentrate, with many children being in a flow state, fully immersed in the activities that they were doing. The sensory elements of the practical workshops enhanced this immersion.

Wellbeing: Children applied their learning, noticing they began to spot plants and fungi after their engagement with this project. Children described the sessions as 'calming' and 'relaxing'. There was pride in the work they had created, and the real-world elements of their samples being looked at in a science laboratory.

Staff

Wellbeing: Staff reported positively on the engagement of their children and found the Artscaping activities had a positive impact on their own wellbeing.

Parents and wider community

Positive engagement: The project and associated pop-up exhibitions provided positive engagement with parents, some of whom don't usually engage with school initiatives. It provided a big celebratory moment to build pride between children and their parents and carers. Parents, carers and children were able to talk to the artists and scientist who were present at the pop-up exhibitions, asking further questions and having discussions. The exhibition was a further way for the children to understand the topic.

Raising awareness: Wilburton have been able to share the samples with the wider community, to raise awareness of mycelial networks and interest in their local environment. The images from the children's samples will continue to be used in the Crop Science Centre's outreach work, so their contribution will continue to raise awareness and consideration of plants and fungi for others.

Turning vision into reality

Processes

Pre-Information: Headteacher David Aston ensured this project was well understood by his whole staff team, drip-feeding key information in advance of the project, and supporting staff to ready their classes for the project through picture-books, games and activities to familiarise pupils with the topic in advance (See 'Tools and resources' for links).

Planning: Artists Caroline and Sally orientated themselves with the school site and the local environment in advance of their workshops at Wilburton. Time was spent thinking through the practicalities of delivering the workshop outdoors, considering exactly what materials would be needed and how to adapt the workshop in challenging weather.

Challenges: Inclement weather – from hailstorms to strong wind – was a key challenge throughout the project. This could have impacted sampling, as there was a frost a few days ahead of our sampling day. Wind made working with art materials outdoors tricky, with artists needing to secure children's artwork to tarpaulin with masking tape. The school's ethos of outdoor learning meant that the children were very accepting of challenging weather conditions.

Opportunities – engaging with your local university and artist community

CCI has established a portfolio of professional artists who bring their own practices and knowledge to schools and communities. They pair specific artists with specific projects bridging creativity, imagination and skill-sharing.

CCI had established links with the Crops Science Centre, but most universities have a public engagement policy to bring their research into their local communities. While many academics are happy to be contacted directly, university communications or public engagement officers are often a good starting point. They will be able to connect schools with relevant academics or research groups and assist with logistics and funding. For a project similar to this case study, any researcher who uses microscopy (or other imaging techniques) to study the natural world would be a good fit, be they soil scientists, microbiologists, plant scientists, etc. Any topic that can reveal and engage the children with a usually hidden part of nature, ideally found locally, would likely lead to an exciting collaboration.

It may be the researcher's first time working with a school, so it is helpful to provide them with the school curriculum and any relevant recent class topics to allow them to pitch activities appropriately. They may also require specific details after the workshop to aid the impact reporting required by most research funders.

Successes

Celebrating together: Celebrating the project with the wider parent community provided a moment for the children to capitalise on their learning and take pride in all they had achieved. Bringing artwork, photographic documentation and the mycelium samples together created a celebratory tone to the end of the project.

Relationships and community: The school's collection of trees and their mycelial network became a powerful metaphor for the children as they connected their individual tree drawings together with their imagined mycelial imagery. These final images became a symbolic representation of the support and collaboration that is in the school community.

Takeaways

Forward planning: When planning a whole-school project on this scale there needs to be long-term communications and planning between all staff, so that there is time for this topic to be relevant to, aligned with and enhancing the curriculum.

Scaffolding information for each age-group: The continuity of this project – from initial picture books and activities to the sampling and then creative workshops inspired by mycelial networks – helped to deeply embed understanding for pupils. Ensure external providers understand key stage levels and tailor information to children's ability.

Be prepared to be outdoors – whatever the weather: support children to get used to working in the elements and ensure they have the right clothing to be comfortable outdoors. Ensure you have additional equipment (e.g. tent pegs, tarpaulin, tape, etc.) to secure artwork when working in changing weather.

Simple, inexpensive materials: Use materials that make connections to the environment. For example, the artists made inks using natural materials (nettle, oak, blackberries, raspberries and minerals); children were offered only three pastels, but shown how to create more colours through blending. The artists used available materials to respond to the topic – using invisible wax drawings to link with the invisibility of mycelial networks.

Encourage individual creativity and response: The artists actively welcomed individual responses to the theme, encouraging children throughout to be curious, and use their imagination. Every artwork was different – the artists were not prescriptive on one outcome. This is like mycorrhizae where every arbuscule (the tree-like structure where exchanges of nutrients happen) is different.

Reach out to local researchers: Many scientists want to engage with the local community and share their research, but lack access. Such collaborative art-science-school projects can bring so many mutual benefits once initiated.

Celebrate through a pop-up exhibition: Bring teachers, parents and pupils together to celebrate their achievements. The work was displayed in the hall, in a temporary pop-up display using the floor and projecting images. It doesn't need to be expensive to be effective.

Tools and resources

Seek from iNaturalist is a useful app that could be used to support children with plant identification.

Wilburton C of E School Values – Intent Statements and Progression https://docs.google.com/document/d/1JXkiYbhZbXaNxV45almSyLenHfZH1JWmbwoehF5pQt0/edit

Boddy, L. (2021). *Humongous Fungus: The Weird and Wonderful Kingdom of Fungi*. London: DK Children.

Gravel, E. (2018). *The Mushroom Fan Club*. London: Drawn and Quarterly.

The Adventures of a Friendly Fungus – Animation
https://scratch.mit.edu/projects/501021929/fullscreen

British Mycological Society – Resources for Primary School Education
www.britmycolsoc.org.uk/education/primary

Making ink from berries – see recipe below.

Making ink from berries – Adult supervision needed

Ingredients

- 1 cup of berries (blackberries or blueberries)
- 2-3 tablespoons of white vinegar
- Pinch of salt
- 2 teaspoons of gum arabic (optional)

Materials needed

- Hot stove
- Small saucepan
- Potato masher
- Sieve
- Jam jar

Method

- Place the berries in a small saucepan with the vinegar. Crush the berries with a potato masher and add a pinch of salt.
- Heat gently and then simmer for 5–10 minutes.
- Take off the heat and allow to cool.
- Press the berries and liquid through the sieve into a jam jar.
- Add 2 teaspoons of gum arabic, if you have any, to increase permanence.
- The ink will keep fresh for a week or so in the fridge.

2 Making learning memorable
BEN ERSKINE

School Name	Fulbridge Academy
Age group taught within school	3–11
Location of school	Peterborough
Any distinguishing features	• Large four-form entry primary school. • Socially and culturally diverse community in an area of high deprivation, with over 30 nationalities represented.

Intent of the curriculum

Our overriding aim is to ensure that we improve the lives of the children. We enable them to enjoy learning and fulfil their potential by developing the resilience, curiosity, knowledge and skills required to be successful. There is a moral purpose and underlying rationale to all we do:

- We ensure the curriculum is fit for purpose.
- Our pedagogy gives children the best chances to succeed.
- Staff have an excellent work-life balance.

At Fulbridge Academy we have designed an innovative, knowledge-rich curriculum that *prepares* children for their future. It is informed by research and shaped to meet the needs of our local community. Our curriculum enables each child to develop an active mind, identity, heart and voice. The knowledge and skills of the curriculum are thoughtfully sequenced so that children remember what they learn and understand the key concepts of each subject.

ACTIVE MIND Challenge Resilience Accuracy	**ACTIVE IDENTITY** Responsibility Individuality Respect

ACTIVE LEARNING

ACTIVE HEART Choice Integrity Awareness	**ACTIVE VOICE** Confidence Collaboration Empathy

Figure 3: *Active learning boards*

Active Learning is a framework that supports our curriculum. It covers all the things we teach and the ways in which we teach and educate the whole child. Active Learning is split into four sections:

1. **Active Mind:** The academic side of all we teach. There is a strong focus on reading because of the way reading supports children to learn through the rest of the curriculum.
   To enable every child to become a fluent, enthusiastic, lifelong reader with a foundation for understanding the world and a positive attitude to learning.
2. **Active Identity:** The children's recognition of themselves in context. Do they have a supportive understanding of who they are, where they come from, their place in the world?
   To ensure every child is proud of who they are and has a positive understanding of their community, heritage and background.
3. **Active Heart:** The children's understanding of other people and how they relate to other people.

To ensure every child understands the importance of respectful relationships and an appreciation of the diversity in the world.

4. **Active Voice:** The children's ability to express themselves, to communicate and to collaborate.

   To ensure every child develops the confidence to express themselves clearly and the empathy required to collaborate with others.

The four aspects ensure that we are looking at the whole child when we are supporting them to fulfil their potential by developing their curiosity, resilience, knowledge, creativity and skills.

Implementation

Making learning memorable

1. We want the children to remember the learning they are taught in their lessons
2. We aspire for the children to have experiences that will live with them for the rest of their lives.

This second part is achieved through trips, experiences and role-play. Woven into the curriculum are opportunities for children to learn through play. They get the chance to role-play events and scenarios linked to their learning. The planned trips support the curriculum, but also allow children to experience things that all children should have the opportunity to experience, for example:

- going to the beach and into the woods (contrasting environments);
- visiting London;
- going to the theatre, a sports stadium, a museum, a place of worship, etc.

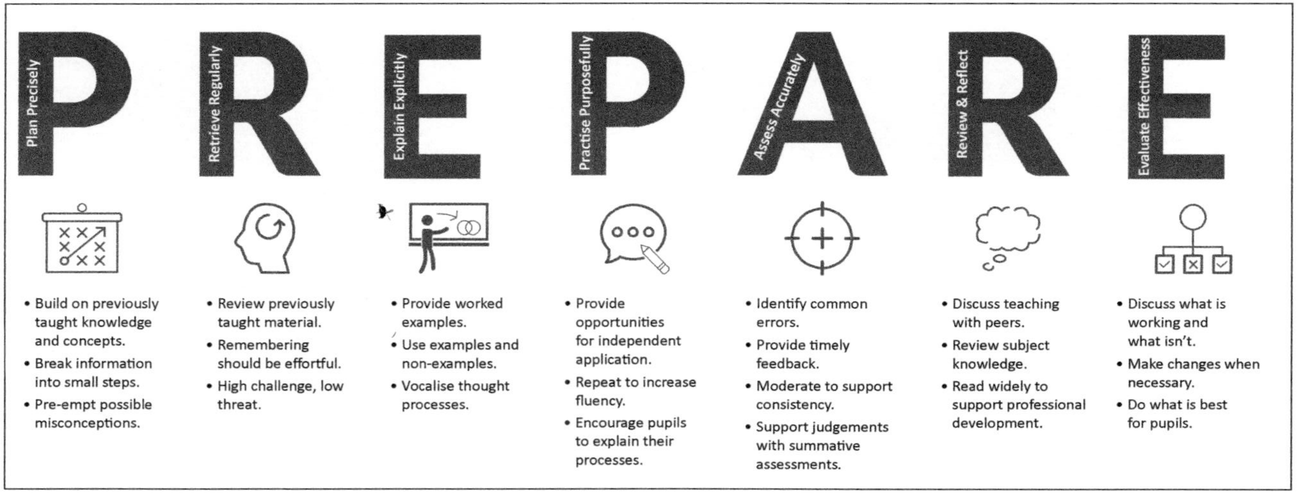

PREPARE framework

Plan Precisely
- Build on previously taught knowledge and concepts.
- Break information into small steps.
- Pre-empt possible misconceptions.

Retrieve Regularly
- Review previously taught material.
- Remembering should be effortful.
- High challenge, low threat.

Explain Explicitly
- Provide worked examples.
- Use examples and non-examples.
- Vocalise thought processes.

Practise Purposefully
- Provide opportunities for independent application.
- Repeat to increase fluency.
- Encourage pupils to explain their processes.

Assess Accurately
- Identify common errors.
- Provide timely feedback.
- Moderate to support consistency.
- Support judgements with summative assessments.

Review & Reflect
- Discuss teaching with peers.
- Review subject knowledge.
- Read widely to support professional development.

Evaluate Effectiveness
- Discuss what is working and what isn't.
- Make changes when necessary.
- Do what is best for pupils.

Figure 4: *PREPARE framework*

Our Active Learning model is complemented by our PREPARE framework.

This supports the implementation of our intent and the aim of making learning memorable. The PREPARE framework is based on Daniel Willingham's Simple Model of Memory (2009).

- First a learner pays attention to information in their environment, something they experience through their senses.
- This information is brought into their working memory where it is thought about deeply in relation to information already held in the learner's long-term memory.
- Through deep thinking and practice this information is stored in their long-term memory: attaching itself to, and changing, knowledge that is already stored there.
- Knowledge in long-term memory can then be retrieved and brought back to working memory to support future learning.
- The ability to retrieve information can be strengthened through practice.
- Information in long-term memory and working memory can be forgotten.

For each of the areas of PREPARE we have a linked WalkThru. From each of the overriding main WalkThrus there is a cluster of WalkThrus that we use as the mechanism to coach and support staff in improving their teaching practice in those areas.

Plan precisely – knowledge must be built on knowledge and concepts already in the long-term memory.

- When planning, we must think of what the students already know.
- Current knowledge needs to be brought to the forefront of their minds so that children are ready to understand a new concept.
- Planning must break information into small steps.
- Our working memory is limited so we don't want to overwhelm it.
- We plan to ensure there aren't too many new things being taught at one time.
- We need to plan for possible misconceptions that children may gain or already have in their long-term memory.

Retrieve regularly

- We review previously taught learning.
- We consolidate the knowledge that children already hold in their long-term memory and show how it is relevant to the new learning.
- Learning should be effortful.
- Remembering is an important part of the learning process.
- Retrieving information from the long-term memory strengthens the memory.
- Retrieval activities must be difficult, but not too difficult.
- High challenge, low threat: retrieval needs to be low stakes, but challenging.

Explain explicitly

- Children are provided with worked examples.
- A worked example is a visible model that is clear and concise and provides the process we want the children to complete.
- We use 'examples' and 'non-examples' to clearly describe concepts; these allow children to connect to something they already understand.
- We vocalise thought processes. By making our own thinking clear we show exactly how to understand a given concept as well as role modelling how to be an effective learner.

Practise purposefully

- We provide opportunities for independent application to give children the chance to think deeply about the learning that is currently in their working memory and begin to store it in their long-term memory.
- We ensure there is enough repetition for children to become fluent in the retrieval; practising something to become fluent reduces the chances of it being forgotten.
- We encourage children to explain their processes. If children think deeply they can verbalise their thoughts and describe their processes.

Assess accurately

- A key part of assessment is to identify common errors.
- This helps us detect the children's misconceptions and provides timely feedback.
- By identifying and pausing the practice that could be ineffective, and explaining the misconceptions, we can increase the chances that the rest of the practice supports learning (these areas are both formative assessments and lead to changes in teaching).
- Summative assessment is completed through moderation and standardised tests. These allow a clear and precise view of children's progress and attainment.

Review and reflect

- As described on page 28 (see 'Turning vision into reality'), the level of reflection, review and discussion is significant, beneficial and has a positive and significant impact on Continuing Professional Development (CPD) provision.

Evaluate effectiveness

- Feedback from all stakeholders is taken into consideration: we always evaluate changes. The choices we have made have involved a lot of thought and research and will not change without good evidence.

Impact

To measure impact, we bring it back to our Active Learning framework. We look at how this framework impacts the decisions on our curriculum, and therefore the children, parents, staff and community.

At this level of review, the impact of the framework on the pupils is evident through how:

- Active Mind supports them to acquire academic content and make it part of who they are.
- Active Identity supports children to understand themselves.

- Active Heart helps them understand others and the wider world.
- Active Voice is supporting their ability to communicate and collaborate.

Every aspect of our curriculum supports one or more of these elements of Active Learning.

These examples from our curriculum are what we consider when we measure impact:

- The history and geography curricula focus on the community the children come from and the wider world they will embrace as they grow up.
- The commitment we make to physical education with specialist teachers. We want children to identify as people who enjoy exercise and sport; as people who see themselves as healthy, active individuals.
- The specialist performing arts teaching supports children to develop an Active Voice, to think about how they can communicate with confidence and collaborate with others.
- Our mathematics develops children's Active Minds through a coherent way of teaching. It supports them in their academic goals. It seeks to identify them as mathematicians and encourages them to see mathematics as a reasoning and problem-solving subject.
- Our reading curriculum aims for the children to become fluent and enthusiastic readers in the wider reading curriculum. The texts and stories that are chosen ensure the children are given a different view on the world, as well as being able to relate to the characters and content. All of the elements of Active Learning are supported in the reading curriculum.

School is not all about data and results; however, these are still hugely important. Good results, especially in the core subjects, will support children's progress through their education journey and as they move into the working world. The children at Fulbridge achieve a high standard of academic success in the core subjects and gain knowledge to support their development in the other curriculum areas.

The parents and community are involved through our parental engagement work. Parents have the opportunity to come in and be part of lessons, listen to leaders speak about what they will see in the lessons, why we teach it, and how as a parent they can help their children at home. Our inclusion team supports families and their children where there is a specific need. This is often highlighted through the Active Learning framework, i.e. this could be related to the child's academic, physical or emotional ability, or concerns around their identity.

Turning vision into reality

The building of the curriculum has evolved over many years. We have worked with organisations such as Creative Partnerships, Whole Education and the Cambridge Primary Review Trust as well as educationalists like Roger Cole, Matilda Jubert, Robin Alexander, Mick Waters and more recently Mary Myatt. We have been inspired by the work of Sir Ken Robinson, Daniel Willingham and Tom Sherrington among others. Since 2020, Christopher Such (author of *The Art and Science of Teaching Primary Reading*) has worked at Fulbridge and has been an integral part of leading on further curriculum improvements and design.

Fulbridge is a very large school and consistency of approach to ensure the curriculum and pedagogy are aligned is a practical challenge. The solution has involved recording CPD sessions so that staff can revisit the previous input if they need to. This exists alongside a robust induction programme for new staff. The CPD we offer has adapted to ensure the key messages are getting to all staff. This is as well as differentiating for individual needs, the needs for a subject or an area of the school.

The amount of planning, preparation and assessment (PPA) time staff receive is above the statutory requirement. The extra PPA time means that they have more opportunity to talk about the lessons, the planning and the way in which the lessons are taught, discussing good practice and how to overcome challenges. Planning is done collaboratively and curriculum leaders support planning meetings where it aligns with a whole-school initiative.

Another aspect is ensuring teachers improve their subject knowledge. As well as in-depth learning about the subject they are going to teach, they use release time to learn about the models and representations that support the teaching of that content.

The community we work in and the world we live in are always changing, so the development of our teachers must not be static either. It is essential for teachers to have the chance to read books, articles and blogs that are relevant to the school's curriculum and pedagogical approach, which also align with our CPD and teachers' appraisals.

We have a CPD library and a CPD section on the curriculum website, containing blogs and podcasts for staff to access. This is supported by high quality in-house CPD. When you combine all these factors it gives staff the opportunity to learn and develop as well as share their own thoughts and ideas, effectively contributing to the school's continuous curriculum development.

This is further enabled by having specialist teachers in PE, performing arts, art and Forest School. We want every subject to be taught with the expertise it deserves.

This has resulted in the curriculum continually evolving; higher staff expertise; a better work-life balance; and a consistent improvement in the lives of the children.

Takeaways

- Have a clear framework that sets out your vision and your curriculum intent.
- Consider the whole child and their individual needs.
- Create a clear and consistent approach to the way all staff implement the curriculum.
- Develop a truly broad and balanced curriculum.
- Consider how subjects interrelate and the progression and prior knowledge needed for this.
- Promote and give time to research and staff development.
- Create a support network within the school with clear pathways.
- Consider the community you work within and how this affects your curriculum.
- Trust staff and develop them as leaders.

3 Releasing the imagination and celebrating the art of the possible
DR JAMES BIDDULPH

School Name	University of Cambridge Primary School
Age group taught within school	4–11
Location of school	Cambridge
Any distinguishing features	• The first university training school in the UK for primary education.

Intent of the curriculum

Our curriculum aims to be bold, free-thinking and rigorous. It is underpinned by a commitment to the values of excellence, equity and learner empowerment. We aim to be:

- **Ambitious:** everyone is encouraged and enabled to achieve and attain highly.
- **Innovative:** the learning community benefits from belonging to a research and teacher education community, both within the school itself and also as part of wider University and school partnerships.
- **Inclusive:** everyone is welcome and everyone included.
- **At the core of our curriculum:** developing compassionate citizens.

As such, our principled approach to designing our curriculum is rooted in democratic notions of education in which:

- children's voice is central
- we empower children to make sense of the complex world they live in (Rudduck and Flutter, 2004)

- we develop their ability to question; to discuss, challenge and contest diverse positions respectfully and compassionately; and to consider views about our world and how we should live in it.

There is a critical thinking nature to the school, so we question assumptions about truth and knowledge. In understanding the multicultural communities we live in, there is a need for children to learn about the diversities that exist in their local and global communities. As inspired by the words of Lord Williams and the Cambridge Primary Review (2010):

If you're going to be a decision-making citizen, you need to know how to make sense and how to recognise when someone is making sense… that there are different ways of making sense, different sorts of questions to ask about the world we're in, and insofar as those questions are pursued with integrity and seriousness they should be heard seriously and charitably.

Lord Williams, 2008, quoted in Alexander (2010, p.13).

- We aim to develop a community of compassionate, active, globally-minded people.
- The values of empathy, respect, trust, courage and gratitude are embedded through learning experiences, with the purpose of living these out.
- Three pedagogical pillars guide our practice: Oracy and Dialogue, Habits of Mind and Playful Enquiry.
- Both domain-specific knowledge and skills and positive dispositions towards individual subject areas are fostered through coherently-planned learning sequences.
- Positive relationships are fostered through the engagement with our vision and values. We enable a space in which teachers and learners can develop the knowledge, concepts and skills to be compassionate and active global citizens.
- Diversities are enabled and celebrated.

Implementation

Curriculum learning as experienced by children is mediated by a variety of factors, not least by educators with responsibility for design and implementation. A curriculum represents what adults infer that children need.

Through their interactions with both the subject content and the diverse set of children they work with, educators interpret and then put into practice many versions of the intended curriculum. This is important for all those involved in implementation: curriculum does not function in a vacuum and can quickly look very different to what was envisaged.

Because of this complexity, there is need to support educators in the developing of knowledge not only for teaching content, but also the pedagogical repertoires that can bring learning alive. Through this development, educators develop a very special type of practitioner expertise that helps to find a journey out of the tensions between children's thinking and curriculum content. Takahashi (2021) draws attention to this space in between the intended and implemented curriculum and explores how the planning stage of lesson design supports educators to be better prepared for teaching sequences of learning. This emphasis on the planning stage, a feature of Japanese lesson study, is an aspect of professional development that is often overlooked. It is one that allows educators the space and time to develop better predictions of what might happen when the lesson takes place; learning to close the gap between what we intend children to learn and what they actually learn.

Curriculum guidance materials are therefore necessary for providing teachers with the information they need and yet are insufficient without the processes by which they can be explored and understood. Materials of high quality give educators a steer not just on what to teach but also how it can be brought about and what progression looks like. For example, learning what the more perplexing aspects of the subject content will be, how these can be anticipated, pre-empted or responded to. Unlike some high performing education systems such as Japan, the extent and availability of these materials in the UK is still limited and puts an unrealistic expectation on schools to produce such intricate and far-reaching knowledge by themselves. A more efficient and sustainable system is to develop strategic and collaborative partnerships between teachers, specialists and researchers, who together create an iterative body of knowledge that can be accessed freely and widely.

At the leadership level in schools, curriculum planning often revolves around coverage and progression mapping. Alongside this and in collaboration with teachers, our leadership team spend time planning in detail the sequences of learning that would form the basis of a project's trajectory. This allows the 'big thinking' to be built on by a group of teachers and then allows them to spend more time on customising this journey to the needs of their classes. These sequences include clear learning intentions, outcomes, core vocabulary (with accompanying flashcards), knowledge maps with core factual information, assessment 'quizzes', enrichment events and opportunities for children to apply and synthesise their learning in playful ways.

To develop these processes of planning, we use a school-wide programme of lesson study and coaching. Lesson study takes place both within and across phases and links to areas of curriculum and school development. As part of lesson study cycles, we work with subject-specialist expert advisors. We release teachers for an average of four planning sessions per year to study subject progression across the primary school and knowledge development across a unit of learning, and to collaborate on planning, observing and engaging in a post-lesson discussion on a 'focus research' lesson.

Alongside this, the leadership team offers more bespoke support to teachers each week, coaching, mentoring, team-teaching and modelling lessons in their specialist area of teaching. Such protected professional development time for teachers allows them to think deeply about subject and pedagogical knowledge, work with a leading expert and then go back to apply these ideas in their classrooms.

Impact

The process of understanding impact is really about tuning in to understand whether children have learned something but also what they have learned. The old adage that nothing is taught unless it is learned reminds us that in spite of good intentions and even with a well-considered curriculum, there is no guarantee that children will have learned what was set out to happen.

William's framework (2011) of five core strategies guides educators within a broad framework to help educators and children understand where they are in the learning journey, where they might go next and how to get there:

1. Sharing learning intentions and success criteria.
2. Feedback that moves learners forward.
3. Questioning that elicits discussion and evidence of learning.
4. Children as owners of their own learning.
5. Peers as instructional resources for one another.

Formative assessment, linked with high quality teaching, is described by William as the bridge between teaching and learning. He rightly puts the emphasis on assessment as something that is adaptive to children's needs and that crucially leads to change – a re-thinking of how can things be done differently so that children can go on to learn better. At our school, each class has a 'responsive teaching journal', and these contain within them a wealth of teaching assessment notes on observations and assessments during lessons. This information is then used to adapt teaching in the same or the next session.

Alongside domain-specific pedagogies of assessment for learning, our subject leaders have developed clear assessment guidance for their subject areas. For example, the use of unit tests or 'quizzes' three quarters of the way through a unit gives information so that teachers can help any children needing further support. Children's recordings provide rich data for teachers and leaders to understand their thinking, what they remembered and what they have understood, in their own terms, as the main points of learning. Working in unison with summative assessments and quality assurance, understanding impact then works at the different levels of short-, medium- and long-term cycles of assessment.

Turning vision into reality

Curriculum implementation needs the whole community to collaborate. From phase leaders being released to collaborate on sequences of learning, to teaching assistants scaffolding dialogue in the classroom; from parents helping to translate vocabulary flashcards for pupils new to English, to the teachers planning and reflecting on children's curriculum progress; everyone is a key player in creating transformative curriculum learning opportunities for children.

There are challenges in working from the National Curriculum, a document that has one page of guidance for one subject and nearly a hundred for another, and schools are left to decipher how to best create structure. How can we think creatively to avoid the trap of trying to cover everything at the expense of depth and meet our broader curriculum aims? How many of these areas need to be taught as distinct themes or projects and how many would be better included as part of immersive days or weeks?

What is clear is that prioritising professional development by giving adequate time in the day is essential, albeit an always challenging undertaking in the complex workings of a school. By protecting educator development as an immovable priority, we protect curriculum development and implementation.

As an education system, much wider collaboration is needed between schools, subject experts, researchers and specialists. We need to rethink the structures underlying knowledge creation, researcher and teacher collaboration, knowledge dissemination and mobilisation. Our work with Japanese Lesson Study suggests to us that the role of expert advisor is one that is missing in our school system and would represent a closer aligning of research, theory and practice.

Takeaways

A curriculum needs clear aims: Does the curriculum lay out a greater purpose beyond a list of content? Does it equip children to grapple with needs of the present and future? When we consider pressing issues such as climate change, technology, health, wellness and citizenship, conventional parameters of a curriculum can quickly be understood as insufficient.

Professional development needs to be prioritised: The vast majority of educators are trying their best with the resources they have available. Rather than adding to the hyper-accountability culture in and around schools with an imbalanced level of support, we need to grow educators through building their capacity.

Values-led: Are the school's values meaningfully embedded and observable in children's curriculum experiences?

Text rich: Text choices that are carefully planned to accompany what is being taught is a time-consuming but key strategy to opening up opportunities of personal, social, emotional and cultural development for children.

Resourced: A resourced curriculum needs time, funding, organisational prowess and systematisation. Resourcing a curriculum needs to be honoured for its importance, as it often mediates and shapes how children access the curriculum in practice.

Where is the children's voice in curriculum planning and what role should it play?: Moving beyond misconceptions and extremes of children deciding the curriculum, adults engage in a perilous endeavour (Fielding, 2007) when they 'speak for others' and assume they know what is best for children to learn. A humble perspective that seeks balances between voice, recognition of diversity and different forms of knowledge, opens up possibilities.

Planned sequences of learning: Expecting teachers to re-write curriculum sequences for every unit is problematic. Instead, curriculum guidance that is created through a collaboration with subject specialists and then customised and iterated by teachers allows for them to spend more time on meeting the needs of their pupils.

Curriculum progression planning and knowledge needs to be applied and embedded into specific sequences of learning: It is through a systematised focus in professional development that this knowledge comes alive and supports transforming theory into practice. It is when progression is partnered with skilful planning, responsive teaching and assessment, that true coherence starts to take shape.

4 A curriculum matched to context
KYRSTIE STUBBS

School Name	Boothroyd Primary Academy
Age group taught within school	4–11
Location of school	Dewsbury, West Yorkshire
Any distinguishing features	• 95 per cent of pupils are of Muslim or Eastern European backgrounds.

Intent of the curriculum

As a headteacher, it was very important to me that the curriculum we developed was one that met the specific needs of our context and community.

The new framework meant in fact that it was easier, rather than limiting, for me and my Senior Leadership Team (SLT) to intentionally create it. There is no 'one size fits all' when we are talking about children and we took this approach with our curriculum design rather than buying one off the shelf.

Our intention was clear.

Creativity

We wanted our curriculum to excite and engage our children, and to ensure we built a love of learning across all subjects so that there were no areas of the curriculum where pupils felt they could not achieve. Essentially, we wanted every child to enjoy every subject and to see its relevance in their own world. We knew that none of the existing curricula that we had looked at did this in the way we needed it to for *our* children, so we knew we would need to design a bespoke curriculum model for our school.

Community

Our curriculum *had* to meet the needs of our community and to understand this we had to first identify and then analyse the barriers that currently existed for our children to be able to learn effectively and for them to achieve outcomes similar or better than national levels from 'well-below' starting points. It was clear from the analysis that our key drivers had to be developing oracy, life-skills and diversity.

We knew that retention of information was a key concern, primarily as a result of cognitive overload due to most of our children being English as an Additional Language (EAL) learners, and the extra demands that put on them when writing. We ensured that all our lessons started with a 'got it grid' approach to ensure we supported building the retention of facts in a way that was familiar to our children. The consistency and simplicity of this approach was key.

Table 1: Example of a blank 'Got it grid'

Last lesson	Last week
Last half term	Last year

Cultural capital

We completed a cultural capital analysis for each of our subject areas so that we fully understood some of the gaps in knowledge and experiences. For example, in geography we knew that we had to build in more opportunities for children to experience different environments as the majority had never left the local area. In music we knew we had to expose children to a more diverse range of musicians due to the cultural barriers that existed; we also wanted to ensure every year group learned an instrument as they did not have this opportunity outside of the school environment.

Cohesion

We wanted our curricula to be cohesive, with seamless threads running through them that ensured learning was deepened and not diluted. For example, the threads of life-skills, diversity and oracy needed to run through and be taught across all of our subject areas rather than be a bolt-on.

Implementation

Creativity

There were some areas we felt needed to be taught more explicitly due to both our community and the context of the curricula to date. We introduced new areas into our curriculum that were taught each week and built on over the years from Year 2 to Year 6. These strands were called our 'Extended curriculum' and focused on the areas shown in Figure 5:

Extended Curriculum Drivers
Aspiration, Diversity & Equity and Cultural Heritage

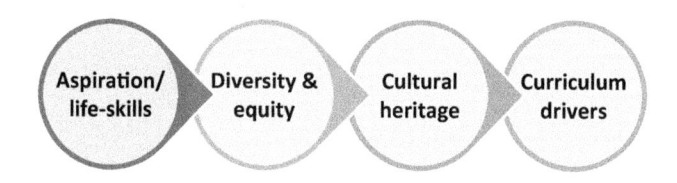

Aspiration/life-skills → Diversity & equity → Cultural heritage → Curriculum drivers

Term	Autumn 1	Autumn 2	Spring 1	Spring 2	Summer 1	Summer 2
Session 1	Inspirational People	Diversity	Mental Health	Migration	Equity	Life-skills: Survival Skills
Session 2	Aspirations	Life-skills: First Aid & Safety	Cultural Representation	Life-skills: Gardening & Growing	Life-skills: Cooking	

Figure 5: *Areas covered by the Extended Curriculum*

This part of our curriculum was, in effect, 'extra' teaching and not part of the National Curriculum; however, we felt that it was an integral part of the teaching we needed to meet the specific needs of our community.

For EYFS and Year 1 we focused on the same areas but in our continuous provision areas, and we developed enhancements to support each strand, mainly through the use of books.

Community

We carefully built in opportunities to close gaps in knowledge across our foundation subjects through weaving diversity and oracy through each unit, ensuring progression and broad coverage. This meant focusing on key vocabulary as well as building in tasks which developed the skills of oracy, such as debate, to deepen understanding. We ensured that children were not limited by having to write in every lesson and instead focused on subject integrity, building the skills of specific subjects. It wasn't that we removed writing completely – we just focused on disciplinary writing linked to the subject, rather than genre, or we scaffolded the writing as part of English lessons.

In each subject we looked at where we could make our curriculum more relevant for our children. For example, in geography we ensured our studies were of Eastern Europe and Asia which allowed children to share their own experiences and therefore feel more involved in the learning. In history, we focused on the experiences of the soldiers who joined the war from India as part of our lessons, as well as the more 'traditional' approach of focusing on soldiers from the UK.

Cultural capital

After completing the cultural capital analysis for each subject it was very clear where we needed to build in opportunities for children to broaden their experiences. This was the important foundation for our whole curriculum: our aim was to close gaps in both in children's experiences and in their knowledge to improve equity. In some subjects this meant exposing them to a wider range of significant people; at the same time we ensured that we focused on ensuring representation of all the protected characteristics within our units of learning.

Cohesion

The key to our implementation was the introduction of 'floor books' across foundation subjects. Floor books are scrapbook-style shared books that a group or class of children use to record, draw, and write their learning in a less formal way, while still demonstrating their understanding. We had seen this approach being used in some excellent Early Years settings and it became instrumental in deepening knowledge and allowing children to develop key concepts without being limited by writing ability. Floor books were introduced for foundation subjects as a way of evidencing knowledge and progression without the need for every child to produce a written outcome in every lesson. These also supported children in making links to prior learning and being able to articulate their learning to others. The depth of learning increased due to fact that more time was spent in the actual learning than the evidencing of the learning! We ensured that standards were set for the collation of these books, for example that each child was represented. We evidenced greater depth and challenge and made sure that pupil voice was captured.

Impact

From the start children were more engaged in their learning: children from Eastern Europe, for example, were able to share their experiences in geography lessons, thus bringing more relevance to their learning. The confidence of some children grew as a result with the added benefit of their vocabulary and language improving at a faster rate than previously. We believed that this was due to both the improved relevance of the content for our pupils and the barriers of writing being removed: cognitive load was reduced and children were able to focus on the retrieval and storage of this vocabulary. This was evidenced when we completed disciplinary writing in our English lessons – due to their improved vocabulary, the quality and quantity of writing improved for the majority of our children.

We found that the introduction of floor books also allowed the children to facilitate and lead much better discussions about their learning and make links to prior learning. The depth of their knowledge was greatly improved due to more of the lesson time being spent learning and less evidencing the learning.

We achieved our aim of children knowing more and remembering more, partly through using the 'got it grid' in each lesson, but also by enabling them to demonstrate their learning in a way that suited them as individuals. This approach also allowed children with SEND to shine, again because of the removal of the writing barrier and being able to demonstrate their learning in different ways. Children with additional needs were just as able to talk through the floor books and their learning as others within their cohort and it allowed them to demonstrate often hidden abilities across the curriculum.

The children also told us that they 'loved' the floor books and were extremely proud as they talked through them with visitors or staff in a way that few pupils had been able to, prior to this approach.

Our extended curriculum was received very positively by the community. Despite some initial concerns around being able to achieve equity in all aspects (for example some same-sex families had concerns), our use of floor books ensured that all people of all faiths in our community were on board and could see the benefits of representation to create a cohesive school community. We could see the impact on behaviour across school, especially from children towards others of different ethnicities and faiths to their own, as we developed their understanding in this more structured and explicit way.

Another benefit was that discussions around personal development were transformed. Children could discuss issues such as discrimination and equity across all year groups and how it related to them and others in their community in a more eloquent and coherent way than when we used PSHE lessons as the main teaching mechanism. The links between other subjects were also clearer, for example discussions around migration linked geography with an understanding of how cultural heritage impacts our history.

Turning vision into reality

One of the key reflections I have taken from the design of our curriculum is that we almost took too long to put it together! We were slower off the mark than we might have been due to worrying initially about moving away from the standard National Curriculum. We were too concerned with the content, and forgot that the objectives in the National Curriculum are not excessive nor explicit in the way they are taught. The way they are taught is very much up to individual schools; we just need to have to the courage to do it. Another time-blocker was that we trialled our approach in one subject rather than having the courage of our convictions to just do it across the board.

Another main reflection I have, when looking at the published curricula that are out there, is that we worried too much about how different ours was and how it would be perceived – perhaps forgetting that we knew our children better than anyone else!

My words of advice about curriculum: as long as you have clear reasons for your content, you can explain how you have ensured the progression of core skills and knowledge and how you meet the requirements of the National Curriculum and the needs of your children. Just go for it!

As I look back, I also think about participation: we might have benefitted from involving parents in the development of our extended curriculum to a greater extent from the start. This would almost certainly have stopped the issues we faced with some of the aspects around equity. I also wish we had shared and collaborated more with other local schools in our community. There were lessons and knowledge we might have shared that could have further improved the curriculum from the start.

I think there is a tendency to wait to launch a curriculum until it is perfect – the very nature of the beast means that it will always be changing and improving over time. Refining a curriculum as you go along is a much better approach than waiting for it to be finished. In education, do we ever really finish anything?

Finally, I believe the concept of floor books is one that needs to be explored further. It continues to be one of the key changes we introduced across the school which had the biggest impact on both workload of staff and on the learning for our pupils. I genuinely think we should move towards this approach regardless of the curricula we teach, to ensure equity by the removal of barriers, reduce cognitive load and deepen knowledge and retention.

Takeaways

- Identify and analyse the barriers that exist to learning before starting any curriculum design.
- Analyse cultural capital issues in subject areas and ensure your curriculum addresses these.
- Be clear on your focus strands and ensure your curriculum is cohesive across all subject areas.
- Be brave – you know your community and you know what content is needed to support them.
- Don't limit children's learning by focusing on writing outcomes.
- Ensure children can see the relevance of the curriculum for themselves.

5 Da Vinci life-skills curriculum and assessment

ROSINA DORELLI AND ZACHARY REZNICHEK

co-founders of Biophilic Education Alliance (BE All)

School Name	BE Hub
Age group taught within school	10–14 (at the time of writing)
Location of school	Cambridge
Any distinguishing features	• Flexi-schooling and project-based learning.

Intent of the curriculum

The purpose of Biophilic Education and the Da Vinci Life-Skills Curriculum (DVLS) is to cultivate confidence in learners. Instead of moving into adulthood with stress filling their minds, we help young people develop the capacity to engage wholeheartedly in the learning journey that is life.

We believe that the current school system does not foster the fundamental life-skills needed to manage and adapt to an increasingly volatile world; it needs rethinking. The fast-changing digital future, artificial intelligence, climate change and extinction events require adaptability, resilience and problem-solving skills that are not currently being provided by schools. Biophilic Education Alliance (BE All) is a model for the future of education to empower the entrepreneurs and world-builders of the future and inspire new ways of learning for all.

Biophilia is the passionate love of life. Biophilic design is being heralded as the architecture for a sustainable future. Biophilic spaces are more organic, have access to daylight, use natural materials, and provide sanctuaries and views. Research suggests that if we live and work in spaces designed for our species to flourish, we can improve not just our physical and mental health, but also our cognitive function. We have expanded this concept to create a curriculum through which all young people can flourish.

Our purpose is to improve students' agency, self-efficacy and wellbeing, as well as supporting them to find and explore their passions and vocations, because we need an extensive variety of skills and knowledge to build thriving communities. A BE All vision for the future combines the knowledge, skills and wisdom of our ancestors with ground-breaking technological possibilities and the ingenuity of loving humans. We aim to nurture a more sustainable, ethical and inclusive outlook on a local and global level.

Community and collaboration are at the heart of our philosophy. We are working with local businesses, farmers, organisations and councils to create real-world projects and apprenticeships so that our students can develop civic responsibility and a sense of belonging to their community. All our DVLS projects equally value the four key domains: **academic learning** with critical thinking and reasoning; **physical and practical learning** with movement and technical skills; **social emotional learning** with self-management and teamwork; and **creative/intuitive learning** with ideation and problem-solving.

Implementation

Our Da Vinci Life-Skills (DVLS) Curriculum figurehead, Leonardo Da Vinci, did not see the world through siloed subjects. He explored everything with an insatiable, childlike curiosity, whether it was science, art, geography, maths or linguistics. He was a polymath and a systems thinker and would have probably struggled in our current system. If he was academic, he would have been steered away from the arts, and if dyslexic he would have struggled in exams. We have designed a interdisciplinary, project-based curriculum to enable all students to flourish, particularly the entrepreneurs, designers and changemakers of the world like Da Vinci.

We provide comprehensive scaffolded teaching resources including schemes of work, road maps of how our learning objectives meet the National Curriculum, slideshow presentations and student portfolio templates. To support the delivery of our curriculum, we provide CPD, Biophilic Education (BE) training and mentoring, and certificates for freelance teachers and schools, both nationally and globally. Our BE training guides teachers to implement not only the DVLS curriculum, but all project-based learning (PBL) and portfolio-based, formative assessment frameworks.

We have created five interdisciplinary pathways that blend the traditional school subjects and embed the learning objectives from the National Curriculum:

The **Personal Exploration** pathway involves individual passion projects and group projects designed by the students with support from their mentors. Learners are guided with leading questions such as: what do you want to do/make/get better at and what problems do you want to solve?

The **Production** pathway creates content for live events such as: a science museum on the human body, a multimedia art exhibition on beauty, a screening of a stop-frame alien animation or a fashion show based on cultural identity.

The **Enterprise** pathway models how to put something useful into the community and encourages students to start an enterprise. They design buildings, spaces or products by exploring industrial and civic design, engineering, robotics and coding.

The **Food** pathway investigates the journey of food from the ground to the plate and waste management. We grow and cook food, find out about the global food trade, nutrition and health. Where possible, we work with the community to form a farmers market and a Community Sustained Agriculture programme.

The **Multiverse Games** pathway uses the robust world-building aspects of role-playing game (RPG) adventures to develop social-emotional learning experiences to explore identity and communication skills in historical settings. Students design characters and their back stories, considering the beliefs, social structures and professions of the time they are in. It is a wonderful team-building exercise that explores a range of life-skills.

These projects are evidenced in digital portfolios and are evaluated by students with support from their peers and mentors. We are developing and evaluating nine core life-skills and 27 sub-skills. We use this same assessment rubric for all our projects, so that students and teachers can explore and develop each skill thoroughly. This is not a competitive framework and there is no pressure to reach mastery in all skills or by a particular age. We are developing the students' ability to evaluate their own strengths and challenges and how to find ways to improve them. Students receive a DVQ (Da Vinci Life-Skills Qualification) and a report in each pathway at the end of each year.

Learners and mentors start each day with a 30 minute 'BE Time' activity, which is a non-judgemental, creative expression time for the students. We follow a different expressive mode each day of the week: visual, movement, sound, silent reflection and storytelling. There are no recorded outcomes from BE Time; it is process-only time for social-emotional development.

Schools can licence the DVLS curriculum on an annual basis for a fixed fee per pupil and a minimum number of mentor feedback sessions with DVLS master mentors. We offer yearly packages, for example a school could deliver our curriculum for their Year 7s to help support the transition to secondary school, or they could continue their licence through to Year 13. Some schools have been interested in running a BE Hub within a school for certain students who are challenged by larger class sizes, or who would benefit from a more creative, entrepreneurial and experiential programme.

We run a BE Hub in Cambridge for the research and development of Biophilic Education and to model our DVLS curriculum and assessment framework for other schools globally. We teach each of our pathways one day a week to enable flexi-learning for home-educated students. For example, a student could attend on Tuesdays and Thursdays to do Production and Multiverse Games projects.

Impact

We have been piloting the DVLS Curriculum at Empathy Middle School (EMS), Bali, Indonesia since January 2022. EMS was a new addition to Empathy Primary School and within our first year we tripled the intake of students and received wonderful feedback from learners, parents and teachers. Learners have been part of co-designing the school rooms and the permaculture garden and have created a monthly farmers market for the local community. We also run a skills share with a large group of local schools to share best teaching practices with NGOs and local social enterprises.

We have found that giving learners more autonomy, encouraging their innate curiosity and sparking their imaginations has increased their engagement and enjoyment of school as well as boosting their confidence, resilience and ability to resolve conflicts.

Some recent feedback and evaluations:

- 'When I fail I want to have that mindset where even if I fail I won't let that affect me and I keep on working to make my project better.' (Aged 14)
- 'I loved to do my PEP because I can do something that I'm more interested in and it's more enjoyable.' (Aged 14)
- 'I'm really excited by what is going on at this school, gosh, I wish I went to a school like this, I'm jealous, you should start an adults' class… we are seeing a positive change in [student]'s attitude… there is more engagement and excitement about school... he's starting to connect more.' (EMS parent)

- 'He liked his American school… but he likes Empathy better. He said he is not afraid to make mistakes at Empathy, which was not the case before.'
(EMS parent)
- 'The absence of the quantitative marks is a breath of fresh air, because sometimes when you give a mark to someone quantitatively, they can be obsessed to score the highest mark by any means necessary and not having that can give some people less anxiety and peace of mind.'
(EMS teacher)

In January 2023, we started a pilot with Chatmore British International School (member of the Council of British International Schools), Bermuda. This too has been a great success. In September 2023, they started delivering the DVLS Curriculum for their high school students. The school founder gave us some very encouraging feedback:

Their curriculum [DVLS] is exactly what we wanted. I'm really excited by what they are doing, it links very nicely into our current curriculum, we are using IPC [International Primary Curriculum] and IGCSE, but this life-skills piece… We are finding our students saying 'This is how I want to learn'.

The Chatmore students, aged 14–18, were extremely positive about trying something new when we worked with them in January 2023. They enjoyed both the BE Time and the projects, in particular designing their own companies, making vegan burgers and going on a RPG adventure in ancient Rome:

- 'I really enjoyed…storytelling because it helped me reflect and think outside the box.'
- 'It gave us time to be creative.'
- 'I was able to use my imagination.'
- 'I enjoyed a pause to listen to nature's sounds.'
- 'The reflection helps me clear my head to start the day in a positive way.'

We are keen for teachers to have more fulfilment in their work and play an active part in the learning process with the students, so we were very encouraged by the Chatmore teachers' feedback:

- 'Students found the geometry in art interesting and it connected them with their landscape and local wildlife. It was clear what the end goal for each *pathway was and this helped students connect their learning with the final goal.'*

- *'Watching the RPG plot unfold was also very interesting... [it] forced the students to think/make decisions on the spot… and together.'*
- *'The Da Vinci pathways offer an opportunity for teachers to bring the practical into their classrooms. The options are varied and at least one would either be suited or be interesting for a student in each classroom.'*

Turning vision into reality

We used the concept of design iteration to build our curriculum. We started with a design brief that questioned what education is for. We stripped the concept back to the beginning: how do we want to educate the young of our species?

We all stem from tribal communities, in which our ancestors sang and danced; adorned themselves; told stories; found, prepared and ate food together; explored the world and solved problems; as well as connected through ceremonies, traditions and spiritual beliefs. Our current education system does not seem to value all the aspects of being human. There is a greater emphasis on knowledge and a mechanistic view of learning and testing, which may not hold its value in a digital future. The digital age presents an opportunity to rethink a system that was designed for an industrial age. When redesigning, it makes sense to hold on to the valuable parts and the things that are working, and rebuild with those pieces, with the creative glue of connectivity, communication and social-emotional wellbeing. We felt that the National Curriculum is an excellent compendium of knowledge, so we coded every learning objective from each subject (Key Stages 1–4). We mapped them onto 40 projects over four years, making sure that there was a scaffolded thread of knowledge and skills that built up in each subject. This was an incredibly complex but rewarding process that we will keep iterating, improving and expanding as we progress. There is so much opportunity to co-create, co-design and co-build with learners, mentors and the community.

Our biggest challenges are changing how the content is delivered and how it is assessed. It is hard to innovate in the restricted environment of memorising exam content, league tables and Ofsted inspections. In secondary schools, teachers tend to stay in their departments and focus on their specialisms and there is a hesitancy to work together, share knowledge and teach a interdisciplinary curriculum. We hope to foster an environment of collaboration and exploration, where teachers are excited to learn with the students and each other. Teachers don't always need to know everything and together they can work out how to find the needed knowledge or skills. If GCSEs hold a general range of knowledge in subjects that are important for every adult to know, then it is a positive thing for all the subject specialist teachers to have that knowledge too.

There is a concern about 'cheating' and fairness in portfolios and course work when the incentives are competitive. We would like to acknowledge that all assessments are inherently unfair and do not reflect the complexity of a person's ability. No one comes to an exam with an equal amount of support or aptitude. We all develop at different rates, some people have the advantage of extra tutoring and others have natural abilities with memory or exam skills. Neurodiversity is a factor that has only recently been interpreted as a gift rather than a disability. In high-stakes competitive educational environments, examiners can be biased in their judgements and grades can vary between different adjudicators. In the workplace, when someone helps you it is considered collaboration. Why then is it cheating in school? Schools and teachers need to be trusted to build reputations of excellence and fairness, so that universities and employers can trust the evidence and reports they receive. We have created a multimodal assessment system that incorporates skill-based course work, low-stakes knowledge testing, and high-value portfolio production that can better evidence the complexity of an individual's ability.

We are advocating for a system of collaboration over competition. Not only do we want to build trust in teachers and students to evaluate their own work, but we also see the opportunities to assess themselves as a way to develop a higher inner standard when it comes to learning. After all, who knows better what is distracting, engaging, motivating and bewildering to a learner than the learner themselves? If learning is to be authentic, then learners themselves need to set goals, determine obstacles, outline strategies and procure resources for their learning. They need to be given the environment to ideate, prototype, try, fail, realise, observe, process, re-approach, iterate, fail again and – through re-iteration, re-processing, and re-creation – finally succeed with great satisfaction, resilience and a growing confidence in their abilities.

Takeaways

- Find real world applications for the knowledge you are teaching to help students know why they need this knowledge. Connecting learning

to local and global issues and enterprises can foster a sense of duty, belonging, community spirit and citizenship.
- Learn alongside your students and let them know how much you can learn from them.
- Find out what each student is interested in, then try to find connections with their interests and what you are teaching them.
- Give students some autonomy and choice in what they learn; allow them to do their own research on topics and follow their own interests.
- Get learners to teach each other. If they each research different topics they can present their work to each other, which also helps support their oracy and public speaking skills.
- Keep the learning exciting by presenting knowledge as an ever-advancing exploration. Students are the explorers of the future and they may uncover new knowledge that changes how we perceive things now.
- Value what students can achieve in collaboration with each other and with professional elders rather than solely what they can do alone.
- Give students some autonomy and choice in how they present their work. Does it always need to be written? Could they evidence their learning in other ways like slideshow presentations, drawing, dance, installation, video or audio recordings?
- Allow for a time in each day where students are not being judged for what they do or make.
- Encourage experimentation and avoid stigmatising mistakes because making mistakes is how we learn.

Editor's reflection on Part 1: Leadership and management – vision and ethos

In this section, the leaders' vision and values, passions and strong sense of purpose have shaped the way that these curricula have been designed and implemented. The case studies are inspiring, optimistic and hopeful. They highlight the importance of working with parents and carers, fostering positive relationships and building partnerships beyond the school grounds as well as an appreciation of heritage and the school's unique context to make learning exciting and relevant.

There is a particular emphasis also on supporting young people to gain the knowledge, self-belief and cultural capital they need to succeed in life. In the Ofsted Handbook, Ofsted says,

> *Our understanding of 'knowledge and cultural capital' is derived from the following wording in the National Curriculum: it is the essential knowledge that pupils need to be educated citizens, introducing them to the best that has been thought and said and helping to engender an appreciation of human creativity and achievement.*
>
> Ofsted Handbook, 2023, point 250

The case studies highlight the importance of creativity, communication and collaboration, and prioritise the co-construction, celebration and future-proofing of outcomes. Cross-curricular links, playfulness, imagination and active learning also feature across these case studies in order to make learning meaningful and memorable. Additional time for PPA, professional development and knowledge transfer between colleagues all help to engage and empower the educators as partners and curriculum co-creators. Thoughtfulness, *slowliness*, risk taking and the courage to borrow from elsewhere and try new ideas are also key elements behind the success of these designs. Moreover, whilst academic skills are important, these are not the only important measures. Through the curriculum, other qualities such as collaboration, empathy, respect, trust, courage, wellbeing and gratitude can be promoted. These attributes serve as a means to revitalise society to one that is imaginative, confident, playful, and fun.

PART 2

Leadership and management – operational excellence

Introduction

Curriculum leadership not only includes vision, ethos, behaviour management, personal development, and producing programmes of study (aspects that have been discussed in the previous section), but it also includes consideration for the day-to-day experience for pupils and all the adults working in the school.

Research shows that the quality of an education system is dependent on the quality of its teachers. School leadership is second only to classroom teaching as an influence on pupil learning. High-quality professional development, effective HR, safe, supportive working conditions, recruitment and induction play an important role in retaining teachers, changing teachers' practices and improving student outcomes.

Staff in any school are its most important and most expensive resource, making up anywhere between 80 and 90 per cent of the revenue budget. Over the years, I have become increasingly aware of the role that good HR plays in ongoing strategic school improvement. HR is complex and challenging, and underpinned by compliance and law. Few school leaders will have time to become as proficient as they need to be in HR as well as being an educator, so it is vital to procure the best HR services possible to ensure processes in the school are managed correctly.

Schools will need to ensure that they have a suite of robust HR policies for performance management, capability, disciplinary, grievance, absence, etc. This is so that all staff are clear about what the expectations are of their role and how they can best individually deliver towards the school's collective aims.

With high rates of staff stress in school due to workload, parental complaints, student welfare and student behaviour, one of the most important policies to put in place is a staff wellbeing policy. Student progress and potential will not be realised if there are no teachers left to teach them.

It has been reported that only 10 per cent of schools have signed up to the Department for Education's Wellbeing Charter (2021), which demonstrates a public commitment to actively promote positive mental health and wellbeing through school policy. This may be because schools have created their own charter or they have effective wellbeing procedures in place already, or it may be that there is insufficient regard for this important issue in some schools. A wellbeing policy is only as good as the actions and ethos that support it. In her excellent book *The Trust Revolution in Schools* (2020), Jeanie Davis sets out a number of practical ideas to implement that will promote a strong sense of trust, belonging, and good psychological safety in schools. This, in turn, will ensure that schools are great places to learn and work in.

Joint professional development is the training that the whole faculty receives, whereas continuous professional development can be tailored to the needs of individuals. To secure successful curriculum implementation it is important to ensure that staff are not overwhelmed by too many competing priorities that they are expected to deliver all at once. Priorities for staff training and delivery should be aligned with the priorities in the school improvement plan, and this can be broken down into a termly operational plan to focus on a smaller number of goals within a shorter timeframe. 'Putting Evidence to Work' is the Education Endowment Foundation's (EEF) guide to school implementation (2019). This sets out six steps for curriculum implementation, in recognition that implementation is a process and not a one-off event.

The first of the six steps is to prepare for change and to ensure that the time and capacity are right in the school so that new initiatives stick and are not seen as just another add-on, at risk of being dropped due to the number of other tasks teachers need to contend with.

Ideally, decisions around staff training will be a combination of what the school needs and what the teacher wants. Currently, a huge amount is expected of teachers, not only to manage and teach a class, but to be subject champions as well, with the knowledge, skills and expertise to write and sequence a programme of study and to also ensure that it is delivered with fidelity to the scheme by other colleagues. Teachers will appreciate not only the opportunity to attend subject-specific training, to ensure they can lead their subject well, but also the time out of class to monitor, evaluate and review how successfully their programme of study is being embedded in the school.

Milton Road Primary School

Teachers at Milton Road Primary School work hard to produce or source well-sequenced schemes of work in their subject area. We publish them on our school website along with the associated policy, vocabulary progression, assessment methodology and the subject-specific adaptions and available provision for pupils with SEND, to ensure that we have an ambitious curriculum for all our pupils.

What has become evident through this process is that the successful delivery of all the subjects is dependent on each teacher following the published progression documents, in a spirit of collective mutuality.

Governors and Trustees play an important role in monitoring the curriculum, including the way that each subject is championed in the school. Most governors are assigned as a link governor to work with subject leaders on a particular area of the curriculum. Governors are volunteers and may not necessarily know how schools work. It can be challenging for them to navigate how schools operate, to understand how the curriculum is organised and to find time to meet and work with subject leads to monitor the implementation and impact of their curriculum area. At Milton Road, we are attempting to overcome these challenges by scheduling at least one 'twilight' teacher meeting per term for all the governors to attend, to meet with staff for tea and cake and to talk with individual teachers about their curriculum area. This will alternate with a morning meeting so that governors can see the school in action and watch lessons being delivered. In addition to visits, every term as part of the Headteacher's Report to the governing board, subject leaders are invited to write a paragraph on their subject under the headings of 'Intention', 'Implementation' and 'Impact'. In this way, we hope, the governors will be able to monitor their subject: the policy, the programme of study and what it looks like in practice.

Along with health and safety, safeguarding is paramount. Safeguarding and protecting the health and welfare of the children is the foundation of the curriculum. The number of different aspects relating to safeguarding and the responsibilities of teachers has increased year-on-year and include duties to: protect children from maltreatment; prevent the impairment of children's mental and physical health or development; ensure children grow up in circumstances consistent with the provision of safe and effective care; and take action to enable all children to have the best possible outcomes.

Ensuring that all staff have received annual training, that they have been appointed through safer recruitment processes, that there is an effective induction process to include information on policies such as the Whistleblower Policy, Lone Working Policy, Acceptable Use of IT Policy and Missing Child Policy (all 2023), is an essential component of overall curriculum leadership. It is also important to ensure that safeguarding and child protection training is not a one-off event but is threaded through the life of the school as part of a school-wide protective ethos.

One of the ways to do this is to ensure that safeguarding and health and safety are a standing item at the top of every meeting agenda. At Milton Road, we hold a team briefing every Friday morning with six key content areas that reflect the strategic and operational work of the school that all staff need to know about, to be updated on or reminded about. These are:

1. Safeguarding and health and safety.
2. Vision, values and ethos.
3. Monitoring, evaluation, recording and reporting.
4. HR and professional development.
5. Events, visits and visitors.
6. Housekeeping.

Another, important aspect in leadership is ensuring that the ethos and practice of the school promotes and ensures inclusion, diversity and equity. Fostering these values ensures that the school not only meets its legal obligation, but is welcoming and responsive and is proactive in ensuring that all children receive the support and resources they need in order to succeed. Over recent years schools have also become better equipped, through training and development, to meet the needs of the children in their care. They are therefore better able to make reasonable adaptions and additions to their practice to support a wide range of social, emotional, health and educational needs.

A note on the case studies

The following five case studies centralise the importance of physical, social, emotional and mental health and wellbeing in school alongside consideration for diversity, equity and inclusion.

The staff in our schools are our most important and valuable resource. Sadly, too many of our skilled, creative and brilliant educators are leaving our profession, with a great number leaving within the first five years after training. More needs to be done about this, both at national level and by individual schools. Teaching is the profession that creates all others, so schools and society need to be more proactive and strategic in order to retain them.

Younger teachers entering the workplace today put a greater priority on their work–life balance and wellbeing, and, rightly, will not tolerate toxic practices. This is excellent for everyone. When leaders prioritise the wellbeing of their colleagues, we create a positive culture and a healthy and happy ethos that is conducive for optimal learning and connection for all: staff, children and families.

One of the most simple but effective techniques that schools can implement is to draw together a Wellbeing Charter listing the working conditions and opportunities available to staff. I first heard about such an idea from Jonny Uttley, CEO of The Education Alliance and co-author of *Putting Staff First: A blueprint for revitalising our schools* (2020). Like the one we have at Milton Road Primary School, a Wellbeing Charter could include a number of elements such as:

- a warm, supportive, kind and caring whole-school culture and ethos
- free teas, coffee and milk
- protected PPA time that can be taken at home
- supportive professional development and access to training and other opportunities, including national professional qualifications
- a yearly planner with clearly publicised deadlines

- a supportive feedback policy to make marking purposeful and manageable
- leadership release time
- additional time given for marking assessments
- limited number of data drops
- a wellbeing and social team
- a trained mental health lead
- an employee assistance programme
- access to a free wellbeing app
- supportive line management
- a buddy system for new colleagues
- a staff handbook
- a suite of HR policy documents
- an open-door policy
- twice yearly check-ins with the headteacher
- on-site car and bike parking
- low stress approach to lesson observations, book looks and drop-ins
- family-friendly approach for colleagues to attend their own children's performances, concerts, university open days, graduations etc.
- consultation and involvement in school organisation and curriculum design
- lots of laughter, friendship and the occasional slice of homemade cake.

All staff, teachers, assistant teachers, office colleagues, site managers or any employee working anywhere for that matter, want to feel seen and valued and that they belong, and above all that their unique contribution makes a difference and is appreciated.

The following five case studies emphasise the importance of relationships, inclusion, diversity and social and global justice and have been co-constructed with colleagues so that the curriculum is meaningful and sustainable for everyone in the school's community.

6 A curriculum of PRIDE
CHRISTOPHER HARRISON

School Name	Grove Road Community Primary School
Age group taught within school	3–11
Location of school	Central Harrogate, North Yorkshire
Any distinguishing features	- Including English, there are 25 different languages spoken by our learners.
- We were the first North Yorkshire school to obtain 'School of Sanctuary' status.
- Approximately 24 per cent of our pupils are 'disadvantaged' and 29 per cent of our children have special educational needs and/or disabilities. We have an on-site, eight-place Targeted Mainstream Provision (TMP) to enable the school to support children with complex communication and interaction needs, in a custom-built extension to the school.
- We are a THRIVE school, which means that all staff have received training on a whole-school approach based on neuroscience, attachment theory, child development and their implications.

Intent of the curriculum

Curriculum statement: Our philosophy of learning, delivered through our broad and rich Grove Road Curriculum, creatively embraces the essence of our vision to instil in our children the knowledge, skills and values to be happy, confident, independent and successful lifelong learners.

Our PRIDE characteristics are the foundations of our curriculum and underpin what we believe makes a child happy, healthy and ready to learn. With these, children are able and willing to engage with the PRIME areas and, in turn, will be able to access the subject specialisms. Every child has the right to a fun, exciting, experience-led education that inspires, challenges and supports them in equal measure. The PRIDE characteristics, PRIME areas and subject specialisms are all interconnected and influence each other.

Our curriculum model encourages pupils to make discoveries, to be excited and to want to find out more. Learning is personalised and achievements are recognised and celebrated. The emphasis is on the development of skills and understanding and on encouraging learners to investigate and expand their subject knowledge through a range of activities designed for the individual. Our entire curriculum is underpinned by our PRIDE values, the core foundations of our school, and these are the key building blocks that we believe enable children to thrive in their learning.

Figure 6: *PRIDE characteristics, PRIME areas and subject specialisms at Grove Road*

PRIDE characteristics
Passion: Think big, dig deep and aim high. We have ambition to achieve our goals.
Resilience: We show 'grit' and a determination to succeed.
Intrepidity: We are brave and bold; we dare to seek challenge.
Dependability: We seek out opportunities to prove ourselves to be honest, trustworthy and responsible.
Empathy: As a team, we support each other – working together and looking after each other with kindness and understanding.

PRIME areas
Developing an identity
Exploring morals and values
Oracy and debate
Emotional regulation
Physical literacy
Problem-solving and creative thinking
Feedback and solution

Subject specialisms
We are *readers*
We are *writers*
We are *mathematicians*
We are *scientists*
We are *geographers*
We are *historians*
We are *artists*
We are *musicians*
We are *designers and creators*
We are *physically literate*
We are *digital leaders*
We are *philosophers*
We are *linguists*
We are *safe and respectful citizens*

Figure 7: *Maslow's hierarchy of needs*

This has been built with reference to Maslow's hierarchy of needs, where an individual must be supported holistically in order to develop higher order skills.

Once children have developed their PRIDE characteristics, they can then access the PRIME areas, which are broken down into key phases and sections in line with 'Development Matters' (DfE, 2020, revised 2023).

Each PRIME area is explored in detail in each phase (Early Years pupils work within Development Matters) and has been broken down into: what a unique child should be able to do at that age and stage; what adults can do and provide based on the positive relationships they maintain with the children; and how the school environments will facilitate this. Each of the seven PRIME areas is broken down further into phases, such as in the example on the following page.

Table 2: PRIDE characteristics broken down by PRIME areas

A Unique Child	Positive Relationships	Enabling Environments	Learning and Development
Every child is a unique child who is constantly learning and can be resilient, capable, confident and self-assured. **Practitioners:** - understand and observe each child's development and learning, assess progress, plan for next steps - support babies and children to develop a positive sense of their own identity and culture - identify any need for additional support - keep children safe - value and respect all children and families equally.	Children learn to be strong and independent through positive relationships. **Positive relationships are:** - warm and loving, and foster a sense of belonging - sensitive and responsive to the child's needs, feelings and interests - supportive of the child's own efforts and independence - consistent in setting clear boundaries - stimulating - built on key person relationships in Early Years settings.	Children learn and develop well in enabling environments, in which their experiences respond to their individual needs and there is a strong partnership between practitioners and parents and carers. **Enabling environments:** - value all people - value learning. **They offer:** - stimulating resources, relevant to all the children's cultures and communities - rich learning opportunities through play and playful teaching - support for children to take risks and explore.	Children develop and learn in different ways. The framework covers the education and care of all children in Early Years provision, including children with special educational needs and disabilities. Practitioners teach children by ensuring challenging, playful opportunities across the prime and specific areas of learning and development. **They foster the characteristics of effective early learning:** - playing and exploring - active learning - creating and thinking critically.

Table 3: PRIME areas broken down by Key Stage phases

Oracy and Debate			
Phase	The Unique Child: What does 'healthy' look like?	Positive Relationships: What can adults do and provide?	Enabling Environments: How does the school environment support this?
KS1	Children can speak clearly and in full sentences, reflecting on the listener's actions and changing their delivery accordingly (e.g. challenging the listener if they are not showing good listening skills). They will track the speaker and they understand how to take turns within conversations in pairs or groups. Children can voice their opinions and are starting to recognise that others may have different opinions from their own. They can listen to points made by others and can ask subsequent questions to seek clarity in the points being made.	Adults will plan regular opportunities to discuss and share ideas within lessons on a daily basis. 'Talk time' will be clearly valued and every point made will be heard in full and respected. Kagan structures (2015) will be introduced throughout the school year, building up a bank talking strategies within the cohort, alongside regular use and modelling of stem sentences.

Adults will model standard English at all times and will sensitively encourage children to speak in full sentences. Phonics lessons and interventions will be used to support children with accurate phoneme pronunciation. | Stem sentences will be clearly displayed and overtly modelled within the classroom environment. All adults within the environment will scaffold standard English. Key vocabulary and spellings within topic foci will be clearly displayed and referred to on a regular basis. |

A curriculum of PRIDE

Table 3 *continued*

Oracy and Debate			
LKS2	Children can speak fluently, reflecting on the listener's actions and changing their delivery accordingly (e.g. challenging the listener if they are not showing good listening skills or projecting their voice more when speaking in front of a larger audience). They will track the speaker and use their body language, such as nodding or smiling, to encourage the speaker to continue without interruption. They understand how to take turns within conversations in pairs or groups. With support, children are beginning to share their own ideas and thoughts while sensitively listening to and challenging those from their peers. They can discuss contentious items as a pair or a group with some support.	Opportunities will be used to discuss and debate preferences within the classroom (e.g. what would you like to play on the ball court today?). Kagan structures (2015) will be used to facilitate paired and group conversations and debates alongside repeated use of stem sentences. Adults will model standard English at all times, often asking children to extend their thinking using conjunctions to clarify and explain their meaning.	Stem sentences will be clearly displayed and overtly modelled within the classroom environment. All adults within the environment will scaffold standard English. Key vocabulary and spellings within topic foci will be clearly displayed and referred to on a regular basis.

Table 3 *continued*

Oracy and Debate			
UKS2	Children can clearly articulate or present their thoughts, opinions and ideas and can reflect on how their life experience might lead to them having certain dispositions or stereotypes. They are able to change their communication strategies accordingly based on the group they are talking to (e.g. pairs, whole class etc.) and they are beginning to experiment with the tone, speed and volume of their voice when addressing others. They can sensitively and clearly challenge viewpoints they disagree with and they will listen to and reflect on challenges made to their own thoughts and ideas.	Adults will plan regular opportunities to discuss and share ideas within lessons on a daily basis. A broad range of Kagan structures will be in place and used at regular intervals throughout the teaching process with increasing levels of independence from the children. Debate club will be offered to facilitate deeper debates and scaffolding to support these, tracked by 'debate webs'.	Debates and discussions will be actively encouraged within the classroom and school culture / environment.

Implementation

Our Curriculum of PRIDE has grown organically with input from the whole staff team. Initially, we had key documentation for our subject specialisms, such as reading and geography, but these were inconsistent across subjects and some were clearer and more user-friendly than others. At this point, we introduced four key documents and formats:

1. Curriculum statements to clarify the intent of that curriculum area and focus staff acutely on how that area of the curriculum sits within the bigger picture. For example:

   Reading
   Our reading curriculum rests on the foundations of diverse, inclusive book spines that are used as windows for our children to gaze on wonderful new worlds, doors for our children to enter magical new environments and mirrors within which our children can see themselves. Decoding, including the use of phonic skills, is equally weighted with comprehension and we ensure that our children master the mechanical aspects of reading while developing and refining their understanding of what they have read.

2. Subject flowcharts to support staff with delivering lessons consistently while supporting pedagogical creativity.
3. Long-term overviews to clearly illustrate the curriculum sequencing to support staff with planning, coverage and avoiding unnecessary repetition, while supporting the development of a consistent, aligned curriculum offer.
4. Medium-term planning templates to support staff with planning in a consistent, low-maintenance format that could be handed over to future teachers.

As we started to accumulate these core documents, we concluded that there was nothing underpinning and binding these curriculum areas together into one simple, coherent format that truly met the needs of the community we serve. At this point, we went back to our school's PRIDE values: passion, resilience, intrepidity, dependability and empathy. These had been successfully introduced the previous year and the children and staff had really bonded with them. It was, therefore, logical to place these at the centre of our curriculum model. Alongside this, we were also looking for ways to integrate the fantastic resources put together by THRIVE and ReflectED as they are key cornerstones of our curriculum offer. At this point, the 'PRIME areas' started to form. With my Early Years background, I have always prioritised children's characteristics of learning and underpinning dispositions. Suddenly, here was the opportunity to deliver that in a meaningful way. Thus, the Curriculum of PRIDE model was formed as an umbrella to encompass all our curriculum work so far.

Across each phase of school, teachers pulled this core curriculum guidance together using a thematic approach to planning, putting together long-term curriculum overviews and half-termly/termly topic webs that advocate creativity, cross-curricular learning and active engagement. We share these with families via the school website to support them in joining their children on their learning journey.

Each topic web is centred on a theme or topic that teachers believe will attract their pupils' imaginations and interests, creating a way in for various areas of the curriculum. Topic webs incorporate a 'Stunning Start' and 'Fabulous Finish'. A 'Stunning Start' is a launch event, often rooted in suspended belief, which engages children in their learning: a focal point for the sequence of teaching that leads to multiple learning opportunities and avenues for investigation. This might include a spaceship crash landing, a letter from the local MP, a special visitor or an archaeological find. A 'Fabulous Finish' is a finale to a sequence of learning that creates purpose and closure to the children's learning, such as a performance assembly where visitors are invited, writing to the prime minister or running a campaign to raise money for the World Wildlife Fund in order to protect wild animals. This format is strongly underpinned by the work of Debra Kidd and Hywel Roberts in their book *Uncharted Territories* (2018).

Creativity and fun in planning for learning is a priority to ensure learning is enjoyable, active and challenging. The social, moral, spiritual and cultural aspects of learning are taken into account, ensuring teaching reflects and celebrates our cultural diversity as a school.

Impact

As a school we have removed formal observations in favour of a number of Paul Garvey's *Talk for Teaching* strategies (2017) as a way of measuring and tracking impact via staff development and monitoring.

This includes:

- teacher-led learning walks and self-evaluation reporting forms (SERFs)
- Twenty20 teaching
- IRIS Champions and film club
- TeachMeets
- pupil voice surveys.

For further details on these strategies please refer to the personal professional development (PPD): Talk for Teaching document available on www.groveroad.n-yorks.sch.uk/teaching-and-learning/staff-professional-development.

All monitoring is mirrored by in-house CPD that celebrates success and gives opportunities to use research-informed strategies to unpick next steps shared with the team. A two-year monitoring cycle is in place alongside a two-year CPD cycle so growth can be facilitated and tracked over time.

We store all our key subject specialism documents online, alongside banks of videos that demonstrate high quality teaching and provision across school. These clips are curated and quality assured by subject leaders before being uploaded (with the permission of the recorded teacher). This bank of quality assured videos will continue as a live document that can be added to throughout the academic year as subject leaders refine their field of expertise. This will, in time, create a bespoke curriculum platform that showcases high-quality teaching across the school over time and can be used to further develop curriculum areas and the pedagogy, subject leadership and curriculum design that underpin our Curriculum of PRIDE.

Via these monitoring systems alongside external scrutiny from our local authority, THRIVE and various other agencies, we have been able to reflect on the impact of our curriculum model in a range of areas:

- Teaching is consistent across the school due to supportive monitoring and subsequent CPD, clear documentation and support, including videos.
- Staff are able to use their planning time more creatively due to the availability of a clear curriculum model.
- Staff have ownership of the curriculum model and actively engage in developing and personalising the systems over time.
- The curriculum is interconnected and children are seeing more benefit from making links in their learning.

- Stunning Starts and Fabulous Finishes have had a significant impact on pupil buy-in while providing opportunities to develop cultural capital.
- Subject leaders have a better overview of their respective curriculum areas and can signpost quality teaching easily via our online platform.
- Families are more actively involved in their children's learning journeys via the topic webs and the learning platform Seesaw.
- Handover between subject leaders is quick and easy due to mirroring of core document formats and clarity of subject specialism curriculum statements.
- New staff and those new to phase integrate quicker and make quicker progress in their teaching due to the ease of access to supportive documents alongside a supportive monitoring structure.

Turning vision into reality

Our Curriculum of PRIDE was launched in the September just before Covid-19 struck. We managed to move many of our monitoring systems onto our remote CPD and monitoring platform, but it really impacted on the growth and personalisation of our curriculum model. The initial delivery of the PRIDE model went very well and was recorded so all new staff, support staff and Governors could have access to it as well. The session was also delivered in a Governing Body meeting so the school Governors have a comprehensive understanding of the model in place. This has been further reinforced by involving the Governors in the monitoring cycle by partaking in learning walks and providing access to the IRIS Curriculum groups online.

The greatest challenge with introducing any whole-school change is maintaining clarity in a large system while ensuring there is buy-in from all staff involved. Messages had to be delivered clearly and staff were involved in every step of the creative process. Subject leaders have grown their curricular understanding and pedagogical awareness throughout the process, however our online monitoring – as strong as it was – was not as strong as all the in-person support offered in 'normal' times.

Removing formal observations had a huge impact on staff buy-in with regard to the monitoring cycle. The changes here have also given staff more ownership of the process, further supporting the drive for self-efficacy across school. It has also created a more sustainable and, in our professional opinions, a more accurate view of our curriculum and staff development over time.

Embedding the PRIDE values was critical before the model was pulled together, but it would have been good to have the overview before the team started to build the key documentation for their respective subject specialism leadership areas. This would have created a more consistent, level starting point within the creative process while highlighting that everything was building on the values that put children at the heart of everything we do in school. It was also challenging at times to find ways to interweave pre-made curriculum resources that we had already paid for. In hindsight, it is better to find models that suit your curriculum, not the other way around. This can also be said for assessment tools, as your assessment strategies need to sit well alongside your vision, values and ethos within and across your curriculum model. We are now at a point where this is working much more fluidly, but it has taken a good deal of trial and error to find the right balance for our cohorts and context.

We are currently unpicking how we can really personalise the offer that sits within our long-term subject curriculum overviews. While it is increasingly diverse, our curriculum does not yet fully reflect or represent the local, national or global communities that we proudly serve. We fully commit to Dr Rudine Sims Bishop's (1990) metaphor of books being windows, mirrors and sliding glass doors, however we aim to take this further with our curriculum. All children have a right to feel seen, heard, respected and loved within their learning journeys and it is our duty, as educators, to make this happen.

Takeaways

- The whole staff team should be involved in the creation of a curriculum.
- Curricula are fluid documents and should grow and change to reflect your current cohort.
- Every member of staff in school needs to understand the curriculum model and how the school values are represented through it, to support consistency and clarity.
- A clear, consistent, robust curriculum model can save a lot of time for teaching staff throughout the course of an academic year.
- A high-challenge, high-support, low-threat monitoring cycle is critical alongside the introduction and implementation of any large-scale change in schools.
- Governors should be heavily involved in schools' monitoring cycles.

7 A curriculum that sparkles
CRAIG CHAPLIN AND PHILIPPA ROLLINS

School Name	Fortuna Primary
Age group taught within school	5–11
Location of school	East Midlands
Any distinguishing features	• Primary special school for pupils with SEMH needs. • Whole-school 'nurture' approach. • Pupils are placed in the school once they have an EHCP and very few actually attend all the way through (the average is just over two years).

Intent of the curriculum

As a special school for pupils with social, emotional and mental health (SEMH) needs, many of our pupils have been unable to fully access the curriculum in their previous educational settings. This may have meant working on a one-to-one basis outside of the classroom, following a bespoke and sometimes reduced or off-curriculum timetable, attending short-term alternative provision or, for some pupils, permanent exclusion resulting in them not attending school for some time.

On top of these experiences, many of our pupils' ability to access the curriculum is impacted by trauma and insecure attachment, developmental delay, neurodivergence and specific learning difficulties.

In combination, our pupils' needs and prior experiences frequently (although not always) lead to them arriving with a poorly established and sometimes negative perspective of themselves and, indeed, schools as institutions.

At the core of our curriculum intent is the ability to engage individual learners with a skills-based and immersive curriculum that places the children at the centre of their learning. An essential component of this is the inclusion of 'sparkles' in the delivery of our curriculum.

For us, sparkles are the additional value-added elements that engage learners by making them feel considered and valued through the curriculum. Sparkles go above and beyond what is expected but, in the specific case of our cohorts, are required. Our aim is that these sparkles sit alongside pedagogical considerations to ensure the curriculum is awe-inspiring, captures our children's imaginations, provokes their curiosity and sticks with them as an experience. Learners in our school should feel delighted and invested in as young people. They should feel that the sparkles we provide are something they deserve to have. They should feel highly valued as service users.

As a whole-school nurture setting, a key consideration of our intent was to consider the underlying knowledge, skills and understanding that should precede the primary stage curriculum specification – the social and developmental milestones as well as the basic needs of learners. In any school it should not be assumed that all pupils arrive prepared to learn and access the curriculum. Therefore, our intent is also to ensure our children are equipped and prepared to be learners.

Implementation

We have taken an iterative approach to curriculum development, drawing on a range of approaches that we have trialled, adapted and embedded to create an effective amalgamation of what works well for us. Over the last 10 years, we have explored visual literacy, immersive learning and real-life projects to enhance and engage pupils in their learning. Learning is tangible and contextualised as much as possible.

Central to our approach is the view that we are a learning organisation. There can be many trends in education, and we as a staff have remained mindful of the need to carefully consider the merit and impact of what we adopt and just as importantly what we choose not to adopt. Central to this is the need to understand the 'why?' of what we do or don't do.

An example of understanding the 'why?' is our approach to having immersive classrooms. In our original implementation, whole classrooms would become rainforests, Egyptian tombs, or disaster zones. It looked amazing but took a lot of resource, time and effort. After some reflection we scaled this back to having an immersive area along one side of the classroom and discovered this engaged the children just as well and created more space (and less visual noise) to effectively showcase children's work using learning walls.

A key consideration of how we implement our curriculum has always been how we create a 'golden thread' to show the interconnectedness of subjects. Like many schools, we had previously driven our curriculum through themes which were usually related to science or one of the foundation subjects. However, school data showed that, despite our efforts, this did not produce the progress in reading that we would have hoped for and it was felt that, as a key component of learning, this had an impact on learning across the curriculum.

As stated in Ofsted's The Reading Framework (2023), 'pupils who find it difficult to learn to read are likely to struggle across the curriculum, since English is both a subject in its own right and the medium for teaching' (page 4). It goes on to say 'whatever pupils' socio-economic background, making sure that they become engaged with reading from the beginning is one of the most important ways to make a difference to their life chances' (page 12).

We have therefore shifted to a curriculum that is book/author led and spans across all subject areas where meaningful links can be made – care had to be taken not to force everything to connect through tentative or arbitrary links. This required careful consideration of how the curriculum was mapped, which was led by our Teaching and Learning middle leader and a senior leader with previous curriculum design experience. A team of two is still a rather small team, however, and there were opportunities to engage with subject leaders and consultants, who added additional experience and perspective to the design of our curriculum.

Like any school, our staff demographics change over time and include everything from Early Career Teachers to staff who have seen 20 or 30 years of curriculum development. Ensuring that our plans included banks of ideas, signposted useful resources and made use of prior learning was therefore an essential aspect of our curriculum design. Making overt what we have already learnt is effective in our curriculum mapping means that this learning can be maintained over time and benefit those at the earliest stages of their careers. This learning is not fixed, however, and can evolve and develop over time as we learn more as educators.

Alongside our academic curriculum sits what is colloquially referred to as our 'play curriculum'. Within our school day all pupils, regardless of age, have opportunities to engage in social and developmental play. The school uses formal developmental assessments (Nurture UK's Boxall Profile) for all pupils to identify developmental and behaviour vulnerabilities that can impact learning and curriculum access. Through a progressive play curriculum, which shows consideration of children's developmental, attachment and trauma experience needs, children can then secure the developmental milestones that are prerequisites for learning to take place. This can range from learning to connect experiences to engaging cognitively with others.

Impact

Impact can often be viewed through a narrow lens in education. When we restrict our understanding of impact to attainment data and pupil's results, we do our school communities a disservice. To paraphrase the nineteenth-century American academic Henry Adams, a teacher's influence is eternal and boundless.

Our curriculum within a nurturing culture and with its sparkles communicates a sense of professional care that all children should experience. The vast majority of our pupils and parents report a newfound love of coming to our school, a sense of belonging and feeling considered. This is supported by the school's attendance data, which has been significantly above the local and national averages for many years, and is more comparable with mainstream primary schools.

As pupils begin to engage with the curriculum, they develop an improved sense of being a learner, their self-esteem improves, and they become more resilient to the challenges of learning. This begins to extend beyond the boundaries of the school grounds and term time. Over time, this allows our young people to make the academic progress that has previously eluded many of them. As a result, they develop a sense of school being an inclusive, caring, nurturing, safe space where they can prosper. Education gains value and hopefully this not only improves the future life chances of our pupils, but also generates an intergenerational effect if they go on to become parents themselves.

As a special school, it is important to be mindful that the complexity of a pupil's needs can impact their rate of progress. We have, therefore, created a bespoke target setting approach that uses a baseline assessment to establish an average rate of prior progress, which can then be used to inform future target setting based on an anticipated rate of accelerated progress.

Due to children starting at the school at different stages of their primary education, the impact of the school's approach can also relate to how long children have attended the school. While school data would indicate that there is a positive benefit for all pupils, generally there is a greater benefit both academically and developmentally for those attending for more than two years.

A key consideration when developing our school curriculum was the impact on staff wellbeing. As with many schools, workload has been highlighted as a concern when staff have been surveyed, although we compare favourably to national averages. Using regular monitoring, a workload action group and a wellbeing lens through which to view curriculum change, we have sought to ensure that our curriculum has a positive impact on staff wellbeing. The impact of this is that we have dropped or adapted workload that was inefficient or did not create enough value (this can be ambiguous and needs to be carefully considered) to warrant the work from staff. Adding sparkles does not have to be time consuming and we have crafted our plans to shift some of the time spent on planning and research onto crafting high-quality resources, organising events and creating immersive experiences.

Turning vision into reality

The decision to change our curriculum was a risk, as the one previously in place was recognised as strong and effective and was well understood by staff. This decision was grounded in our desire to get the most from our curriculum and ensure it was delivered in the most holistic way possible for the pupils we serve. We therefore started with a rationale for change that took a deep look at what the intent of our curriculum truly needed to be.

Change can be hard to navigate and requires a degree of re-learning, and new learning takes time and energy. There was, therefore, a conscious effort to ensure the teaching staff understood the rationale for our curriculum intent by considering it from the specific context of our school. The head of school, Hannah Keegan, led an INSET day where all the staff were given the ingredients to make themselves an ice cream sundae and, once finished, they each shared their creations. There was then reflection on why nobody had just chosen plain vanilla ice cream. Time was then spent discussing whether vanilla was enough for our pupils or if they needed more due to their specific needs and prior experiences.

The school's Teaching and Learning middle leader worked alongside the senior leadership team and subject leaders to ensure that there was a guiding coalition with a clear vision of what we were setting out to achieve as a school. Having a clear vision of what we wanted facilitated clear inputs, although some subject leads recognised that they required subject-specific CPD to ensure they could advocate for best practice in their areas. This was particularly pertinent following on from the Covid-19 pandemic, when subject leader development had fallen down our list of priorities.

In parallel to this, the school established a child development middle leadership position who worked alongside the senior leadership team and a play therapist to design a play curriculum related to the developmental stages provided in Nurture UK's Boxall Profile. Much like the work on the academic curriculum, this work was iterative and is seen as an ongoing work in progress that becomes more refined over time.

A key consideration across both work streams has been ensuring that we develop streamlined and efficient systems of working that do not create unnecessary workload. This requires regular evaluation and a genuine learning culture. Our curriculum will be refined and evolve over time, adaptations will be made and sometimes decisions we have made won't go the way we expected. Middle leaders and senior leaders ask questions because they are generally intrigued to hear the answers and are not stubbornly tied to previous decisions if new information indicates the need for change. We can try something and either keep it, change it or bin it depending on what we have learnt as professionals. We use SWOT analysis (Strengths, Weaknesses, Opportunities and Threats) after each term to evaluate the curriculum to structure this process.

As is likely to be the case with any curriculum development, deciding how prescriptive to be was a key consideration. Finding a balance between rigidly setting out what to do and allowing room for individual creativity was carefully considered. In both our academic and play curricula there are suggested activities that can be delivered as written or adapted to suit the needs of a class. Our aim was to support as much with the upfront, standard work of planning to allow more time for staff to be creative around the core learning and add those sparkles.

Takeaways

- Consider national and statutory guidance relating to the curriculum as a universal starting point for curriculum design, not the limit of it.
- Ensure time is spent considering what developmental and social skills are required for learners to engage with your curriculum. Ensuring pupils can attend to a teacher or member of support staff, for example, should be a priority.
- Consider the 'why' of what you are doing – the answer should be that it enhances teaching and learning within an established and shared culture.
- Make sure that your curriculum is data-informed – this should not just be assessment and obtainment data; it should also include pupil and staff views. This should be collected regularly to monitor impact over time.
- Having a framework such as a SWOT analysis can help evaluate the curriculum and develop it over time.
- When leading change, make use of appropriate change management models (Kotter's 8 Steps for Leading Change is a useful framework).
- Ensure there are efforts to maintain and sustain organisational learning, through clear documentation, succession planning and regular CPD opportunities.

Tools and resources

Anna Freud Centre Wellbeing Measurement Tool for Schools – useful for measuring impact of change on staff wellbeing
www.annafreud.org/resources/schools-and-colleges/wellbeing-measurement-framework-for-schools

Nurture UK's Boxall Profile – Tool for assessing developmental gaps that could impact learning
https://new.boxallprofile.org/#how

Kotter's 8 Steps – A summary of Kotter's 8 Steps to Change framework
www.kotterinc.com/methodology/8-steps

SWOT Analysis – A summary of how to use the SWOT analysis framework
www.investopedia.com/terms/s/swot.asp

8 Intentional inclusion = conscious curricula
NICOLE PONSFORD

> **Nicole Ponsford**, FRSA is the co-founder and CEO of the Global Equality Collective, whose mission is to give organisations and schools all they need to break their own new ground in diversity, equity and inclusion.

Intent of the curriculum

The curriculum is the beating heart of teaching and learning in our schools. Not only is it how we measure achievement, but it the means by which our students learn about themselves – and others – 195 days a year. As an examiner, Head of School, Head of Department and school improvement coach, I know the intent of the curriculum is to help us recognise student attainment (in all guises), but it goes way beyond this – the curricula we design will not only shape our learners' sense of self but well beyond school life and in our society as a whole.

If we can agree that the intent of your curriculum is to bring *new knowledge* to your students so they understand their identity and place in the world, develop the cognitive skills and abilities they need today and for their future – and to support society in moving forwards – your curriculum needs to be intentionally inclusive.

By designing a curriculum full of 'mirrors and windows' (Styles, 1988) for all our students, we can enable and empower them to be without barriers, hateful beliefs and restrictive stereotypes; in other words, the person *they can be* if you ensure your curriculum is designed with them in mind.

Knowing where you want your curriculum to go is very important.

You need to do this before you start work on the actual curriculum. Being able to articulate your curriculum choices and the thinking that got you to your final decisions is good practice, so a well thought through and strategic curriculum, which teaches content in a sequential and meaningful way, should be part of your curriculum design conversation.

So, how do you embed equity into the curriculum, so it is at once authentic, accessible and evidence-driven? Easy. Identify and then understand your 'why'. Use these levers to create your bespoke roadmap, your conscious curriculum.

Implementation

How do you deal with the complexity that is intersectionality?

How do you recognise differing identities in our curricula from a historic point of view, and ensure this fits with your curriculum roadmap?

How do you take a strategic approach to inclusion that both understands your school culture and the curriculum?

Take a breath. This is tricky – but necessary – stuff. Take away any big 'buts' you have and reflect on why you *wouldn't* bring equity into your lessons and DEI (Diversity, Equity and Inclusion) into your curriculum. For some the 'why' is pioneering, simply facing towards our next 100 years of formalised education. For others, it seems an unending can of worms. However, isn't it time we risked feeling a bit uncomfortable in order to get it right from the start? We start with the facts.

Culture is the first factor to bring in here.

DEI in education is all about infrastructure and culture – the culture of inspections, qualifications, politics and a whole pile of messy and distracting elements that can derail even the most passionate of champions. As a result, teachers and curricula can often be on the back foot when matching school demographics with the current imposed traditional curriculum content and individual teaching and learning design in schools. Ultimately, what do your school leaders want when it comes to inclusion in the curriculum? If the culture of your school is not inclusive, if it is not welcoming and equality is not wanted, if accessibility is not at the core of your vision and values, the odds are that curriculum decisions and budget will not be too.

Don't DIY your DEI

Equip yourself first. Understand your school's infrastructures and systems: leadership that can support key decisions; teachers who are trained and knowledgeable; designated funding; accessible tools; and clear delivery methods – with a twist of flexibility thrown in to take risks in order to improve.

Plan > Do > Review > Assess > Repeat

The first step, therefore, is making sure your *system* is just that – a series of working parts – which will help all stakeholders get this right.

Then look to your curriculum through a whole-organisation improvement lens. Reflective approaches, like the GROW coaching model (Sir John Wittmore, 1992), can support this or be a means to capture leadership, staff and student voice.

Next, look to gain incremental steps through a solid action plan (based on evidence). Create the tracks you want this to run on and drive your school towards that culture and curriculum of inclusion and belonging you know it deserves. This includes understanding the lived experience of your stakeholders, their privileges and disadvantages (or opportunities!) and how those will work alongside the current curriculum. Next, use a needs analysis or audit which includes support staff and students as well as curriculum staff, to find where you intend your curriculum to sit.

Then we look to the experts for learning. Who? Your leadership is probably not as diverse as you would like, so there will be gaps in their understanding and privilege, which leads to bias and inequitable decisions. Academic research, when it comes to DEI, is sparse and ill-informed. Current intersectional academic evidence and research is barely existent. The literature out there is only just starting to use technology to understand intersectionality at scale. While it does, we can dig merely a few demographic factors deep; nothing like the complex lived experience that we know our students understand. Therefore, listening to those with lived experiences and speaking to experts can empower dynamic curriculum design. From this you can create bespoke and personalised curriculum models based on your unique school demographics.

Impact

Once you have this information, you can move to the 'what' and 'how'. You can look at hyperdiversity and how to *utilise* it. You can bring in demographic diversity, cognitive/neurodiversity and cultural diversity. From accessible technology for all learners, to role models that represent your families, to curricula that represent your global majority stakeholders, you will build a curriculum that represents the diversity and inclusion in your setting. You will create a curriculum that supports a sense of belonging for your students. In doing so:

- This will engage students in the curriculum as they see themselves and their lives represented.
- This can also improve attendance as the curriculum becomes relevant to your learners.
- It promotes critical thinking for your students (and staff!).
- Improves career progression with a subject-based curriculum that identifies the needs and interests of your students, alongside understanding structural issues.
- Wider stakeholders like families and external teams will be supportive of this design, due to inclusion of SEND provision or anti-discrimination approaches.
- Your setting will be safer – disclosures from students around DEI can come from diverse curricula but can now be supported by professionals.

DEI needs to be based on the lived experiences of the school's demographics so you can identify the gaps and opportunities to bring in new knowledge (which is what the curriculum ultimately is, right?). Ensuring evidence leads your action and drives change means that you have a foundation to build your road map and can be confident that you are on the right track to create exciting and engaging lessons, making school an exciting and safer place – where everyone belongs.

Turning vision into reality

There will be resistance to change from some, complaints of being time-poor and under-funded. However, creating a curriculum that is conscious in its intent to include more students and close equity gaps will change your system. It will challenge attendance data, it will encourage subject engagement and it will future-proof your vision and values. Time wasted in catch-up, low-level behaviour issues, parental complaints (at best) and not keeping the best interests of your students at heart is the alternative path.

When any system improves and changes, there will be old-fashioned rebukes – dead wood who deny 'change is good' – so expect pushback from some. This might be based on creating new content for lessons, or the political or cultural challenges that diversity and inclusion can bring to the surface. Get ready to be uncomfortable.

However, relying on your data, evidence and voices from within your organisation can illustrate and drive change. Be open to a system of change: offer opportunities for staff and families to understand and also gain ownership by co-designing your next steps. Allow reflective periods to assess and take stock of what is working at this point, what needs flexing, or promoting – or binning. Bring a growth mindset to the process of redesigning a curriculum with intent. For that *is* the intention.

The schools and Trust that I work with know that organisational change takes two or three years. When it comes to curriculum reform, it can help to take sections as a starting point, such as an initial year group or subject, and then make improvements each year. Having designated (and valued) members of staff to lead on this, and others to review and offer professional development both within and outside of your organisation, can help identify any problem areas or additional opportunities. This could include creating better equality in your sports provision, supporting all learners with exam provision or careers advice based on your subject. It could be working more directly with exam boards or your trust. It could be by diversifying your textbooks or bringing in a more diverse student workshop or guest speakers. Whatever it is, it must be conscious and intentional. *This* is what will help you rise from the pitfalls and turn problems into opportunities. Every time.

Takeaways

- Curriculum data – how does this personify the demographics of your school and help improve curriculum design (and for whom)?
- Staff voice – from curriculum staff to support teams and wider staff, how can they all support conscious curriculum design?
- Student voice – how do you understand student voice when it comes to the curriculum?
- Individuals in the curriculum – key historical figures, local role models, core texts and class reading books can all help expand the indirect observed lived experiences and cultural capital of your staff and students.

- Wider curriculum – bring in data to understand the reach and impact of the demographics of your students and understand what you are making accessible and to whom.
- Assistive Technology (AT) – how are you using AT to support curriculum access and understanding to all of your students?
- Community and curriculum – how does the curriculum relate to your community and what action do you take on this?
- Consider how assemblies add into the narrative and any new knowledge you are focusing on.

Tools and resources

Global Equality Collective Platform – World's first Diversity and Inclusion platform for education
GEC Collective – 300+ DEI experts in education
www.thegec.education/collective
GEC Community – 13,000+ DEI experts, change makers and growing community for education
GEC Resources including access to the UK's largest DEI collection of books
www.thegec.education/resources
GEC Manifesto and Values
www.thegec.education/manifesto-values

9 Shaking up the curriculum
SARAH WORDLAW

School Name	Streatham Wells Primary School
Age group taught within school	4–11
Location of school	South London
Any distinguishing features	• A curriculum which is actively anti-racist, anti-homophobic, anti-sexist and anti-ableist.

Intent of the curriculum

We live in a society that is not equal. Marginalised groups are further marginalised by systems of power and access to services and opportunities. We have a unique position as educators to use our sphere of influence to raise consciousness and make a difference. It's our responsibility (and privilege) to ensure the next generation is more enlightened than we are currently and to teach young people that there are no outsiders in our society irrespective of race, disability, sexuality, religion or gender identity. To fight for institutional change to both recognise and eradicate discriminatory beliefs. It is a fact that no child is born racist, homophobic or sexist. These are behaviours that children learn early on, from outside influences. A curriculum which is diverse, inclusive and representative is imperative to building and changing our society for the better. With that in mind, a curriculum should actively teach about, represent and *deliberately* include different races and ethnicities, people with disabilities, the LGBTQIA+ community, different religions, women's history and rights and different cultures.

This should include ensuring a well-rounded British history curriculum, including Black British, British Asian, women's and queer history and associated role models. It should include learning both *about* and *from* people with disabilities. It should include challenging European bias and heteronormativity. It should include developing richly diverse music, arts and PE curricula. I believe curriculum intent should use these areas to teach about social justice, sustainability and human rights and develop children's voices to articulately justify their thoughts. It should aim to raise awareness and empower children, particularly from marginalised communities, and ultimately foster active, well-rounded citizens who can think critically about the world around them.

Implementation

Developing a diverse curriculum is not an easy feat. It takes time. It is a journey, not a destination. There is no eureka moment – 'We are diverse now!' – it is a process and commitment which is ongoing. Start with auditing where you are now; progress can only be measured if you understand where you started.

Ensure that all stakeholders are involved, and that commitment to change is a whole-school priority. This includes the staff team, governors, parents and children.

Next, audit where you currently are. Which subject or which area would you like to start with? Is it that you want to develop a less white-centric history curriculum? Or is it that you would like to develop LGBTQIA+ inclusive teaching across the whole curriculum. Clarify your vision, and once you have… audit, audit, audit.

Look at what you are currently offering using a variety of evidence, including:

- curriculum maps
- children's work
- pupil voice
- learning environments.

For a school to be truly inclusive, the ethos and culture surrounding the curriculum should also be reviewed and audited for the following:

- The hiring and training of staff.
- Does the school leadership model a commitment to anti-racist values?
- Is training on offer to address racial equality?
- Is there a whole-school approach to racial equality and are all staff on board?
- Is the staff team diverse and do global majority staff members feel their opinions are valued?
- What are the links between race and wellbeing?

- What are the links between race and 'behaviour'?
- How can you use your local community to frame discussions around protests, struggles or campaigns led by global majority communities in your area?
- How diverse are the toys and dolls around the school (particularly in EYFS)?
- Diversity in displays around the school. Can you eliminate segregated areas like 'boys' library corner' or 'books for girls'?
- All policies (most specifically anti-bullying policy, behaviour policy and child protection policy) should include a statement about zero tolerance for:
  - homophobic, racist, transphobic, sexist and ableist language
  - racial, gendered and/or homophobic harassment.
- The language surrounding gender and sexuality used across the school – Stonewall's primary curriculum (2019) has fantastic glossaries for staff and pupils.
- Wider community: ensuring that you invite a range of people to run assemblies, career and whole-school events, and actively include people of different ethnicities, female role models and those who are LGBTQIA+.

There is a range of great audit tools and questions on The Key website. These can be used to structure auditing. The tools are a way of reviewing where you are currently with your curriculum and should give you an idea of what needs to be developed. These audits can be completed in whatever way suits you and your position within the school. They could be done in a staff meeting as discussion points, or as a fact-finding task. However they are done, the purpose is to help reshape and restructure the direction of your subject. It is important to include different stakeholders in auditing as well, as different people will bring different perspectives to the table and those professional conversations around this are crucial.

When auditing, you might find particular strengths in one area and a different area that needs development. Share your results with the team, discuss how to move forward, and what specifically to focus on. Once you have an idea of where you currently are, you can think about the school vision and priorities moving forward.

To move forward, you need to shape your curriculum intent clearly, so the work that comes next has a clear direction. Curriculum intent simply means the what, why and how of your curriculum. What exactly are you intending to do with your curriculum, why do you intend to do that and how do you plan to get there?

You must first consider the purpose of your curriculum:

- What strong educational principles does the school and leaders believe in or practise?

  Examples of educational principles are:
    - language-rich
    - twenty first-century skills-rich
    - knowledge-based
    - skills-based
    - both knowledge- and skills-based
    - human rights and activist curriculum (my personal favourite!).
- What do you want your curriculum to achieve?
- How would you like children to leave your school?
- A child who starts in Reception and leaves in Year 6 will have what skills?
- How do we prepare children for life beyond primary school?
- What values do we hold?
- What do you believe is right for the children?
- What pedagogical approaches and evidence-based research should we follow?
- What should the curriculum *not* be?

The answers to these questions guide deep discussions surrounding your aims. Once you have your educational principle(s), you can build a curriculum statement around this. Don't just follow trends; they go out of date. Think about the true educational principles and evidence that guide your practice.

Impact

So, you have designed your new curriculum and you now need to know the impact. How well is it being taught and what impact is it having on children's learning – and lives?

Impact can be measured in a variety of ways, and it is important to use both quantitative and qualitative data to get a fully rounded view.

Go back to your intent, and your initial audit. Ask yourself: Have you started to do what you aimed to do? I deliberately use the word 'started' because, as I said before, diversification is a journey, not a destination. Have you made progress since your initial audit? Evidence for progress could come from:

- attainment and progress data
- behaviour incidents
- pupil voice
- attendance data
- parental engagement.

Ultimately a richer, more diverse curriculum results in children becoming critical thinkers, which will positively impact their attainment and progress – but in addition, it will develop their sense of self and confidence.

As educators, we know that education is powerful: it is a chance to change life opportunities for young people, in particular those from marginalised communities. We too are on a learning journey with developing our understanding of the world, our subject knowledge and our own ability to critically think so we can deliver the absolute best for those we teach. Diversity, inclusion and visibility in the classroom are a constant journey. We all have our own biases – conscious and unconscious – based on our own experiences of lives and personal education. It is important to be able to become more self-aware, to question, discuss and respectfully challenge each other on thoughts, beliefs and understanding of the world, so we can grow as individuals and furthermore as educators. The long-term impact of a diverse curriculum is better opportunities for marginalised groups, levelling the playing field.

It's our responsibility and privilege to ensure the next generation is more enlightened than we are currently; to teach young people that there are no outsiders in our society irrespective of race, disability, sexuality, religion or gender identity. To fight for institutional change to both recognise and eradicate discriminatory beliefs. Racism, homophobia and sexism are behaviours that children learn early on from outside influences. This is another reason why diverse and inclusive teaching is imperative to both build and change our society for the better.

Turning vision into reality

Developing a new curriculum, one that is more diverse, is an incredibly rewarding process and it can enable practitioners to make a real difference in children's lives. One of the biggest pitfalls in developing a new curriculum is trying to rush or do too much at once. This ends up with leaders and staff becoming exhausted and the curriculum not having the intended impact. Another pitfall is to deviate from the intention – be crystal clear about what you are trying to achieve before jumping in. And don't forget the key competencies children must learn for each subject in order to make the most progress as learning. A progression of skills, built from year to year, is essential for your changes to be effective.

One of my biggest indicators of success were the last Year 6 class I taught, because they were able to critically think about the world around them, question inequalities and, as a result, make incredible academic progress. Children in this class called out racism on a school trip to a residential centre. We went to a climate change protest in central London. Many went to the Black Lives Matter protests. The pupil leadership team were interviewed by Sky News on the war in Ukraine and how to treat everyone with respect. Despite the pandemic, this particular class made enormous academic progress, and this was also evidenced in their KS2 SATS. They were an amazing bunch of fierce young activists; I know they have bright futures ahead of them, and I like to think that they will go on to pass the boldness, knowledge and bravery to question the powers that be, and to challenge generations younger than them in the future.

Takeaways

- Decide on your intention, involving all stakeholders.
- Audit, audit, audit – find out where you are now.
- Take your time, don't do too much at once. Remember it's a journey, not a destination.
- Check out existing resources to build upon such as those from the Historical Association, The Black Curriculum or Stonewall.
- Use lots of different ways to measure progress, not just attainment.
- Celebrate the successes!

Tools and resources

Historical Association
www.history.org.uk/primary/categories/classroom-resourcesks1
The Black Curriculum
https://theblackcurriculum.com/freelearning
Stonewall
www.stonewall.org.uk/resources/creating-lgbt-inclusive-primary-curriculum
Wordlaw, S. (2023) *Time to Shake Up the Primary Curriculum*. London: Bloomsbury.

10 Change at pace
TOM TURNHAM

School Name	Lyndhurst Primary School
Age group taught within school	4–11
Location of school	South East London
Any distinguishing features	• A two-form school. • Students advocate for all communities to celebrate the diversity which comes from being a global citizen.

Intent of the curriculum

We believe that all Lyndhurst pupils should have a lifelong passion for learning. They should be taught the skills they need to identify and overcome any individual barriers to their acquisition of knowledge. This will be achieved through a holistic, evidence-informed pedagogy that holds inclusivity at its heart, where teachers model that they are also learners and are compassionate while having high standards. Our sequential curriculum is rooted in our local area and allows learners to apply our core values while gradually expanding their world schemas. This will develop staff who are creative and engaged and pupils who are proactive, informed and confident in celebrating individuality.

Implementation

We try not to reinvent the wheel so we have separated subjects into those that are simply about the acquisition of skills and knowledge and do not need to be personalised to our context: phonics, maths, reading comprehension, French, PSHE and science. For these subjects we use quality purchased schemes of work so that staff can focus on the delivery rather than the planning. For the subjects in which we believe need to be firmly rooted in our community and values, we have developed clear progression of skills documents that outline what will be covered and when. These, combined with medium-term plans created by a central team of interested teachers, allow us to have a rich curriculum without significantly adding to workload.

We are building a solid bank of quality lesson resources to support the plans. Arguably the most important part of 'quality first' teaching is the explanation – if we have slides and images that enable teachers to have access to quality explanations, we are improving outcomes for all students.

We've taken the decision to prioritise our history and geography curricula as we feel they best exemplify what we can achieve but we are also making small changes to our art curriculum. As Mary Myatt is often telling us, curriculum change is a slow process that shouldn't be rushed. We agree with this although we know that, as is true in our case, sometimes change must happen at pace to ensure that pupils are getting what they deserve. We have tried to balance this by thinking about what we will focus on in our CPD sessions. These are now not subject-specific and focus instead on areas such as explanations or modelling so that the impact of any upskilling can be applied across subjects (it also has the benefit of altering the culture of a team). The real curriculum work is happening behind the scenes, with senior leaders supporting middle leaders in making the change at pace. As new units are ready we can work with teachers in each phase group to ensure that they are on board with the new units. In this way, we can manage a lot of curriculum change at a rapid pace without staff and pupils feeling like they are spinning out of control.

The hardest part, of course, is the interim period where you have plans that teams are excited and passionate about but pedagogy that is still catching up, or staff who are still getting on board with the changes. At this point it is vital that you remain true to your key messages – but not by email.

Something we found useful early on was to ban emails about curriculum. We discussed this with our middle leaders and decided there was no reason for them. They agreed that messages about curriculum sent in circular emails not only have no impact to teaching but also are detrimental to staff wellbeing. New information would be sent as part of our weekly staff bulletin and could include a link to an information/briefing document that would be saved in our shared drive; training would happen in meetings so didn't need to be emailed; and feedback should be personalised so didn't need to be emailed.

As a time-starved middle leader, it's easy to send an email that alienates staff. We wanted to avoid that at all costs.

Impact

It's early days for us, but we have seen that staff are already excited about our changes. They can see the links to the locality and to our values and, most importantly, they are excited because the curriculum is bespoke to them. Pupils are excited as their knowledge is specific to their area; they can talk about local buildings and place names, which creates a connection to the place where they live. They are also not missing out on core knowledge that is vital for success in the future.

I don't think we have yet seen the true impact on staff as we are still in the first stages of our curriculum. I am confident, however, that in year two or three we will start to feel a real difference as we are able to draw on a set of quality plans and related resources that only need tweaks based on how we will deliver them to our current cohort. We know that this will improve workload, while not resulting in the feeling of disassociation that only using schemes can bring. We also know that as we spend time reviewing and refining our resources, we will improve the quality of our teaching, raising the bar of our least able staff and supporting their development. The idea is that no teacher will have to spend Sunday evening researching how to teach a concept or idea. The work will have been not only done but improved on over several years, so we can be confident that we are using an effective method of transferring information and one that builds on knowledge gained in previous years.

Turning vision into reality

It was hard! The first step for us was to give our middle leaders back their power – they needed to know that it was their curriculum and that they had the power to choose the content, but most importantly they had to be able to justify their choices. Engaging staff in that debate was transformative: they felt like experts, they sought new information and many rediscovered their passion. The next step was to capture that in a consistent and manageable way. We chose to use progression maps so that we had a shared language. A teacher could look at any subject and understand how to read the document. We spent time as an entire staff, working in groups, determining the strands for each subject and what the core knowledge or skills needed to be for each strand in each year group (and term). This became the backbone of our curriculum. As a leader this was the hardest part. Some staff clung to old units and tried to build a curriculum around what they have always done (sometimes due to fear about telling a teacher they would lose a loved unit); some fixated on topics rather than skills and knowledge. This involved lots of one-to-one time with middle leaders discussing their subjects, reassuring them that I would back their decisions and reminding them that it is their curriculum and they are responsible for it.

Of course, this resulted in a lot of new short-term planning and, more importantly, a lot of anxiety about working over the holidays to catch up. I set clear instructions. Don't work over the holidays. We will create time to support the planning as we are making the decision to prioritise curriculum development. We had structured INSET and staff meeting time to work on plans. We set clear deadlines and expectations so that staff could see that we meant what we said.

We are still on the journey and not every teacher is fully on board yet. We have pockets of resistance; our next step is to work with those teachers to help bring them around. We are not sending emails about it, making threats or passive-aggressive comments in staff meetings, but we will make expectations clear for the next term and meet face-to-face with staff who are finding it hard, for whatever reason, to meet those expectations. After all, this is about developing staff.

Takeaways

- Empower your subject leaders; they are your biggest tool.
- Have a consistent format for your progression of skills and knowledge.
- Ensure that everyone is clear about what skills and knowledge are covered in each year group.
- Regularly sit with your subject leaders and talk about their subject.
- Every term, look at exercise books with pupils to see what they say is actually happening in class.
- Plan for the resistance – know what the barriers will be and address them head on.
- Ban subject leaders from sending emails about curriculum.
- Prioritise! Don't do everything at once.

Editor's reflection on Part 2: Leadership and management – operational excellence

The passion, determination and commitment of the leaders in this section is uncompromising. They build their curriculum around strong, well-defined educational principles. They want to secure the best outcomes for every child; they are conscientious and ambitious; they want to make the world a better place; but they don't pretend it is going to be easy!

As Sarah Wordlaw says in her case study 'Shaking up the curriculum': 'We have a unique position as educators to use our sphere of influence to raise consciousness and make a difference.'

The case studies emphasise the importance of embedding a set of purposeful values, which help to define the school culture and set the foundations upon which the rest of the curriculum is built. With middle and senior leaders contributing to the process, these designs help to engage learners with skills-based and immersive curricula that places the child at the centre of their learning. Inclusion, diversity, equality, equity and representation are considered to be imperative if we are to build and transform our society for the better. These leaders know that the curriculum must evolve over time so that it remains relevant to the learner and that effective assessment ensures the learning is pitched correctly; in this way we can ensure that every child will succeed.

Well-constructed, thoughtful and diverse curricula allow young people to understand the inequality and injustice that many people face and provide them with the skills, competencies and compassion to challenge the status quo. A curriculum that draws on the expertise and lived experience of the school's stakeholders ensures that all voices are heard, increases representation and provides improved opportunities for marginalised individuals and groups to succeed.

A conscious, humane, inclusive and diverse curriculum also offers benefits for educators. Removal of formal staff observations in favour of measuring and tracking impact via continuous professional development (as referenced in the 'Curriculum of PRIDE' case study by Christopher Harrison) is positive for staff workload and wellbeing. Impact can be measured using both quantitative and qualitative data, such as attainment and progress data, behaviour incidents, parental engagement, and staff wellbeing surveys.

Aspirational, empowering curricula help to ensure that everyone involved feels that they are contributing to something bigger than themselves and that they have an important role to play in shaping a positive future for everyone. Such a feeling is inspiring, energising and good for the soul!

PART 3

Quality of education

Introduction

Central to the Ofsted Education Inspection Framework (EIF) is the 'Quality of Education' judgement, which comprises of the three I's of 'intent, implementation and impact' (Ofsted, 2019).

This model reminds me of Simon Sinek's book *Start With Why* (2011), published a decade prior to the Ofsted EIF, and specifically of the model of the three concentric circles with 'Why' in the centre, 'How' in the middle circle and 'What' in the outer circle. Since the publication of *The Power of Why*, many organisations, including schools, have used this framework to consider their purpose, their goals and how they will achieve them.

Whether it is the Simon Sinek model or Ofsted's three Is model, this three step approach is an invitation to schools to think carefully about what it is they are trying to achieve through their curriculum, how they will go about it and what the outcomes will look like for their children. This process, starting with intention, ensures that the design of the curriculum is considered and planned, not haphazard and not left to chance. Curriculum intent is about curriculum design, the manner by which schools provide a broad and balanced, ambitious curriculum for all their pupils, one that opens windows to the world and doors to future opportunities.

The EIF was based on a great deal of research, including visiting schools to understand how they were setting out their curricula, with many school leaders citing context as a driver for priorities. In some instances, this concerned Ofsted as they perceived it to be an excuse for complacency and lack of ambition.

The EIF draws on neuroscience, human cognition, memory and the process of learning. In the EIF, Ofsted quotes Sweller et al. (2011): learning is defined as 'an alteration in long-term memory. If nothing has altered in long-term memory, nothing has been learned.'

For learning to take place effectively it should be well-sequenced so that new learning can be built on prior knowledge, like building blocks carefully stacked onto each other. This careful sequencing minimises knowledge gaps that can impede success. Learning is achieved most effectively when it is built up over time, allowing pupils to understand increasingly complex ideas and take on more challenging activities. When children are not successful it is because a concept, an idea or some key knowledge has been missed, so pupils are not able to make the necessary connections because the foundational knowledge is not secure. It is the teacher's job not only to ensure the learning is well-sequenced, but to systematically assess where learning has not been fully understood; to provide effective feedback and to take remedial action to close the gaps.

Ofsted's guidance on inspecting the curriculum (2019) states: 'Leaders and teachers design, structure and sequence a curriculum, which is then implemented through classroom teaching. The end result of a good, well-taught curriculum is that pupils know more and are able to do more. The positive results of pupils' learning can then be seen in the standards they achieve. The EIF starts from the understanding that all of these steps are connected.'

The white paper published under the coalition government in 2010 was one of the first times the Department for Education stated its intention to 'make it easier for headteachers and teachers to find out about improvement services on offer as well as making high-quality research, good practice and free resources easily available.' Since then there has been a (mostly positive) proliferation of education research to support teachers in making choices to ensure that teaching and learning happen in classrooms as optimally and efficiently as possible.

Milton Road Primary School

At Milton Road Primary School, despite the many time constraints, we aim to make the best use of available research to inform our pedagogy. Like many schools, we use a wide variety of sources, including the Education Endowment

Fund, The Great Teaching Toolkit, books such as *Teach Like a Champion 3.0* by Doug Lemov (2021), and *Think!: Metacognition-powered Primary Teaching* by Anoara Mughal (2021), as well other sources including blogs, tweets and videos.

At the end of every term, teachers assess the children's knowledge and skills against the key objectives in each programme of study. We use different ways to assess dependent on the subject. For reading, grammar and maths we use National Foundation for Education Research (NFER) standardised tests: Progress in Reading Assessment (PiRA), Progress in Grammar, Punctuation and Spelling Assessment (GAPS) and Progress in Understanding Mathematics Assessment (PUMA). For other subjects, teachers may use quizzes, or written summaries, or final completed design products. End of term Expert Showcases are excellent opportunities for the children's work and progress to be assessed, and self-assessment is also a critical part of this. Throughout the term, the children document their learning by uploading photos and commentary into their Learning Portfolio on our learning platform SeeSaw.

Teaching children to be effective learners means empowering them to explain not only what they have learned but also how they learned it. We want the learning experiences for our children to be as exciting and as broad as possible and, like many schools, educational visits are an important aspect of the curriculum. Each year group's Learning Adventure is mapped out to include the places and extra-curricular experiences the children will enjoy along the way. At the start of term, our children will receive a tangible map of the places, people, stories and skills they will encounter as part of their Learning Adventure.

To do this we have worked with Emma Bennett, a Cambridge artist and editor of the *City Art Book* series. Emma has created over 150 illustrations for each of the experiences and children can tick off each of these as they encounter them as part of the curriculum. We hope that in addition to being a beautiful souvenir of the child's Learning Adventure, the maps will also serve as an *aide memoire* to help them retain learning and knowledge and make connections.

A note on the case studies

Each of the five case studies in this section focuses on a discrete subject area, with history, computing, English, physical education and the arts all being celebrated.

There are explanations here of why discrete subject knowledge and specific skills are so important, and useful guidance on how to secure high standards and continuity as well as how to develop the confidence, skills, knowledge and understanding of other teachers in the school.

Each of the contributors is an inspiring expert in their field, so I am delighted that they have shared their case studies with us.

11 Curriculum continuity from KS1–5 – history as a case study
ALEX FAIRLAMB

School Name	Kings Priory School
Age group taught within school	4–18
Location of school	Tynemouth, Tyne and Wear
Any distinguishing features	• An all-through school, from EYFS to Year 13.

Intent of the curriculum

Transition between schools and key stages is a complex beast. In terms of a child's cognitive development, there is no reason why there should be a transition gap. However, the gap exists and it continues to impact the progress of children academically and emotionally in future years. There are many issues that contribute to this gap, one of which is a lack of curriculum continuity between key stages and institutions, in particular in foundation subjects such as history and geography. Individual institutions themselves will be working hard to ensure that curricula are sequenced (for example, from Key Stages 3–5), but the disconnect between primary and secondary curricula means that often KS3 can begin without a complete understanding of the readiness of pupils and without knowing in sufficient depth the concepts, skills and vocabulary that has already been taught in primary.

Typically, aside from the KS1–2 National Curriculum, secondary practitioners often have little knowledge about what pupils have studied before they enter their classrooms in Year 7. This can lead to low expectations of pupils in terms of skill development (with some Year 7 history lessons focusing on teaching chronology, what is a source etc., which they have already been taught since Year 1) and assumptions that history has been taught in either a cross-curricular topic format or in ways that are not true to the discipline, such as writing a letter to the king about how London should be rebuilt after the Great Fire. While primary practitioners can follow the KS1–2 National Curriculum with fidelity and have the KS3 curriculum to consult, they often don't have knowledge of the specific concepts, vocabulary and skills that need to be in place in preparation for the differing secondary schools' curricula their pupils transition into.

Moreover, secondary colleagues are not exposed often enough to the incredible teaching strategies of primary practitioners and have limited awareness of the quality of learning and work that primary pupils undertake and produce. There is much for secondary practitioners to learn from primary practitioners and adopt into their own practice; observing primary colleagues helps to raise expectations of pupils in Year 7+ (low expectations is a cause of the transition gap). Meanwhile, primary practitioners are expected to be the experts of each subject they teach, yet they often won't have the time and disciplinary knowledge (unless their degree was in the subject) to craft curricula and assessments that secondary subject specialists hope could be constructed. This can lead to the opinion of secondary colleagues that they must 'start from scratch' in subjects such as history, assuming that 'proper history' as a discrete discipline has not been studied at primary in a meaningful way.

Therefore, at Kings Priory School, we have embarked on a Curriculum Continuity programme where primary and secondary practitioners are working together to co-construct curricula and assessments from KS1 through to KS5. The aims of this are to:

- Ensure continuity of the curriculum and pedagogy: build on prior knowledge and skills, sequence learning from KS1 and avoid repeated content.
- Ensure that there is no misalignment of KS1–KS2 and KS3+ teacher expectations of pupils and their learning as this could limit challenge.
- Create opportunities for cross-phase moderation.
- Ensure that pupils who are not making expected progress in subjects are accurately identified and that this information is shared across key stages to ensure a continuity of intervention and knowledge of the pupil.

- Empower and enable practitioners to create curricula and assessments collaboratively to ensure a shared understanding of the demands of the discipline.
- Share good practice and expertise across key stages.

Implementation and turning vision into reality

Embarking on curriculum continuity is an ambitious endeavour, but one that is entirely worthwhile. To prepare and plan for this, the subject lead for history in primary and the subject lead for history in secondary worked together with myself (as Assistant Principal of Teaching and Learning and as a history teacher). To begin, we agreed the vision for our history curriculum and ensured that we had read and understood the National Curriculum documentation of all key stages and reviewed independently the existing curriculum, drawing on CPD from places such as the Historical Association to support with this. In our vision, we ensured that we had a common language and understanding of what history is and the nature of it, including how it is constructed and communicated. We were acutely aware of the need to ensure that our curriculum not only ensured a progression of knowledge in a coherent, sequenced series of narratives over time (substantive history), covering a breadth of substantive concepts (empire, society, democracy, etc.), but also that it included the progression of disciplinary skills (second order concepts).

To ensure a sequenced and coherent curriculum, it was important for us to meet regularly to review the endpoints of the history curriculum and then audit and map where content, skills, concepts and vocabulary were currently taught to build towards this end-goal. From this, we were able to determine what content was to remain and what content we needed to review or change, as well as identify how we could build the second order concepts and disciplinary skills of pupils over time. From this, we were able to construct a progression model of content that mapped where golden threads of concepts wove through. We also constructed a skills progression model, which would enable those designing the schemes of learning to know the expectations of how pupils' skills should be developed within each key stage, how it builds on prior skill development, and how it ensures readiness for future skills development – as one continuous flow or crescendo. Having the skills progression model has meant that when designing our schemes of learning (SoL), we make sure that disciplinary skills are developed in a manner that is true to the discipline of history. Using sources as an example, this includes task design, language used (such as 'reliability', 'provenance'), and approaches to modelling this skill. This means that in Years 3–4, teachers are able to develop pupils' ability to know the difference between 'description' and 'inference' (having secured knowing what a source is and how to describe sources in Years 1–2) and begin to thread in tasks which then develop source evaluation skills, such as reliability tasks. Within this, pupils are explicitly taught how historians use sources to forge interpretations. The shared construction of this model has ensured that, for each disciplinary skill, the curriculum is rooted in the demands of the key stage and is also challenging in terms of preparing pupils for future endpoints.

Each practitioner's pedagogical knowledge of pupils within the key stages was central to this. It would have been a mistake for the secondary lead to plan the schemes of learning for primary practitioners, because the secondary practitioner would not have the experience or knowledge to appreciate how a Year 1 pupil learns. Likewise, a secondary practitioner's knowledge of the intricacy of the discipline, such as the nuances of teaching sources and the subtle microsteps that go into teaching them (including misconceptions), is vital.

With our narratives over time, we thought carefully about which content and concepts should be introduced at what point, and how we can ensure that narratives began in Year 1 and continued through the remainder of the progression model, building over time to Year 13. We wanted to make sure that not only was there horizontal progression, but also vertical progression, with concepts such as empire being taught in KS1 to enable KS2+ to build on this concept and develop across and within different periods. The current KS1–2 National Curriculum sets out a series of markers that should be in a history curriculum, such as studying a significant national event and the lives of significant individuals. We felt that one of the issues with KS1–2 is the fact that this often leads to isolated topics where an event is studied as a whole topic and people are then studied as a whole topic, without exploring substantive concepts and the wider history of the time. This disconnected ticklist approach can result in topics that are not sequences and confusing chronology for pupils – such as pupils moving from Grace Darling to the Great Fire of London then Tudor Kings and Queens.

Instead, we decided to implement the approach used by secondary practitioners of having broader periods of study (which in primary would mean incorporating one or more of the National Curriculum requirements within a wider topic) underpinned by an overarching enquiry question, rooted in scholarship. To ensure pupils develop a secure understanding of chronology, the curriculum is designed in chronological order, with frequent retrieval of previous time periods and tasks that require pupils to situate the current topic within the wider expanse of history. For example, in Year 2, rather than studying Grace Darling (an individual) and the Great Fire of Newcastle (a local event), we have instead created a SoL that explores the Industrial Revolution on a national and local level, encompassing significant individuals and a local event within this. The result is that we can build on pupils' prior knowledge of Queen Victoria, developments during her reign and the condition of society at that time (Comparing Queens, Year 1) by exploring in greater depth the impact of the Industrial Revolution during her reign. By having the Industrial Revolution as a broad topic, underpinned by an enquiry question, we are able to explore significant individuals within this period alongside local and national events. This gives greater opportunity for Hill's (2020) idea of world building:

> *Many of them, it seemed to me, were mainly matching up information that they had encountered as words on a page, but which effectively constituted little more than 'knowledge fragments' that did not sit within a coherent picture. In other words, I was doubting whether my pupils were able to conjure images of these places in their minds, and draw conclusions based on what they could see within them. In practice, this begins with identifying core features and building blocks of these imagined pasts, and subsequently positioning, emphasising, linking, and revisiting them in thoughtful ways.*

The result of doing so is that we can build not only on the narrative of the Victorian era begun in Year 1, but also on concepts such as monarchy, society and empire, which were also part of the Year 1 SoL. Moreover, we have identified which narratives and concepts are to be built on in KS2+. For example in Year 6 and into our KS3 and KS4 curriculum, we study Crime and Punishment, including an in-depth study on Whitechapel in the Victorian period.

Woven within this is the core strand of 'communicating like', with disciplinary literacy embedded throughout. Pupils are explicitly taught key vocabulary (such as 'monarchy' in Year 1) and 'reading and writing like an historian' is modelled, so that they can read sources and interpretations effectively, as well as write reasoned arguments and responses in the manner of an historian. Additionally, opportunities for structured talk where they can debate, as historians do, are built in with prompts to support the use of disciplinary language and content. The collaborative approach to this has meant that shared principles and common approaches are used from Year 1+, enabling practitioners to build on learning secured earlier in the curriculum model.

The greatest challenge that we have experienced has been finding the time to create the vision. We meet regularly to calibrate the progression model and map out next steps, but the time to action those next steps has to be balanced against the other demands that being a practitioner in a busy school present. To avoid the project becoming overwhelming, we identified short-term SoL to focus on developing for this academic year, and which topics would be developed in the next academic year. This would then ensure that we were not overwhelmed with the labour of SoL development and did not cause too much cognitive overload for primary practitioners delivering adapted and new units. It has provided reflection and evaluation time so that any creases can be ironed out for subsequent SoLs.

Impact

In 2023 we started a phase of initial implantation, with Year 1 and 2 pupils studying their first topic of the new curriculum model in the spring term and Year 4 studying their new Roman unit in the summer term. We began our moderation process in the summer term.

In terms of pupil outcomes, the language that the pupils are using has developed impressively. Year 1 pupils, who had read Floella Benjamin's *Coming to England* (1995) at the same time, told me that they had been studying 'formidable monarchs'. Pupil voice surveys told me about the challenges Elizabeth I faced due to people at the time considering women to be too weak to rule, and how she paved the way for later female monarchs like Victoria and Elizabeth II. Taking up the opportunity to deliver a lesson to Year 1 (as a secondary teacher), we studied Victoria and the pupils were able to compare similarities and differences with Elizabeth II in terms of length of reign and technological developments during their reigns. Their retrieval of the reign of Elizabeth II, built into the lesson, was strong and they were able to describe how far the role of a monarch had changed over time.

Primary practitioners have shared how they were initially worried about the high expectations set out in the SoL, but that the pupils have risen to this challenge and experienced great success with their learning. They have given feedback about how the pupils are finding the content interesting and that they can see, through formative assessment, how their knowledge is developing in broader ways than with the previous schemes of learning. They have also shared how they appreciate the input from secondary in terms of ensuring that the skills of history are embedded into the curriculum. They have been really positive about the resources being created for them by the team overseeing the project so that they can focus on adapting the lessons to meet pupil needs and use the time to engage in CPD around the teaching of history.

Within secondary schools, history and geography practitioners have attended meetings and CPD where the 'Curriculum Continuity' project has been shared. This has then led to departmental discussions about how to build on, and not repeat, content, and raise the expectations of what can be delivered from Year 7+. They have been impressed by the language that children will be learning in KS1–2 and their knowledge of the content, skills and concepts that have been taught. Geography practitioners are currently working on adopting a similar model of curriculum design.

Our practitioners will be providing in-depth feedback about the SoL to drive developments for the second iteration. Additionally, with future SoL, such as on the Ancient Greeks, colleagues have asked if they can take part in the planning so that they can develop the skills of constructing a primary history SoL with the substantive concepts and disciplinary skills as instrumental pillars of this.

Takeaways

- Meet with primary colleagues. This can be challenging if there is a large range of feeder primary schools. However, arranging a face-to-face meeting or sending out a survey to gauge what content is taught and when can be useful for identifying how curricula can connect. Within multi-academy trusts (MATs), organising a subject lead to coordinate this would be useful. For those not in MATs, identifying two or three feeder primaries to work with would be a great starting point, which could be scaled up over time.

- Devise observation opportunities for CPD: secondary colleagues visit primary schools to observe, engage in book looks and speak with pupils; primary colleagues visit secondary schools to see secondary subject practitioners' pedagogical practice and where the learning they begin leads to.

- Subject-specific CPD. Supporting primary colleagues with access to subject-specific CPD through organisations such as the Historical Association, or working with secondary schools to provide this. This could be in person or recorded (to support phase meetings and prevent issues of cover).

- Create opportunities for supporting with subject-specific assessments and then engaging in moderation. Secondary colleagues can work with primary colleagues to devise assessments, and then also help to moderate. This will raise the expectations of secondary colleagues who will see the quality of the work that primary students can produce. Likewise, primary colleagues can also moderate KS3 assessments so they can see how prior learning is developed, and to hold secondary practitioners to account by identifying if pupils are not being challenged sufficiently compared to their work in primary.
- A long-term view. It can be tempting when embarking on an ambitious project to want to achieve things quickly. This can give rise to issues in terms of workload, cognitive overload for practitioners, and a lack of time to evaluate each step to then help to inform future steps. Embarking on a long-term plan of 2–3 years means that the project has a greater chance of succeeding.
- Seek external expertise as part of the project. We were fortunate that Shareen Wilkinson, Executive Director of Education at the LEO Academy Trust, delivered disciplinary literacy training to our primary and secondary colleagues. This was very important as the expertise of an external person adds weight and value to the project, and can provide phase-specific training in terms of how subject pedagogical principles can be pitched appropriately in different key stages. This also helped to forge a relationship of sharing good practice, including linked reading lists, which has heightened the quality of our reading offer.
- Investing in resources. To support the construction of a curriculum and SoL development, ensuring that practitioners have access to texts, articles and webinars is essential.

12 From digital consumers to content creators
ALLEN TSUI

School Name	Willow Brook Primary School Academy
Age group taught within school	4–11
Location of school	East London
Any distinguishing features	• Proud to have achieved the prestigious Artsmark Gold Award, which recognises and celebrates the school's commitment to embedding arts and culture at its heart. • All our class names are based on famous London landmarks or institutions.

Intent of the curriculum

As subject lead for computing at Willow Brook Primary School Academy since the summer of 2020, I was tasked with writing the Statement of Intent for computing. This process went through a number of iterations until it was formally signed off in January 2022 and published on the school's website. The statement of intent describes why computing is important. It states:

> *In an era when technology is ubiquitous to so many every day, digital literacy, computational thinking, the ability to understand data science as well as engaging with such technology safely and securely are vital lifelong skills whose priority must be on a par with reading, writing and functional arithmetic skills.*

Implementation

I am very fortunate that, since 2016, the school has established a provision that computing be taught by a specialist whose timetable is scheduled as part of the non-contact time or planning, preparation and assessment (PPA) provision across the whole school. Some might criticise such an approach as a risk of deskilling primary teachers and potentially confining learners' development of their digital literacy skills to one lesson per week. To counteract such concerns I have offered a programme of professional development for colleagues interested either in improving their subject knowledge or in taking a more active role in teaching computing. The children at the school also have access to a class set of tablets at least twice a week beyond the timetabled computing lesson. This enables them to practise and consolidate what they have learnt during computing lessons by applying those skills in the context of other parts of the curriculum.

In terms of curriculum structure, the aims and subject content statements contained within the statutory guidance published in 2013 have been meticulously broken down, robustly scrutinised and mapped to the set or framework of 'I can…' statements for the primary computing curriculum distributed by the National STEM Learning Centre. These statements, originally produced by the e-Learning and Information Management team at Somerset County Council, were written as 'end of year expectations' to support assessment from Reception to Year 6. Applying this competency-based approach means that anyone should be able to understand the skills and knowledge being covered in every lesson.

The statements themselves can be grouped into five themes: Computational Thinking, Digital Citizenship, Computer Programming, Creative Media and Information Science. This differs from the model of best practice that Ofsted advocate of 'Information Technology', 'Computer Science' and 'Digital Literacy', since the five block approach enables online safety as well as the impact of big data on our lives to be taught more explicitly through the sequence of lessons with a half term (six weeks) devoted to each.

Each lesson broadly follows a six-step structure. Every lesson is initially framed around a 'Big Question' to enable learners to focus on the acquisition and accumulation of skills and knowledge. For example, to be able to 'describe different parts of the internet' in Year 5, the big question will be 'what is the internet and how does it work?'.

The skills part of the lesson will focus on the practical 'know how' for the lesson and be based on the 'I can…' statements published by the National

STEM Learning Centre. The National STEM Learning Centre is one of the three organisations, along with the Raspberry Pi Foundation and British Computer Society (BSC), the Chartered Institute for IT, that in 2018 formed the National Centre for Computing Education which was funded by £84 million from the Department for Education. The framework statements have also been meticulously compared with those used or published by the US-based Computer Science Teachers Association (CSTA) as well as the International Society for Technology in Education (ISTE). By taking such a globally aware approach means computing is taught to international standards, exceeding National Curriculum expectations.

In terms of key content, all learners are expected to demonstrate that they know and are able to articulate this learning, using the correct terminology and context, to their peers and the wider community. This is expected to be achieved through the production or publication of a collection of digital artefacts created by the children.

For those who show ability to work at greater depth, there will be opportunities to extend learning. Some children consistently demonstrate their capabilities to securely achieve learning targets meaning, according to the National Curriculum, they are two years above their 'age related expectations'. This may be due to the fact that, far from the narrative of 'lost learning' and the clamour for a 'catch up curriculum', the digitally dependent home learning structures so many of us had to become quickly accustomed to during 2020 actually *accelerated* digital literacy skills for many. Having a secure subject knowledge to GCSE standard and beyond allows me to support those learners who are consistently exceeding National Curriculum expectations. At Willow Brook we have a Digital Leadership programme where children work towards the British Science Association CREST Award alongside the Arts Award Certification, both of which are usually reserved for early secondary school students.

Impact

Computing is an exceptionally popular subject among children in most primary schools and Willow Brook is no exception to this. Computing's popularity is such that it has, for some children, it outranks PE, which had long been the most popular lesson in the timetable. The impact of computing is measured through a combination of the Digital Leadership programme, who are tasked to evaluate teaching and learning across the school, and pupil voice surveys, which we expect the children to complete on a half-termly basis.

The feedback and level of engagement with parents and carers from our series of after school curriculum meetings was also exceptionally positive. For children who are secure in their Digital Literacy skills and therefore engaged in every lesson, teaching is effortless. Our Year 5 pupils, for example, are able to independently log in to a Chromebook they have individual use of and simply begin the task that has been set for them via the online learning platform they are directed to use.

Having such a powerful and positive impact on teaching and learning doesn't mean we shouldn't continue to raise standards and provide learning opportunities that stretch, challenge and secure greater depth of knowledge for all learners. This is why all children are introduced to filmmaking in the Creative Media part of the computing curriculum, where they create their own short animation or video. The film or video idea will also provide the opportunity for everybody to write a book, which will be 'published' in electronic form to create a whole-school library and legacy of the children's learning.

Beyond the immediacy of the school community my expertise, as well as the expertise of my colleagues for teaching other STEM subjects, was recognised in September 2022 when the school received the Primary Science Quality Mark award for Outreach. This means that our school's teaching and learning has been recognised as being of such exceptional quality that the school has the capability and capacity to support other schools to achieve the same. Since becoming subject lead for computing in the summer of 2020, I have also been the local computing school Community Lead, facilitating networking opportunities to share and pool resources as well as supporting others with developing their teaching practice. From the feedback across the wider Computer Science teaching community, such opportunities are a source of invaluable support for other schools. Colleagues across the community readily admit they do not have the expertise to consistently teach computing to the global standards Willow Brook does, due to cost and time constraints specifically linked to the size of their schools.

Looking beyond the current academic year, the long-term goals are to achieve the National Centre of Computing Education Computing Quality Mark in recognition of the innovative and aspirational standards of teaching computing that our school is capable of delivering.

Turning vision into reality

How was all this achieved? With the support of the Computing at School's Community of practice and the very generous programme of the National

Centre for Computing Education. I had the inherent advantage of having been 'thinkering' around technology since 1982 and almost 24 years of applied use of technology in the workplace, from data processing to commissioning and managing the installation of Wide Area Networks for over 8,500 staff in 100 locations across England and Wales.

Through this experience, I would always advise colleagues, whether new to the profession, in middle leadership roles like mine or senior leadership, to apply what was known in the Civil Service as an 'intelligent client' role. What this essentially means is that it is unnecessary to be an expert in the field. This notion is perhaps more pertinent to primary teachers, given the expectations to be a generalist. What is more important for the intelligent client is to know what questions to ask and who to ask them to. On a practical level, for example, you don't need to understand the technical elements of the BBC micro:bit software to know that the Micro:bit Foundation website has a wide range of wonderful resources and teaching ideas to enable children to be introduced to physical computing.

I have also been fortunate to work for a leadership team both at school and at Board of Trustees level who have a 'can do and want to' attitude. This has enabled me to take on the role of specialist subject lead for computing with greater autonomy. The opportunity to work across schools, for example, teaching up to A level, has undoubtedly been a real boost to both my subject knowledge and pedagogical practice.

Being a subject specialist in such a technical field can feel quite professionally lonely on occasion. This is where the power of social media and memberships to various networks or organisations are supportive. Writing this reflection, I realised that I have been an active member, or had memberships of, more professional organisations and associations offering post-nominal letters than I have in my full name. I also realise that even though I have over ten years' teaching experience and am acknowledged as having greater depth in subject knowledge, I am still on a learning journey and welcome the opportunity to hear other teachers speak of their experiences, since it will often spark new or refreshed ideas to benefit my own teaching practice.

So what of the pitfalls, challenges and setbacks? Time is a huge constraint and perhaps greater than the lack of funding or resources. Having a decent technical support partner who completely understands the needs of your school and the expectations of your senior leadership team is critical. I know from life experience that poor professional relations with external providers will only lead to frustration, be time consuming and financially draining.

However, hearing the children's groans of disappointment when they realise that the computing lesson is over and the way they speak enthusiastically with everyone they meet about what they learnt in computing is a huge testament to success!

Takeaways

- Join the Computing at School network. It is completely free to join and there is no expectation on anyone to undertake an active role. Computing at School (CAS) is one of only three organisations recognised by the UK Council for Subject Associations as the body of experts for teaching Computing that does not charge for membership. Existing members have a wealth of experience and many readily share their ideas.

- Make use of Teach Computing services and resources. This is the platform created by the consortium of the Raspberry Pi Foundation, National STEM Learning Centre and BCS. The National Centre for Computing Education (NCCE) was funded by the Department for Education until 2021 to undertake its work to improve the subject knowledge of teachers and establish high quality Computing teaching resources.

- Make greater use of social media. Both Computing at School and Teach Computing have an active presence on various social media platforms in addition to their websites. Unsurprisingly, many teachers make use of social media to both improve their personal learning network and share and search for teaching ideas.

- Take an 'intelligent client' approach. No question is ever too foolish to ask. There are many across the wider teaching community who are amazingly generous with their time and will happily share their wisdom in a very supportive way.

- Preparation is everything. Never rely on any computing lesson being delivered exactly to plan. Something will inevitably fail beyond anyone's control. Have two layers of backup plans. Exhausting though this might sound, ultimately it is well worth the effort should it not be possible to teach the lesson originally intended.

- Scaffolding is key. Make no assumptions about what the children are able to do, especially when a lesson expects the children to be able to complete a series of tasks before they even get to create the artefact which is the core of the lesson. Where possible, simplify the login or sign in procedures

so that valuable lesson time is not wasted on trying to log in or sign in to devices.
- Make saving and sharing work part of the early routines. For computing lessons, failing to do so is the equivalent to throwing written work away in book-based lessons.
- Get management or leadership buy-in to your teaching plans. Secure their agreement early on for what they expect 'outstanding' computing to look like, especially progression and assessment.
- Secure parental engagement: a lot of learning happens beyond the classroom and on devices the children may have at home. For children who don't have access to technology outside school, be prepared to run before school, lunchtime or after school clubs to give them the opportunity to practise their Digital Literacy skills.

Tools and resources

Wakelet – To support my role as subject lead for computing, I have organised and openly share the resources I have created or produced into an online portfolio via Wakelet.
https://wakelet.com/@TsuiAllen

13 Opening doors to ambitious English
BOB COX

> **Bob Cox** is an educational consultant and award-winning author of the *Opening Doors* series of books. Bob facilitates a huge UK network of schools developing rich English pathways, a community learning how to open doors to opportunity via equity and excellence.

Intent of the curriculum

Shared in every way by our network of schools is the intention that ambition in English can become the norm, rather than an exception. Day-to-day learning dialogues and expectations are the ones needing the most attention: the ranges of questions; the challenge of the resource; finding meaning in reading aloud; quirky or stylistically interesting language challenges. Inspiring talk in assemblies about aspirations and dreams should be matched by the sequencing of English objectives into progressive patterns to facilitate top class reading and writing every day.

Key questions are common:

- Have we ensured there is structure for coherence and space for creativity?
- Do equity and excellence permeate the daily opportunities?
- Are aspects of English taught, repeated and embedded in a range of fascinating ways that improve written outcomes progressively?
- Is planning pitched high, but with scaffolds and interventions as appropriate?
- How can reading, writing, speaking and listening – the four modes of language – be integrated into quality text to quality writing journeys?
- Is assessment used to improve standards as well as for benchmarking?

These key intentions presuppose another vital one: that rich, complex and beautiful texts will stand at the centre of English and that they should include quality picture books, contemporary children's literature and classic texts linked from past to present and around the globe. At the centre of the curriculum should be a range of poetry, building through the primary phase and transitioning into Key Stage 3.

These texts are the hub of English to provide models and examples through which fluency, oracy, vocabulary, reading, writing and comprehension can be taught and explored.

Implementation

Implementation of these intentions has been varied and context-specific but that's how it should be. Make your plans according to your school's priorities, not to a standard approach. Every school is different. What unites our schools is the sharing of high aims, the belief in the entitlement of rich resources for every child and a dogged determination to make a difference.

'Why should our children miss out?' one teacher said to me.

In my many travels, I have seen that it is the mindset that matters most! When teams grasp the vision for exciting English, the details of curriculum development come quickly. Detailed processes become worthwhile and therefore energising instead of draining. Big principles of 'quality text to quality writing' can be implemented as 'flight paths', with new knowledge acquired en route.

- Plan from and beyond the top. You will not require extension tasks bolted on anymore, because the thinking is different. Start with a concept in English like 'building suspense' and weave in opportunities for comprehension explorations and writing taster drafts early on. See the free unit linked in the Tools and Resources section for more help, including setting out your questions radially around a big challenging one. Each pupil can build towards understanding and applying the concept in appropriate stages. Teachers have told me that pupils finding English hard have had morale lifted by answering 'questions' like everyone else, rather than 'easy questions'! Linear layouts – starting with easy and moving towards very hard – tend to involve advanced learners in too many questions they can answer without struggle while those finding it hard rarely experience the notion of a tough, conceptual question.
- Our schools pitch high constantly and then offer access and interventions when there is a need. The support is still there in the form of visual literacy, small slivers of text before longer text, music and drama. Of course, teacher

explanations deepen learning and love of the text: the minutiae of day-to-day life in a classroom is the most influential on learning!
- The text is at the centre of all these learning opportunities. If it does not have scope that manifests itself in new vocabulary, unusual styles and the chance to explore reading for meaning, then progress will flatten. So, auditing the texts and linking text choice to concepts or aspects of English has been critical to many of our schools.

Turning vision into reality

Implementation has been a combination of more focus on principles and rationales for English teaching and the development of tools, which we call the 'opening doors' strategies, for unlocking knowledge. These allow pupils to access conceptual understanding in manageable chunks. Turning that vision into reality has included these strategies:

- Taster drafts, which are time limited or word limited and introduced early in the process. They give all pupils a chance to imitate an author's style and receive feedback. Some schools use daily tasters: challenge is not only in the length of text!
- Linking in more whole text reading, which is one of the most important things a school can do. It works like this: Let's take the concept example of 'building suspense'. After focused language study inspired by a text like Tom De Haven's *Green Candles* (1997) – which we call the 'zoom in' effect – pupils will love being recommended whole text reading selections with the same concept in mind. Choose picture books, children's literature, classics and poetry to give regular reading bonanzas! Our schools then quiz pupils on aspects of suspense building in their reading. Therefore, I'd advise lots of book talk and quality reading in class. The time invested is time that will be paid back long-term in pleasure from reading and English progress.

Writing improves when stimulated by a diet of great books and poems and linked reading is a system including choice and coherence. Even parental volunteers for reading to pupils can be asked to use some of the linked reading books. The link with the concept provides a depth hard to find with topic work where sometimes English is a neglected partner: a text used artificially simply to complement, for example, the study of the Stone Age, does not add to depth of understanding. Some of our schools, when they have utilised topic work, have always ensured that English teaching has depth and richness within it.

To build an ambitious English curriculum into reality takes the mixture of vision and techniques as I have described; but I can't tell you enough how one school has differed from another. Don't be fooled or disappointed by the notion of an endgame either. By its nature, developing a curriculum is cyclical, evaluative and relies on constant tweaking and adaptation. I've always thought it misleading to buy a package and feel that the job is done! A challenging curriculum is feeding the curiosity of the teachers as well as the pupils and ongoing incremental development gives huge job satisfaction. None of it needs major transformation; it's just more creative tweaks once the concepts for teaching and texts for vehicles are in place.

Thinking of curriculum development as a work in progress is a mindset which will help you through. The work of a school is never finished.

Impact

Don't take my word for any of this! Here are some snippets to give you an idea of the way The Maltby Learning Trust built quality text to quality writing thinking (from my 2023 book, *Opening Doors to Ambitious Primary English*):

> *Our initial aim was to expose children to a breadth of challenging classic texts, switching them on to the wealth of literature available and breaking down the perception that it is 'not for them'.*

> *When the approach was first broached with teachers, there were preconceptions that the extracts would be inaccessible for 'our children', but the results have been transformative.*

> *As teachers became more proficient at applying the 'opening doors' approach, we found that their choices became more ambitious. At Ravenfield Primary Academy, children in Year 6 compared and analysed the language choices within a range of historical speeches from Shakespeare and Elizabeth I to Winston Churchill. Archaic language and motivational aspects were carefully unpicked to enable the children to understand the context and meaning. Taster drafts allowed them to manipulate language from across the speeches, sparking their imagination to create motivational speeches of their own.*

This ambition for excellence has led our English driver group to collaboratively create a canon of literature: a bank of high quality texts and link reading built around the Opening Doors spine to support and enhance the approach.

Jade Petch, Rachel Hanby, Rebecca Moore and Holly Hewis for The Maltby Learning Trust, South Yorkshire

Of course, barriers to progress will revolve around the management of change and the desirability of harder, complex texts becoming a regular diet. Strategies to overcome this include piloting units, feeding back on reading and writing progress, and English leaders producing framework year by year drafts of concepts, texts and success criteria. Overall, routes to ambitious English involve more reading and mastery of texts but less planning. Ranges of questions are easy to pick from the mind when responding to pupils' comments if a teacher is clear about why the lesson is being given and absolutely in command of the reading matter.

I rarely find resistance or barriers reported coming from the pupils! Just as they love 'Jabberwocky' and 'The Highwayman', they will relish whatever a teacher puts before them as long as it's presented with the usual enthusiasm and high expectation. The access strategies are critical though. They represent what teachers have always done: made complex concepts seem manageable and part of the next stage of learning. Crown House pupils' work webpage has many examples of pupils' work like this one from a Year 1 pupil. It's a very powerful way of demonstrating the impact of quality text to quality writing routes and inspired by Christina Rossetti's 'Hurt No Living Thing':

The woodlouse was very crawly
He crawled right up my arm
Some kids are scared of these bugs though
He didn't do me any harm
It is very hard to pick them up
They can curl into a ball
They could fall off anyone's hands
They could hide behind a wall
My stripy woodlouse was very cute
Marty was his name
I had released him
When it started to rain
My mum didn't want him
Living in our house

Our home is just for people
And not for my woodlouse!

By Jonah Gordon-Walker, Wheatfield Primary, Wokingham. Reprinted with permission.

Takeaways

If I had to summarise the big principles stimulating change across schools as curriculum thinking deepened they would be:

- Repeat concepts but ensure the core text and big objective gets harder.
- Include a wide range of readability across the linked reading and organise a flow of books from the library to the classroom.
- Move from 'doing' a text to teaching aspects of English.
- Audit not just the texts on show but also how they are being utilised in lessons. Choosing texts for each year is not a curriculum but it might be a starting point.
- Increase reading aloud opportunities via complex texts for progress in fluency and comprehension.

Tools and resources

Free resources plus the *Opening Doors* series of books
www.searchingforexcellence.co.uk
A free unit which includes an example of the radial layouts (p. 80)
https://searchingforexcellence.co.uk/wp-content/uploads/2021/10/green-candles_od-6-9_sample.pdf
Thirteen-chapter book exploring in detail our schools' journeys with us to an ambitious English curriculum plus extensive book lists, evidence informed work and research
www.crownhouse.co.uk/opening-doors-to-ambitious-primary-english
Routes and an online library of pupils' work – click on each book and see links between each unit and some terrific writing!
www.crownhouse.co.uk/bob-cox

14 Curriculum planning in PE – what children need vs what teachers want

IAN ROBERTS AND HEATHER MACNEIL

School Name	Kingsfield Primary School
Age group taught within school	4–11
Location of school	Chatteris, Cambridgeshire
Any distinguishing features	• A vibrant and diverse school that is highly inclusive. • The ethos is based on developing each child's ability to self-regulate.

Intent of the curriculum

There was a concern that the Physical Education curriculum at Kingsfield Primary School was very fragmented and piecemeal. Historically, the school had relied on a third party coaching company to facilitate the PE teaching, and the curriculum offered had reflected what the coaches wanted to teach. Formative assessment was not evident whatsoever; pedagogy was didactic and one-dimensional.

The school made a decision that Physical Education was to be taught entirely by classroom teachers, with no input from third parties.

The intention was:

- To develop a curriculum reflecting on the learning needs of the Kingsfield School Community. This curriculum needed to reflect statutory

requirements and translate into coherent and progressive sequences of learning both within and between Key Stages.
- To embed assessment for learning within this curriculum map.
- To create a community of practice within the school where teachers work together and reflect on what good and outstanding pedagogy looks like.

We agreed that physical literacy is our main goal. We wanted to plan a curriculum offer that would unlock children's desire, interest, confidence and competence to take part in physical activity throughout their life. We believe vehemently that the experiences and skills they gain within education will pave the way for their adulthood.

Implementation

In planning our new PE offer, we established five key working principles using the acronym SPACE (Specific, Pedagogy, Assessment, Content, Extension).

Specific: We were determined to create a physical education curriculum that is specific to the Kingsfield Primary School and Fenland context. We were determined to reflect, plan and implement a PE curriculum to reflect Kingsfield's unique context and circumstances.

Pedagogy: We were further determined to consider the PE curriculum more holistically, and to be driven by what the children need to learn, rather than by what the teachers want to teach. By doing this, we wanted to move away from PE that was entirely driven by sports, and indeed by content.

Assessment: Planning clear learning intentions, or outcomes, linked to the National Curriculum for Physical Education (2014), became a priority. We agreed to develop appropriate and sequenced learning activities across years, key stages and the curriculum map. Formative assessment (AfL) would then be embedded within all lessons.

We reflected on the opportunities that PE would offer children to demonstrate their learning across three broad domains:

- thinking (cognitive and creative skills)
- social (attitudes and behaviours)
- physical (physical skill or motor development).

These gave us a starting point to design a bespoke curriculum, especially in terms of providing an overview of the knowledge and skills to be learned.

Content: We separated the curriculum into six horizontal schemes of learning, year by year. We then started with the youngest age group, considered the learning domains and what the priorities were at each stage of the year. So, for example, in September when the children have had a long summer break, we asked if the focus should be on group work and team-building rather than the previous games unit, as has always been the case.

We then reframed the year-specific Schemes of Learning into series of units. We then decided, in a simplistic way, what the primary and secondary learning focus would be for each unit, and what the generic theme of the unit was. To show our 'working out', we used a colour code for reference.

For each unit, we added a red mark for physical, yellow for social and green for thinking. For example, in the first units of Year 1, as indicated in Figure 8, we felt the primary focus should be social learning, with physical skills as secondary,

Long Term Curriculum map for Physical Education

Time		Autumn 1	Autumn 2	Spring 1	Spring 2	Summer 1	Summer 2
R	1	Exploring the continuous provision (Assessment)	Games Activity Fundamentals 1 (Cambs Scheme)	Gymnastics Fun Gym Shapes (Cambs Scheme)	Dance On Parade (Cambs Scheme)	Games Activity Fundamentals 2 (Cambs Scheme)	Athletic Activity Foundations and link to Sports Day
R	2	Exploring the continuous provision (Assessment)	Enhanced Provision Playground Games (SWP)	Enhanced Provision Hula Hoops and Skipping Games (SWP)	Enhanced Provision Circus Activities (SWP)	Enhanced Provision Games Activities	Enhanced Provision Athletic Activities
Yr 1	1	Games Activity Fundamentals 1 Multi-skills (Cambs Scheme)	Outdoor Games Playground Games (SWP)	Gymnastics Jumping Jacks (Cambs Scheme)	Gymnastics Travelling Linking Actions (Cambs Scheme)	Games Activity Attacking and Defending (Using Space)	Athletic Activity Fundamentals and link to Sports Day
Yr 1	2	Gymnastics Rock and Roll (Cambs Scheme)	Games Activity Throwing and Catching	Dance Moving Words (Cambs Scheme)	Games Activity Multi-skills Bat and Ball	Dance Weather (Cambs Scheme)	Games Activity Fundamentals 2 Multi-skills (Cambs Scheme)

KEY: Social | Physical | Thinking

Figure 8: *Proposed curriculum map, page 1*

as shown by the yellow and red marks. Having established what the learning foci for units would be, this informed our decision about what the theme would be as a vehicle to bring this learning to life. This is shown in the FMS/multi-skills:

This planning process was repeated for each year group and each respective unit, constantly considering progression and coherence, with concepts and themes revisited and built on over time.

As can be seen within figures 8 to 11 each year group's scheme of learning links to create an integrated curriculum map, where connections can be made both vertically and horizontally, and the learning concepts can be effectively developed.

In these figures, the breadth of learning is quite clear from the sheer range of experiences offered, and the balance can be seen through the 'mosaic' of colours shown.

Extending: We were determined to reflect on how out-of-class learning opportunities could be promoted, how inclusive is the extra-curricular or enrichment programme that is offered and how to embed cross-curricular links with other areas of the school curriculum.

A prime example has been the incorporation of a Water Safety unit in Year 2 (Figure 9). Chatteris is a Fenland community, and the fens carry inherent risks for obvious reasons. Kingsfield does not have a swimming pool, but we developed a 'dry-side' unit to build understanding of the dangers and how to act and

Yr								
Yr 2	1	Games Activity Fundamentals 1 Multi-skills (Cambs Scheme)	Outdoor Play Activities Trails, Trust and Teamwork (Cambs Scheme)	Gymnastics Point of Contact (Cambs Scheme)	Games Activity Invasion Games	Gymnastics Ball, tall, wall	Athletic Activity Fundamentals and link to Sports Day
	2	Circus Skills (SWP)	Games Activity Attacking and Defending (Sending and Receiving)	Dance Activity Magical Friendship (Cambs Scheme)	Water Safety Dry Water Safety Activities	Dance Great Fire of London (Cambs Scheme)	Games Activity Fundamentals 2 (Cambs Scheme)
Yr 3	1	Games Activity Ball Handling (Cambs Scheme)	Sustained Activity Physical distance and circuit training skills	Gymnastics Patterns and Pathways (Cambs Scheme)	Games Activity Net and Wall Games	Gymnastics Handling Apparatus (Cambs Scheme)	Athletic Activity Fundamentals and link to Sports Day
	2	Dance Activity Machines (Cambs Scheme)	Games Activity Striking and Fielding (Cambs Scheme)	Dance Activity Solar System (Cambs Scheme)	OAA Communication and Consideration (Cambs Scheme)	Swimming	Swimming

Figure 9: *Proposed curriculum map, page 2*

Yr 4

1	Gymnastics Rotation (Cambs Scheme)	Games Activity Invasion-making choices (Cambs Scheme)	Games Activity Table Tennis (Resource Pack)	Dance Activity Cold Places (Cambs Scheme)	Gymnastics Principles of Balance (Cambs Scheme)	Games Activity Net Games (Cambs Scheme)
2	Dance Activity Haka (Cambs Scheme)	Sustained Activity Physical distance running and circuit training	Swimming	Swimming	Athletic Activity Pentathlon (Cambs Scheme)	Athletic Activity Fundamentals and link to Sports Day

Yr 5

1	Games Activity Table Tennis (Resource Pack)	Games Activity Invasion Games (Football) (Cambs Scheme)	Gymnastics Pair Composition (Cambs Scheme)	Games Activity Invasion Games (Netball) (Cambs Scheme)	Dance Activity On the Beach (Cambs Scheme)	Athletic Activity Fundamentals and link to Sports Day
2	Swimming	Swimming	OAA Cooperation and Communication (Cambs Scheme)	Gymnastics Press and Go (Cambs Scheme)	Athletic Activity Heptathlon (Cambs Scheme)	Games Activity Striking and Fielding (Cricket and Rounders)

Figure 10: *Proposed curriculum map, page 3*

Yr 6

1	Games Activity Invasion (Tag Rugby) (Cambs Scheme)	OAA Cooperation, Communication and Consideration (Cambs Scheme)	Gymnastics Group Work (Cambs Scheme)	Games Activity Net Wall (Tennis)	Games Activity Striking and Fielding (Cricket and Rounders)	Athletic Activity Fundamentals and link to Sports Day
2	Dance Football (Cambs Scheme)	Sustained Activity Physical distance running and circuit training	Games Activity Invasion (Hockey) (Cambs Scheme)	Gymnastics Body Symmetry (Cambs Scheme)	Athletic Activity Decathlon (Cambs Scheme)	Swimming (Booster and life-saving skills)

Figure 11: *Proposed curriculum map, page 4*

behave in or near water, through scenario-based lessons – a textbook case of applying what the children need to learn.

Impact

Kingsfield Primary School now has a physical education curriculum that enables all children and young people to receive an enjoyable, meaningful and memorable learning experience.

The curriculum is flexible, broad and balanced and will support all pupils to develop relevant knowledge and skills and ultimately achieve success.

According to the Education Inspection Framework in England (Ofsted, 2019), 'good intent' (i.e. the knowledge and skills to be developed at each stage) has the following four features:

- ambitious for all pupils
- broad and balanced
- coherently planned and sequenced
- successfully adapted, designed and developed for pupils with special educational needs and disabilities (SEND).

Kingsfield now has a PE curriculum map that reflects this, and senior leaders and Governors can clearly articulate how physical education fits into the wider planned learning experience for children and young people. More specifically, the development of physical literacy has been positioned as a key aim to help equip learners with the necessary knowledge, skills and values to lead active lifestyles.

Turning vision into reality

Successes

- Teachers appreciate the colour codes for each unit, enabling clarity in their personal planning.
- Planning is more progressive and cohesive, meaning skills are built upon each year.
- The curriculum has a greater variety of content which meets the needs of the children.
- A balance of learning opportunities is bespoke to the needs of the children throughout the year.
- PE has been a vital tool for re-engagement following the Covid-19 pandemic. Our curriculum has helped develop resilience, collaboration, trust and respect, alongside the physical aspects.

Takeaways

Plan a PE curriculum that is child-centred and focuses primarily on developing learning, rather than on teaching the activity content. It must be a priority to provide authentic, meaningful and high-quality learning experiences through a broad and balanced curriculum offer, where all children and young people are supported and challenged to achieve their full potential.

- **Specific:** Ensure your planning takes your school into consideration. This would fall under your intentions of what you intend to do, but also how you are able to implement it. Creating a PE offer specific to your school and context should reap a greater impact.
- **Pedagogy:** How do you intend to run your PE offer? What style of teaching does your school favour? Implementation of this will be down to a number of factors. Getting it right should have a holistic impact.
- **Assessment:** How and what do you intend to assess in PE? How does this inform teaching? Implementing this well should be apparent when you see the impact to a child's development. Assessment for learning must be a tool in order to improve progress.
- **Curriculum:** How will you offer your curriculum? Will teachers decide the activities or will pupils have a say? Will you create a broad and balanced curriculum that works for *your* children in *your* school? Be mindful of the large number of common invasion games that crop up. Is there a clear pathway of learning across the curriculum map and schemes of work?
- **Extension:** How will you promote physical activity and sport throughout the school and community? Will you link your curriculum to your extra-curricular offer? Will local clubs promote their sports and activities?

Tools and resources

Questions to Ask When Designing Your Curriculum – afPE
www.afpe.org.uk/physical-education/wp-content/uploads/Questions-for-Designing-your-Curriculum.pdf
Glossary of Terms – afPE
www.afpe.org.uk/page/Glossary_of_Terms

End of Key Stage One and Two Expectations in Physical Education: Head, Hands, Heart – afPE
https://cdn.ymaws.com/www.afpe.org.uk/resource/resmgr/images/posters/head-hands-heart-web.pdf

15 Arts-rich ambition
NANCY WAYMAN

School Name	The Belham Primary School
Age group taught within school	4–11
Location of school	South East London
Any distinguishing features	• A creative school in the heart of Peckham. • The visual arts, design and technology, music and drama all play valuable roles in helping our children develop skills for life. • The school recently opened in 2015.

Intent of the curriculum

One of the four strands of our school vision is a 'Glittering Curriculum', which is devoted to children developing a love of learning as a result of stimulating learning experiences via an artistic, innovative and far-reaching curriculum. Our aim is to develop creative, independent thinkers who have a strong sense of themselves and their roles in the community. This is made possible with a strategic view of the arts within the wider culture of the school: both art and music leads are part of the senior leadership team.

We established our school in 2015 with an ethos of the arts as central to education. An early School Development Plan stated that 'school leaders wish to foster a culture that places wellbeing and creative problem-solving at its heart for pupils and staff members'.

This is still alive in our intent today which says, 'Our curriculum offers a responsive and imaginative approach to developing skills and knowledge... and takes advantage of a broad range of experiences and opportunities.

[It] encourages pupils to become informed, inquisitive and engaged global citizens'.

Implementation

We believe that the most effective learning takes place when there is considerable emphasis on active involvement; the emphasis is on understanding and explaining rather than rote learning, and the curriculum is designed in a way that new learning progresses and builds in small steps on prior learning.

With that in mind, we have designed our curriculum around termly key themes that run vertically through the key stages such as: Changing Civilisations; Society, Laws and Beliefs; and Migration and Settlement. Connections between subjects are integral as they help children develop and expand their understanding of the world around them. Where possible we teach thematically with children, while keeping them aware of which subject 'hat' they are wearing for each session.

There are discrete music and art sessions taught weekly, as well as singing, in addition to other work that often includes arts outcomes (for example, pen and ink drawing to illustrate the children's own writing in English). We promote the value of cross-curricular work and support teachers to focus their planning to find connections across subjects when they work towards goals such as the 'Spring Showcase'. Here, all the work over the term that contributes to the theme is exhibited or performed to parents along with music or songs that reinforce the learning. Other focus weeks across the year that draw together STEAM (science, technology, engineering, the arts, and mathematics) subjects or humanities objectives also require teachers to consider planning in a cross-curricular way to support children's curiosity and engagement in learning about the world. These weeks incorporate both new knowledge and the development of skills, sometimes in mixed age groups, to enable children to learn from one another and develop themselves as teachers as well as learners.

Impact

Children are confident and articulate about art and music and can relate their opinions to their own and to others' lives. On a recent visit to Tate Britain, Year 5 children knew of the work of Chris Ofili and could also discuss their awareness of his subject, Doreen Lawrence, and make connections to their own experiences. Numbers of children drawing at lunchtime in an area of the library devoted to this have exploded and a songwriting club has sprung up in the music room as a result of a Year 6 unit on songs and orchestration. A mixed-age group of children took part in the world premiere of Alex Paxton's new work 'Candyfolk Space-Drum' with the London Sinfonietta, and were able to throw themselves into the performance – not only conventional singing but noise-making and gesticulating as well – and respond with passion and energy to the conductor and composer. The school's work was recognised with the Platinum Artsmark award due to this weaving of the arts into the children's everyday lives, sharing our practice and making connections with other organisations in the process.

Parents and carers are happy as they believe children really are benefitting from a broad and exciting curriculum offer where creative pursuits inform and support other curriculum work, and are not eroded as children progress through the school and focus on more conventionally measurable outcomes.

To ensure rigour, class teachers ensure that children have covered the relevant skills from each subject's progression of skills document. Subject leaders complete subject 'curriculum health checks' at varying points over a one- or two-year cycle, which are presented to the governing body. These not only allow for reflection against their subject but also for the governing body to act as a critical friend. Senior leaders and governors monitor how successful the school's curriculum delivery is through visits, pupil voice sessions, book looks, learning walks and the annual presentation of the health checks from subject leaders.

Turning vision into reality

As part of our school development plan, the art and music leads decided to embark on the Artsmark Award process. This meant giving an honest appraisal of where we were and how, in practical terms, we proposed to improve the delivery of an arts-rich curriculum in our school, in addition to sharing and disseminating excellent practice across a wider community of schools and other organisations. We had no trouble in getting the buy-in of the rest of the school's leadership team and quickly found a school governor who was interested in supporting and promoting our vision for an arts-rich curriculum. Expectations for the timetable were communicated to teachers, and sessions such as whole-school singing enabled us to offer teachers a small amount of extra planning time. For one term a year children take dance (provided by

Dance Educates), which also enables teachers to gain experience through observing how Dance Educates teachers work or by taking a small extra planning session in that time.

Devoting this much curriculum time to music and dance means that, when it comes to concerts, exhibitions or assemblies, both children and teachers are confident to generate ideas for performance or display and are familiar with the experience of sharing creative solutions. The Christmas shows in 2020 (during a period of restrictions on collaborative working due to Covid-19) utilised the children's visual arts ideas, incorporating their responses to traditional carols – recorded by children along with professional musicians – in paint, silhouette, animation, drawing and dance. They were also testament to the bravery of the teachers, their willingness to have a go and, having given the children the tools, to just go with the process and allow it to develop.

One of the difficulties of insisting on so much timetabled arts time is how to fit all the essentials into a week. Part of the solution is to use specialist teachers (music and PE) to cover PPA time. This can also cause problems though as it means there is little flexibility in the cover timetable. If we were to remove them from the PPA schedule, specialist teachers would become prohibitively expensive but keeping those sessions restricted to PPA cover means that any special events (trips, concerts, themed weeks) have to work around those sessions. This does become challenging at times. We are always looking at ways to incorporate the arts across the curriculum to support children's learning so that we are not only depending on discrete sessions.

We made time within our CPD calendar to allow teachers to consider their plans and how to make meaningful links between subjects and over-arching themes. We structured the long-term planning sessions so that teachers were able to plan in a step-by-step way (starting with unit titles, then knowledge and skills progression statements and finally looking at specific lesson objectives) and would not be swamped with new requirements in this more thematic curriculum aim. Subject leaders were encouraged to think about ways to bring in parents and engage them in the learning taking place at school, particularly during themed weeks. An engineer parent has worked with our science lead to run 'Bridge Building' family workshops and children cast cuttlefish jewellery with a parent who is a professional jeweller.

We found a number of opportunities for performance or exhibition during the school year. All children in Key Stage 2 take part in a devised Christmas production using music, movement and drama to tell the nativity story. Children grow in confidence through their time at the school as they learn to perform in low stakes settings: assemblies; Remembrance Day (trumpets play the Last Post in the playground before the two minutes' silence in music to the rest of the year group); Christmas lunch music from choir; and posts on the school portal.

As well as gathering work across the year for a big, public art exhibition (where children exhibit alongside professional artists), children are able to explain and show their work – from any part of the curriculum – in weekly assemblies to the school and to parents. At these assemblies, children play instruments as the rest of the school enters. These are not only children who excel but children, nominated by the instrument teachers, who have worked hard and accomplished a next step in their learning. In Year 6, children perform together in a show at a commercial theatre. They are instrumental in all aspects of the show, including artwork and the creation of projections as well as props. In past productions they have worked alongside teachers and professional technicians, where they were praised by theatre staff for the quality of their work. A large number of children have had their work selected for the Young Artists Summer Show at the Royal Academy over the last few years.

The Spring Showcase performances have allowed teachers to stretch their own creative muscles, not bound by the conventions of specialist music lessons. Excellent examples have included: work on rivers incorporating 'The Water Cycle Song' by Beccy Owen; literacy work based on the book *A River* by Marc Martin (2015); artwork by textile artist Caroline Dunn; science experiments on condensation and evaporation in Year 3; and work on the environment in Year 4 based on 'For Forest' by Grace Nichols; and diagrams and models, poetry and miniature galleries inspired by Slinkachu. As children become used to working in this way and we build up expertise among our staff, we can support each other year after year. This also helps teachers who are not confident in their own abilities with regard to this sort of creative teaching and learning.

Takeaways

- To do this, the school's strategic view needs to espouse a truly broad curriculum, including the arts, as being essential to children's learning in education and life. This is supported by having an Arts Governor and arts teachers on the SLT.
- Arts need to be embedded into school culture, not only curriculum. A truly arts-rich environment is only possible when it is part of the school culture, the everyday and the special celebrations, as well as the curriculum offer.

- Curriculum time needs to be given to arts subjects – it doesn't happen if you haven't taught knowledge and skills discretely too.
- Provide plenty of opportunities for concerts and exhibitions where creative work is shared.
- Low stakes opportunities are necessary too – process and progress are essential to how children grow to feel confident about themselves as creators.
- Make specialist support available for teachers to build their confidence and give examples. (Do you have local arts hubs, galleries or orchestras that have education departments?)
- Use your local environment – who or what do you have around you to inspire the children?
- Be brave – what's the worst that can happen? Demonstrate to children and staff that there is joy in creating, no matter the outcome.

Editor's reflection on Part 3: Quality of education

When the Ofsted Handbook was introduced in 2019, it caused considerable concern for many schools and teachers, notably in primary schools. Previously primary school teachers were encouraged to be subject generalists as they might be responsible for teaching all 12 subjects. Primary teachers have always been pedagogic specialists for the primary phase and have great expertise in child development for the 4–11 age range. However, with the new framework and the emphasis on subject 'deep dives', primary teachers had to quickly become subject specialists in at least one area of the curriculum, and for that to be to a similar level as their secondary specialist counterparts. This is on top of teaching all the other 11 subjects as well as the pastoral responsibilities for 30 young children day-in-day out! This was a huge ask but, as ever, primary teachers rose to the challenge admirably and successfully. Particular recognition of this, however, must go to colleagues working in small schools, where a teacher might have to take on four or even five subject disciplines!

The case studies in this section offered a number of suggestions for how best to manage the requirements of teaching a knowledge-rich curriculum:

- Alex Fairlamb advocates for forging strong relationships between schools and sharing good practice. He recommends that primary and secondary schools coordinate and collaborate on pedagogy, curriculum content, the key skills to be taught, as well on cross-phase moderation in order to ensure a smooth transition and progress through the key stages.

- Allen Tsui recommends making good use of networks and reminds us, 'No question is ever too foolish to ask'. He says that scaffolding is key to a successful lesson. Teachers should make no assumptions about what the children are able to do and should also look out for time-saving techniques such as making logging in as simple as possible. Allen also suggests breaking down the curriculum and mapping it into a set of 'I can…' statements. This would help anyone delivering the curriculum to see and understand the key skills and knowledge to be covered in every lesson.

- Bob Cox says it is important that an ambitious curriculum for English should be the norm, rather than an exception. He advises lots of book talk, brilliant assemblies, quality reading in class and an inspiring diet of great books and poems. Bob says that a challenging curriculum not only feeds the curiosity of the teachers but also contributes positively to their ongoing professional development as well as creating huge job satisfaction.
- Ian Roberts and Heather MacNeil saw physical literacy as the main goal for their revised PE curriculum. They were clear about the challenges when they started but say they wanted to plan a curriculum offer that would unlock children's desire, interest, confidence and competence to take part in physical activity throughout their life. This comes from a vehement belief that the experiences and skills children gain within education will pave the way for their adulthood.
- For Nancy Wayman a 'Glittering Curriculum' is one that emphasises active involvement over rote learning; it is one that offers stimulating learning via artistic innovative experiences. The aim of the curriculum is to develop creative, independent thinkers who have a strong sense of themselves and their roles in the community. The feedback from parents and carers is very positive as the children are happy and benefit from a broad and exciting curriculum offer.

It is abundantly clear that each of the contributors of the case studies above are passionate and knowledgeable about their curricula and their enthusiasm is inspiring. They make the case clearly that the learning should be well-sequenced, and must be what the children need to learn, rather than what the teacher wants to teach. With the right mindset and a rigorous approach I have no doubt the standards the children achieve in any one of the five disciplines will be very high!

PART 4

Behaviour and attitudes to learning

Introduction

The Ofsted EIF states that inspectors will make a judgement on a number of different aspects that the school deploys to implement the curriculum intent, including the teachers' skills and ability to 'create an environment that allows the learner to focus on learning.'

Ensuring that children are ready to learn and have a positive attitude to learning is critical. Teachers and leaders cannot underestimate the importance of establishing effective routines, setting a good example, having high standards and high expectations of everyone.

Milton Road Primary School

At Milton Road, we start by getting the environment right. There is a distinct 'House Style' at Milton Road, which is based on the house at Kettle's Yard. The house was once owned by Jim and Helen Ede. Jim Ede was an assistant curator of the Tate Gallery (now Tate Britain) in London, who championed the work of contemporary modern painters, such as Pablo Picasso and Piet Mondrian, not only at the Tate where he worked but also in his own home, for which he acquired works by Henri Gaudier-Brzeska, Ben and Winifred Nicholson, Alfred Wallis, and Joan Miró, among others. It was part of Jim Ede's philosophy that art should be shared with others in a relaxed environment, so he would often give personal tours to students; invite them for tea and even loan out pieces from the collection so that students could hang them in their rooms during term time. In 1966, Ede gave the house and collection to Cambridge University, leaving it exactly as it had been curated and how it had been as their family home.

What makes Kettle's Yard so attractive and unique is that not only is it filled with beautiful sculptures and paintings, but there are also carefully selected found and natural objects including lovingly placed stones, shells and plants. The exquisite art of this environment is the thoughtful, gentle juxtaposition and arrangement of objects so that the overall effect is of elegance, beauty, grace, calm and charm. This is the feeling we are trying to capture as part of our school ethos. Apart from the occasional splashes of green in the library, most of the walls are gallery white and the doors a minimalist soft grey. Although relaxed and comfortable, nearly every plant, chair and object in the school has been carefully selected, and has its place as part of the overall curated ambience.

The calm elegance of Kettle's Yard is the exact atmosphere that we want to instil at Milton Road. We are looking for a happy, calm, purposeful school where children feel safe, inspired and ready to learn. Although we are a non-uniform school, one of the things that we do to keep our school attractive, clean and calm is to insist that all our children wear slippers or indoor shoes. Research has shown that when children feel relaxed and safe, they are more ready to learn. With plants, bunting, fairy lights, low level lighting and gentle music playing, our environment hopefully communicates that something wonderful is happening here.

Slow down and make building relationships as important as building projects.
Greg Mortenson, *Three Cups of Tea*, 2006, p.150

Once the school looks right, we want the school to feel right. Taking an attachment approach, our school culture is inclusive, considerate, compassionate and relational. Our pedagogy is inspired by the work of a number of educationalists including Paolo Freire, bell hooks, Michael Fullan, Valerie Hannon, Louis Cozolino and Ron Berger.

We have adopted some of the pedagogic approaches of EL Education where Ron Berger is the Chief Academic Officer (see eleducation.org). As such, our curriculum aims to balance high standards and beautiful work with excellent knowledge and skills, as well as developing positive pro-social character traits.

An important element that we have wholeheartedly adopted from Ron Berger's approach is the philosophy of CREW (see pp. 3–4 for further explanation). We use the mantra 'we are CREW not passengers' to underpin all our work. Many schools will also correctly emphasise the importance of team work ('team work makes the dream work!') as there is significant research that says that ensuring good psychological safety and mutual respect is essential to ensuring an organisation is able to function effectively and fulfil its potential.

Milton Road Primary School was built in 2004. The founding headteacher, deputy and members of the governing body researched optimal learning spaces to inform the design of Milton Road and this included visiting various European schools. The result was a very generous and attractive building. In addition to classrooms, there are shared group rooms, wide learning corridors, a central courtyard, three halls, a large open field and an orchard. Schools today are rarely built with this level of generosity, thought or magnanimous consideration for the staff and children!

Figure 12: *We are CREW not Passengers*

A particularly lovely feature of the school is that outside every classroom there is a 'pod' area. This is a large semicircle with a curved wooden bench able to accommodate all 30 of the children in the class. This is where the children assemble at the start of the day for registration and where they can finish up the day, evaluating how it has been. This resource lends itself perfectly to the CREW time and relational approach that Ron Berger advocates.

Part of CREW at Milton Road is about taking care of the school, each other and the environment and through this demonstrating one of our core values – responsibility. The children wipe the tables after lunch and tuck their chairs in; they are responsible for keeping their pods and the surrounding parts of the playground litter free; for gardening the plots outside the classroom and every week there is a whole-school 'Tidy Friday'. These actions contribute to our ethos and our five 'Take Care' agreements. We:

1. Take care of ourselves.
2. Take care of each other.
3. Take care of our learning.
4. Take care of our school, community and world.
5. Take care for the future.

These agreements are listed on the fingers of a rainbow hand, which are displayed in classrooms and around the school.

Like many schools, Milton Road is very concerned about the increase in poor child mental health, which has seen a significant rise since the Covid-19 pandemic. The Good Childhood Report 2023 shows how anxious our young people are for their families, about their current financial situation and about the future. The authors conclude that the need for improving children's wellbeing is urgent.

At Milton Road, we have an in-school councillor for one day per week; an Emotional Literacy Support Assistant (ELSA); a beautiful therapy dog who visits every Thursday; a nurture room called the Hive; and we ensure that our Social and Emotional curriculum includes a whole-school approach to children being able to articulate their emotions and co- and self-regulate. 'The Colour Monster' posters based on the book by Anna Llenas (2015) are displayed throughout the school; we use Goldie Hawn's MindUp™ programme to deliver mindfulness; and as a school community we proactively look for 'glimmer' moments.

Deb Dana, a clinician and consultant specialising in working with complex trauma, coined the term 'glimmers' as an antithesis to the word 'triggers'. Her work draws on the American psychologist and neuroscientist Stephen Porges' polyvagal theory. Dana's book *Polyvagal Exercises for Safety and Connection* (2020) includes a number of activities that can be used for calming and stilling. During a recent Joint Professionals Training day with my colleagues, I invited them to take a brain break and suggested that they take their shoes off and find a quiet place to stand bare footed in the school grounds for a few moments, feeling the coolness of the grass beneath their bare feet, feeling the breeze on their cheeks, breathing in the air and listening to the sounds of the birds in the trees. It was interesting to observe how different colleagues reacted to this: some instantly took themselves off and engaged immediately with the activity; others huddled in the safety of small groups, a little off task, catching up about the holiday they had just had. After a gentle nudge, everyone took these few minutes of peace, as did I. I noticed that, even though I was trying to demonstrate the benefit to stopping and being still for a few minutes, my mind was initially racing thinking about what we would be doing next and when would be the best time to stop for coffee. Finally, after a few minutes, I settled into the activity. It really felt like a luxury, just to stop, stand and stare. When we returned to the hall, everyone agreed that this was something that few of us made time for and yet it felt so pleasant and so necessary.

What is this life if, full of care,

We have no time to stand and stare?

W. H. Davies, 'Leisure', 1911

A note on the case studies

The five case studies in this section emphasise the importance of playfulness, risk taking, exploration and adventure. Being in nature is seen as a key learning opportunity for children to discover and understand the world around them as well as to discover what they are capable of themselves. Teachers are there to guide and support the learning but there is an emphasis on professional autonomy so that the adults are also part of the learning journeys.

16 Outdoor learning
CHRISTIAN KITLEY

School Name	Manor Lodge School
Age group taught within school	3–11
Location of school	Shenley, Hertfordshire
Any distinguishing features	• Independent and co-educational. • A strong reputation for music, drama and sport. • A beautiful site in open countryside, nestling within fields, woodland and wildlife.

Intent of the curriculum

Through our outdoor learning curriculum, we aim to immerse children in the natural world around them and develop skills that complement and enhance those learned in the classroom. We have designed the curriculum to be broad and varied in order to appeal to all children but without sacrificing depth of knowledge or skill acquisition. As outdoor learning does not have a National Curriculum framework, we have no specific skills or knowledge that we have to cover, which opens the door to a very flexible, innovative and unique curriculum. During the year, our aim is to develop soft skills in the children such as teamwork, resilience and creativity through planned and spontaneous activities. The curriculum is roughly divided into six areas and aims to be broad enough to engage children of all interests and abilities in their outdoor learning lessons.

These six areas will be explored in more detail in the following sections but briefly they are: Bushcraft (including tool work), the Natural World, Art, Outdoor Cooking, Wellbeing and Traditional Crafts. Within each area, different skills are taught and practised but there is significant overlap between them, particularly thinking about the soft skills of creativity, teamwork and leadership for example. The curriculum aims to allow children to develop and showcase their skill sets across tasks that may be new or unknown to them previously, exposing them to a range of ideas and learning experiences that they would not have the opportunity to explore within the confines of the classroom.

Implementation

The children have a dedicated outdoor learning lesson timetabled for one hour every week throughout the school from Nursery up to Year 6. On top of this, all teachers are strongly encouraged to utilise the outdoor spaces for their lessons as much as possible. While not part of the distinct outdoor learning curriculum, these outdoor learning sessions add to the children's interest in the outdoors and help develop our school culture of learning outside the classroom. Across the school, the dedicated outdoor learning lessons are led by myself as Head of Outdoor Learning, a Forest School Leader, and a specialist Outdoor Learning Teaching Assistant. The Forest School Leader is supported in their sessions by the class teacher of the group being taught. Having a dedicated team for Outdoor Learning ensures that we are focused solely on delivering high-quality, innovative lessons and can spend time testing out new ideas to ensure that our curriculum is ambitious and exciting.

In Reception and Year 1, we tend to follow a more Forest School-style approach to learning, allowing the sessions to be child-led as much as possible. The emphasis here is to immerse the children in the outdoors, to develop a connection with the world around them and encourage them to learn new skills safely. They follow the same six areas mentioned above although there is more flexibility with what they choose to do in any particular lesson. There will often be several activities prepared for the children to choose from, in addition to a free play option. We have found that blending a child-led approach with a more traditional skills teaching approach has the best effect for this age group in terms of enjoyment and skills learned.

From Year 2 onwards, the emphasis shifts towards more teacher-led lessons, although there are still lots of opportunities for child-led learning to take place. The beauty of not having a National Curriculum to follow is that we can be very flexible in what to teach and when. Therefore, our planning will change year on year as we get to know the changing interests of the children we teach and adapt lessons to capture their interests. The older years (Years 4–6) is where we start to develop their basic skills further, enabling them to make, discover or understand something far more complex.

Throughout their outdoor learning lessons, the children are encouraged to understand risk and how to manage it. In the Early Years this might manifest itself in a child working out how high an object they can jump off safely without injuring themselves. You might see them going up in increments, one branch of a tree to the next, for example. In the older years, we encourage children to think about what sort of rules should be in place for certain tools or activities before we give them our actual rules. With each new tool or activity introduced, the children understand risk better and how to minimise it.

Along with some examples, the six areas of learning we use are:

- **Bushcraft:** using tools like saws and knives, fire lighting, shelter building and survival skills.
- **Natural World:** exploring nature through bug hunts, fungi, bird watching and tree identifying.
- **Art:** natural art work, observations of seasonal changes, photography, artistic whittling and carving.
- **Outdoor Cooking:** cooking sweet and savoury foods using a range of methods, foraging, food preparation and planting and growing food.
- **Wellbeing:** a variety of meditation, reflection and mindfulness.
- **Traditional Crafts:** thatching, metal casting, blacksmithing and woodland management.

While I use these areas or themes in my planning, lessons or activities, they often overlap and all of them encompass a wide variety of skills.

Impact

The impact on the children has been incredible, especially their attitudes towards nature and the outdoors. They display a really positive attitude towards learning, and they are able to see how the skills they learn outdoors are transferable to indoor lessons and vice versa. Their resilience and perseverance have shown a marked increase too; they have to come to lessons prepared for all weathers, as only lightning or very high winds stop us from going outside for outdoor learning lessons. They love the sense of freedom they get from being outdoors in a lesson; they get incredibly creative building new spaces within the woodland and coming up with stories of what their space or structure is. There is definitely a building of trust that goes on during these lessons, particularly lessons involving tools, heights or fire: not only the idea that they trust us as teachers to keep them safe from something they could regard as being potentially dangerous, but also the idea that we are trusting them as children with tools or activities that they perceive to be 'for grown ups'. The trust develops both ways and I strongly believe that it has helped to build solid relationships.

The parents have bought into the outdoor learning concept and everything that comes with it. A lot of our parent events are held outdoors in our grounds, which has helped us build a culture of outdoor learning that isn't just restricted to lesson time. We have tried to involve the parents as much as possible in our outdoor learning journey: we have had lots of parents support us in building and creating new outdoor learning spaces, for example. These regular sessions to build allotments, an orchard and a Japanese garden have not only created incredible learning environments for the children, but also allowed us to develop a deeper relationship with many of the parents. It also means that we are able to share our vision with them and it has resulted in a high level of parental engagement and support for outdoor learning and the school more broadly.

The impact on staff has been equally high. Having a dedicated outdoor learning team has helped to develop not only the outdoor learning curriculum, but we have also been able to support and advise other teaching staff on how to take their learning outdoors and utilise the outside spaces. In developing my outdoor learning curriculum, I have been able to link in with other curriculum areas and work together with that particular subject lead to enhance what we are both able to offer to the children. Staff have been growing in confidence during the implementation of the new outdoor learning curriculum and the development of our school culture as a place for outdoor learning. We are also seeing more teachers metaphorically breaking down the classroom walls and taking their teaching outside whenever there is a learning opportunity.

Turning vision into reality

The trickiest part of implementing this curriculum was also the most fun part: designing a programme that had no existing framework which I was able to make entirely my own. It was difficult in the sense that I wanted to make it fun and engaging for the children but also offer skill acquisition and progression with very little existing provision to draw on. However, this has also been one of the most enjoyable aspects for me as I have been able to create a curriculum that is completely unique, drawing on a range of ideas from varied sources. Some lesson ideas come from others on social media, others from activities I've seen at country shows or even just inspiration from a walk in the woods. The flexibility and lack of National Curriculum constraints has definitely made my outdoor learning curriculum a pleasure to create. My main thought when creating this curriculum has been to give the children experiences that they would not normally be exposed to. Sometimes this could be traditional crafts that are in danger of being lost, at other times it might be a particular method of outdoor cooking, but I always aim to give the children something to take away from the lesson and an enjoyable experience.

I have been very lucky to have the complete support of the headteacher and governors at my current school which has enabled me to be ambitious and really push the boundaries of what is possible in terms of outdoor learning within a school setting. Our commitment to outdoor learning is a big selling point of the school and this has certainly helped when it comes to budgets and requests for new learning spaces.

I believe that having a clear vision is really important when it comes to designing and implementing a new curriculum. This doesn't necessarily mean knowing what every single lesson or activity will be for a whole year in advance, but what you want your outcomes to be and what the benefits are to your children. One of the ways I have ensured the outdoor learning curriculum is supported across the school is by making clear links between other curriculum subjects and transferrable skills. This has helped other members of staff and parents see the value in a subject that is still fairly uncommon in schools and has helped promote what we do to the school community.

One of the biggest opportunities has been our smallholding project that we have built in collaboration with the parents and local community. With them, we have built an allotment garden and orchard, along with areas for chickens and beehives for the children to use in lessons and clubs, as well as for the community to use. This has allowed us to expand our teaching about food growing cycles and set up a farmer's market to sell our produce, meaning that the project can be self-funding and promotes the environmentally friendly benefit of reducing food miles.

Another benefit of the outdoor learning curriculum is being able to share our experiences and ideas with other schools. We have hosted other schools and events for teachers to come and take inspiration to create or enhance their own outdoor learning curriculum and this is something really positive to have come out of our programme.

Takeaways

- Be brave! Push the boundaries of what you think is possible and don't be afraid of things not going to plan.
- Inspiration comes from all around you – take ideas from social media, events you attend, and especially ideas or interests which the children have.
- Have a clear rationale and vision of what you want to achieve in terms of outcomes and/or experiences.
- Get the support of your colleagues, both teaching and non-teaching; discuss your vision and listen to their ideas.
- You don't need acres of space to have a successful outdoor learning curriculum; be creative with what you have. Just leaving the four walls of the classroom is often enough to get children thinking in a different way.
- Don't allow your curriculum to stand still, there are always tweaks or even bigger changes to be made. Changing or adapting your curriculum doesn't mean it hasn't gone well or isn't good enough, just that you are striving to make your curriculum the best and most up to date it can be.
- Speak to teachers in other schools or settings to see what they do. Most will be very happy to share ideas and processes with you and you may be able to build relationships that will benefit you and the children you teach.
- Be creative with your resources. You don't need to spend much money to create amazing experiences for the children: some bugs and leaves or a tarpaulin sheet cost very little but can be used in a multitude of ways to excite and engage your class.

Tools and resources

www.schooloutdoorlearning.com
www.muddyfaces.co.uk
www.outdoor-learning.org

17 Going beyond the National Curriculum with an explorer curriculum

JOE HALLGARTEN AND JO FRANKLIN

School Name	London East Teacher Training Alliance (LETTA) is a growing MAT currently consisting of two primary schools, Stebon and Bygrove
Age group taught within school	4–11
Location of school	East London
Any distinguishing features	• We run a popular School-Centred Initial Teacher Training (SCITT) alongside 20 partner schools and are a registered provider of apprenticeships.

Intent of the curriculum

Background: how can the National Curriculum avoid becoming the whole curriculum?

The biggest risk to successful curriculum design in English primary schools at the moment may be around the teaching and learning of the National Curriculum. Since the new National Curriculum was introduced in 2014, primary schools are rising to the challenge of a more knowledge-rich approach and designing curricula that are carefully sequenced. If, as expected, the National Curriculum remains relatively stable over the next few years, primary schools' confidence in demonstrating Ofsted's holy trinity of intent, implementation and impact is likely to increase with age and experience.

A far greater risk, one that has been there since the start of the National Curriculum in 1988, is whether schools have space to carry out any significant learning that does *not* relate to the National Curriculum. Since its introduction in 1988, every minister and official has suggested that the National Curriculum should never be the be-all and end-all of a school curriculum. Schools must have their own agency, not just to deliver the National Curriculum in their own way, but to agree and teach additional knowledge, skills and dispositions that they value. Rumour has it that Kenneth Baker (1987, quotes in McNeill, 1991) thought this should be up to 20 per cent of a school's time and Michael Gove (2011) put the figure at 50 per cent. This rhetoric around curricular freedom has never matched the reality. This is largely a result not of an overloaded National Curriculum, but of an assessment and accountability system that forces schools to narrow their curriculum offer. What might primary schools do to break this vicious cycle?

Spotting the gap between the National Curriculum and our vision

At LETTA last year we faced a dilemma that I believe many primary schools face. Our National Curriculum teaching was already strong and getting stronger. Our schools teach the National Curriculum through termly themes, largely in subject-based lessons. Since the initiation of the new National Curriculum in 2014, we have made significant improvements to the design and implementation of this curriculum. Our subject leads, who work across both our schools, have regular opportunities to develop their subject-specific knowledge and to collaborate as a curriculum team. Our subject 'health checks' help subject leaders to monitor how well the planned curriculum lands in the classroom and whether children are building knowledge and skills in each area over time. When it comes to our National Curriculum delivery, we are both confident about our current approach and committed to continual improvement.

However, like most schools, our school has a vision for our young people that goes far beyond the knowledge and skills that the National Curriculum specifies. This is articulated through our four promises we make to our pupils.

Our vision is that every child in every school in the LETTA Trust:

1. Loves learning, achieves their very best, has fun at school and feels excited about the future.
2. Knows how to make friends and get along well with people; to treat them with fairness, compassion and respect.
3. Grows healthy and strong, believes in themselves and has the confidence and resilience to follow their dreams.
4. Feels part of their community, proud of their school and inspired to make a positive difference in the world.

Although we have strong buy-in from our staff and wider community to this vision, we know this isn't enough. However brilliant our delivery of the National Curriculum; however many out of school and after school opportunities we offer (including residentials and visits); however our school's culture – from assemblies to lunches to play times – tries to ensure that this vision is 'caught' as well as 'taught'; all this is still inadequate for the task of developing the young citizens we want our children to be and become. To come closer to achieving our vision for all pupils, we need two things: precision and space.

Precision: turning our vision into behaviours

Just like any set of curriculum goals, our vision needs some specificity in terms of outcomes. Without this, there is a risk that our vision is simply a vague set of platitudes. So we sought to agree and define the particular dispositions – habits of mind and character – we want our children to develop. Through conversations with staff, we identified nine such behaviours:

1. **Curiosity:** the desire to learn, ask questions, understand and try new things.
2. **Creativity:** problem-solving, innovating and inventing across all subjects.
3. **Determination:** not giving up, bouncing back, trying again and staying focused.
4. **Kindness:** making people feel good, sharing, giving, selflessness (crucial to wellbeing).
5. **Confidence:** self-confidence, confidence your voice will be heard, confidence in your ideas.
6. **Fairness:** to include equality as children progress.

7. **Leadership:** organising, taking responsibility, communicating.
8. **Teamwork:** understanding yourself and others.
9. **Citizenship:** local, national and global – making the world a better place.

This, to some extent, was the easy part. Many schools have similar lists. Much more difficult is to consider what progression in each behaviour should look like, breaking down each behaviour into smaller, clearer and, where possible, age-related steps that can be taught and modelled across the school. The aim here was not to create any assessment framework (although this may come at some point). At this stage, we wanted all staff to: understand each behaviour; share a common language to describe and model them; understand what progress in each behaviour might look like; and recognise and celebrate progress. A 'behaviours working group' consisting of staff with a diverse range of experiences worked on each behaviour in turn. Informed by our collation of a vast educational and psychological literature on each behaviour, we agreed on a small number of key 'I show that…' statements for each behaviour, dividing most statements into one of three age categories: EYFS, Years 1–3 (deliberately straddling key stages) and Years 4–6. We also gave concrete examples of what children might be doing when demonstrating each behaviour, and specific actions that adults can take to encourage and model each behaviour. This was a tricky task. Our final document from this is in no way perfect, but does give us a starting point from which to improve through testing and practice.

Space: dedicating in-school time to move beyond the National Curriculum

There is, of course, no dichotomy or tension between the subject knowledge and broader dispositions for learning. There are deep interconnections. The teaching of subject knowledge will inevitably develop some dispositions and ignore others, depending on pedagogical approach. The teaching of dispositions has to happen within a context that demands the application of knowledge. However, a simultaneous prioritisation of both is just very difficult. If, in a maths lesson, it's a competition for prioritising between fractions and fairness, counting and collaboration, knowledge and skills tend to trump dispositions and behaviours.

Although many schools do integrate knowledge and dispositions through subject-led or transdisciplinary approaches, we decided on a different approach. A genuine focus on these nine behaviours needed dedicated time outside of the National Curriculum. Although some knowledge might be learnt along the way, the behaviours would come first. Prior to the Covid-19 pandemic, our schools already had one afternoon each week doing a version of Scouts – putting children in mixed age groups to achieve badges such as 'athlete' or 'cook'. We used the opportunity of a pandemic pause to begin a radical redesign of this time. Working with staff from across both schools, including subject leaders, newly qualified teachers, Early Years practitioners and midday meals supervisors, we created our Explorer Curriculum.

The LETTA Explorer Curriculum

Fridays in LETTA schools look and feel different from the rest of the week. Children are in mixed age groups, collaborating on projects which, where possible, address real-world challenges. These enable pupils to broaden their horizons, develop their character, and explore their personal interests and talents. Much of this takes place outside classrooms, using the outdoors, the local neighbourhood and other parts of London as resources for learning. All school staff (as well as parents and others in our community) are involved, and older pupils are given genuine leadership responsibilities.

During each project, children have the chance to complete 'Destinations' and exhibit the processes and outcomes of their project to others. They have opportunities to develop the outlined behaviours, reflect on their learning and receive meaningful feedback from peers, school staff and other adults. These projects complement our existing knowledge- and skills-rich curriculum, which is taught through subject-driven termly themes.

The Explorer Curriculum provides opportunities for pupils to develop character behaviours and discover the passions and interests that will enable them to thrive, as children and as adults. It gives us the chance to develop and embed these character behaviours in a more focused, systematic way and makes a significant, unique contribution to achieving our vision for every child in our trust.

On Fridays our children are learning, deeply and with purpose, about themselves, the world around them and their place in that world. At the same time, they are having lots of fun!

Explorer objectives

The Explorer Curriculum's main objectives are to provide learning opportunities that enable children to:

- develop their understanding of and achieve progression in the nine LETTA behaviours
- broaden their horizons and connections to the outdoors, their locality and the wider world
- explore their personal interests and talents.

In addition, its secondary objectives are:

- to enable children to learn new knowledge or apply existing knowledge to solving real-world issues
- to give our staff opportunities to build different relationships with children and explore and demonstrate their own talents and interests that go beyond what their current roles allow
- to improve connections with our parents and with individuals and organisations in the broader community of Poplar and London.

Implementation

The Explorer Curriculum – the structure

Beware, potential chaos ahead! The organisational structure of the Explorer Curriculum turns the rest of our school week on its head, in three ways.

Firstly, the pupils are in mixed age groups or 'Explorer Families' which they will remain in throughout this six-year period. Years 1–3 are the Adventurers and Years 4–6 are Pioneers. Each family has between 20 and 30 children and they have all named themselves after places in the world. Older pupils in the family are given leadership responsibilities in the design and delivery of sessions.

Secondly, all staff, from school leaders to midday meals supervisors, are assigned to a family. The leader or 'Guide' could be any member of staff. Each family has at least two staff and, over time, may also include parents who can support on a regular basis. This curriculum needs all hands on deck!

Thirdly, while each family has a classroom base, it is unlikely to spend much time there. The badges demand a flexible approach to the use of spaces, in and out of school. This is without doubt a logistical challenge.

The destinations

The organisation of our destinations is crucial to the success of the Explorer Curriculum. We have created 18 projects, selected to ensure pupils enjoy a range of experiences and can develop a range of behaviours. Over a child's time in school, they will participate in all 18 projects, plus three of their choice (yet to be designed). Each project requires a minimum of four sessions, each lasting a minimum of 90 minutes. Many will require longer than this, including a whole day out of school.

We have created session plans for each project, scaffolded to enable adults to lead sessions with minimal preparation, but also to empower staff to adapt and innovate; redesigning plans to suit their own levels of confidence and particular passions. Each project ideally starts with a preliminary session for Year 6 or Year 3 pupils to support the planning, design and leadership of activities.

Table 4: The Explorer Curriculum projects

Term	Amount of time	Destination cycle A	Destination cycle B	Destination cycle C
Autumn 1	1–2 weeks	Family induction		
Autumn 2	4–5 weeks	Y1–3 Star Spotter Y4–6 Night Navigator	Y1–3 Crafter Y4–6 Legacy Makers	Y1–3 Good Neighbour Y4–6 Local Hero
Spring 1	4 weeks	Y1–3 Stallholder Y4–6 Entrepreneur	Y1–3 Local Activist Y4–6 Global Activist	Y1–3 Poplar Guide Y4–6 London Guide
Spring 2	4 weeks	Choice*	Choice*	Choice*
Summer 1 and 2	6 weeks	Y1–3 Outdoor Adventurer Y4–Y6 Outward Bounder	Y1–3 Den Maker Y4–6 Bushcraft Survivor	Y1–3 Gamesmaker Y4–6 Sports Day Planner

*Choices include: Conservationist, Free Spirit, Wellness Guru and Scout-style badges.

In the first session pupils have the opportunity to agree on a particular behaviour they wish to focus on, as a family. In the final session, pupils reflect on their focus behaviour. Most projects have an opportunity for pupils to share the outcomes of their work with others and access some meaningful feedback. Destination Entrepreneur, for example, ended with a fair where VIP visitors came to view pupils' products and award prizes.

Over time, we wish to work with external partners to redesign existing projects, create new ones, and lead the delivery of both. For instance, the Local Hero project was redesigned in partnership with the Mayor of London Game Changers programme. Staff from this programme lead two of the four sessions and provide advice throughout. Schools like ours receive a multitude of offers from people and organisations who wish to work with our children to focus on a particular agenda. At times, these can feel like random acts of kindness. From now on, where possible and appropriate, we will work with organisations to structure any offer around the delivery of an existing or new project.

Explorer pedagogy

LETTA already has a strong set of principles for learning, which the Explorer Curriculum aligns with. However, we also recognise that, to ensure that the Explorer sessions enable a focus on our behaviours, cross-age learning, and high quality input from a diverse range of staff, we need to adopt a different pedagogical approach, one we adapted from Cambridge University Primary School:

1. Prioritising activities that enable oracy and dialogue.
2. Making deliberate space for metacognition, reflection and feedback relating to our nine behaviours.
3. Building challenges where pupils can only succeed through teamwork and interdependence.
4. Creating opportunities for playful inquiry, which recognise the intrinsic value of play, but also stretch and challenge the way that children approach tasks and develop new ideas.

These four principles inform both the design of our projects and the teaching of our sessions.

Turning vision into reality

The journey so far

For those senior leaders implementing the Explorer Curriculum, the autumn term felt very operational: organising children into mixed-age families, thinking about provision for pupils with additional needs, allocating spaces and people and then communicating, communicating, communicating. We also decided to design and order Explorer passports for each child complete with individual stamps for each destination. This took time and money. We were worried about staff wellbeing. Would this be a step too far in the uncertain world of Covid-19 related absence and catch-up?

Three weeks in, however, walking the corridors on Friday afternoon, it felt peaceful and purposeful. We began to see behaviours like teamwork, determination and creativity emerging in these newly formed mixed-age families. Very soon, parents were telling us it was the thing their children were most excited to talk about at home. By Christmas, as each family reached their first destination, we celebrated together and the Local Heroes event provided festive entertainment for elderly residents in our local care home. Outcomes like this one really make a difference to our community. Some of these residents had had no visitors since the start of the pandemic.

Impact

Adapting first, asking questions later

Like with any aspect of our curriculum, we care deeply about the impact on our children. We feel we need a year of intuitive adaptation, where we are free to tweak our model in response to circumstances and pupil and staff feedback. At the end of the year, we will carry out a survey to understand people's perceptions of the curriculum, then change our plan for in response.

Takeaways

- Get your subject-based curriculum right first!
- Create some separate space for this. Integration isn't everything.

- Keep it simple – there are many, many behaviours with value but you need to prioritise.
- Don't worry about measuring impact in the first year.
- Involve as many staff members as you can in designing the curriculum.
- Plan the implementation carefully and make sure a senior leader is overseeing this phase.

18 Learning adventure curriculum

JONATHAN LE FEVRE

School Name	Pilgrims' Cross C of E Aided Primary School
Age group taught within school	4–11
Location of school	Andover, Hampshire
Any distinguishing features	- A school where children learn to love, laugh and learn, developing healthy and heartfelt relationships so all children gain a true sense of belonging and self-worth. - A warm and inclusive school. - High levels of deprivation and SEND need.

Intent of the curriculum

As a learning community, we discussed what we wanted for our curriculum and the statements below detail the intent. We added UNICEF's Sustainable Developmental Goals (2015) to help our children develop their understanding of how they can make a 'Positive difference in the world', which is within our school vision statement:

> Our 'How'
> Transformational Learning Adventure Curriculum
> Where all children dare to explore
>
> **1.** Generates curiosity and thirst for learning.
> **2.** Encourages collaboration alongside independence.

> **3.** Develops integrity.
> **4.** Builds resilience and independence.
> **5.** Solves complex problems.
> **6.** Results in understanding of technical vocabulary.
> **7.** Caters for and develops all multiple intelligences.
> **8.** Develops spirituality.
> **9.** Results in mastery in understanding of knowledge and skills, including digital understanding.
> **10.** Helps children understand, appreciate, take responsibility and love the world around them.

Intent of the curriculum

Mapping out of the curriculum

We have a combination of internally-planned subjects like geography, which includes place-specific content, and external schemes of work for subjects such as computing. However, for each subject we have mapped out the progression of knowledge and skills in a spiral-type system so main themes are returned to throughout the year and from one year to the next. We group subjects together to create a Learning Adventure where subjects are linked so children can make connections in their learning and at times pulling subjects together (this is locally called 'Blended Learning').

We have also chosen texts carefully to complement the knowledge being studied within the Learning Adventure as well as supporting the English reading and writing focus. We have tried to ensure we have some diversity within authors and cultures across our English curriculum.

Each Learning Adventure starts with a launch day, which creates a level playing field for all children, so they can *all* enjoy and participate in a shared experience and we can also include some of the prerequisite vocabulary to support the learning being focused on within the Learning Adventure. These launch days provide us with an opportunity to assess prior learning linked to previous Learning Adventures and set the scene for the half term.

We conclude the Learning Adventure with a 'Learning Destination' which is a combination of the learning in different subjects and a celebration of the children's understanding. This gives the children a real feeling and sense of meaning for their learning, where children talk with great enthusiasm about *why* they are learning, as well as what knowledge and skills they have acquired. An example of a Learning Destination is a Royal Banquet for Year 1 children, with food they have made in DT, dancing from PE, performance of their music and recital of poems with their parents.

Mini Learning Adventures

For each subject we create Mini Learning Adventures, which are short sequences of learning that follow the stages of learning below:

In summary, we plan learning sessions that ignite previous learning, explicitly making links across different subjects (**Prepare**), we then give the children opportunity to become fluent (**Trekking**) and then apply their learning (**Investigate**). The explore stage helps to develop the children's understanding and gives them a real purpose for their learning. An example of an explore task for a maths Mini Learning Adventure has been to design a futuristic house using 3D shapes, as the half term Learning Adventure was themed around the concept 'Our future is bright' (Year 6 to 7 transitional Learning Adventure). These designs were sent to the local authority architects department and they enhanced them using design software.

Our " How " - Transformational Learning Adventure Curriculum
- where ALL children DARE TO EXPLORE

Preparing
Context - reason
Introduce
Explain
Demonstrate
LOTS OF TALK
Explore of previous learning

Investigating
Multi step Problems
Complex application

Practice
Become Fluent

Simple application

Trekking

Exploring
Mastery with Greater Depth

PLANNING FOR MASTERY gives the children the opportunity to develop their understanding.

Preparing
Purpose
To level the playing field, re-ignite previous learning, engage the children in the mini learning adventure, introduce the tier 3 vocabulary,

Trekking
Purpose
To enable the children to learn the individual skills and acquire the appropriate knowledge so they are fluent in their learning.

Investigating
Purpose
To enable the children to start to apply and master their understanding (application of skills and knowledge)

Exploring
Purpose
To enable the children to fully master their understanding in different contexts and combine different areas of learning.

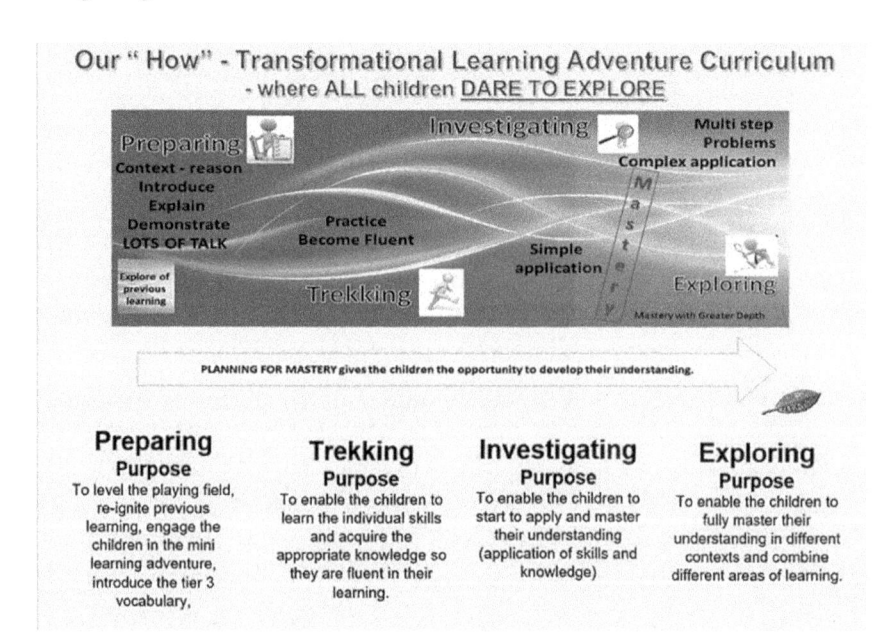

Figure 13: *Learning Adventure curriculum stages*

As mentioned previously, the Mini Learning Adventures, where possible, coincide with the overall theme of the Learning Adventure, which really helps the children make links within their learning. However, we ensure that different subject knowledge and skills are rigorously taught and, where necessary, out of context. We also choose several subjects to include a Sustainable Developmental Goal to discuss its relevance at an appropriate time within the Mini Learning Adventure.

Finally, to complete the Mini Learning Adventures we enable the children to reflect on their learning within specific subjects. We do this by simply focusing on one of our many 'Learning Animals' – in this case 'What happened, Wallaby?':

Figure 14: *Example of a Learning Animal*

We focus on one or two of the questions and the children respond in a variety of ways – group, individually, discussion, written etc. The purpose is for the children to reflect on what they have learnt and share this with one another, thus reinforcing the learning and helping with the retention of knowledge and skills.

We have also together developed an intent for the teaching and learning of the curriculum, which we refer to as 'Great Guiding'. In summary, this includes ideas to make learning more adventurous and also includes a feedback model, which demonstrates how we use modelling and metacognition to guide the children within their learning.

Impact

We have children who want to learn, who demonstrate high levels of resilience in their learning to achieve the learning destinations. We have a curriculum which is inclusive so all children can access it and contribute to the collective understanding. We also have children who can articulate their knowledge clearly and apply their skills confidently.

We have staff who are inspired to create wonderful Learning Adventures which are interesting to teach and have real purpose.

We have parents who love what we do and share how their children love to come to school and are enthusiastic about their Learning Adventures.

Some comments from parents:

The school is a wonderful example of 'getting it right'. The teachers and support staff truly care about the children and have a passion for teaching which in turn creates a fabulous learning environment.

Both my children have flourished in PC's care. The teachers and head have a very strong 'children first' ethos, which as a parent, is reassuring.

Pilgrims Cross has given our children a fantastic start in their learning for life.

The school genuinely wants to provide the very best experience for the children. So much time, effort and love are put into the school day and the adventures that are created.

Turning vision into reality

1. We developed the intent for the curriculum.

2. We used educational research to refine the intent and implementation model for the curriculum to ensure knowledge and skills development.

3. We try to ensure all procedures and process to enable the curriculum to be implemented and explicitly share how things are linked and can enable our intent.

4. We have also created an intent and implementation criteria for teaching and learning (locally known as Great Guiding). This has been helpful in explaining how to implement the curriculum in a way that engages children and reinforces their learning. This is based on educational research and best practice.

5. We have reviewed the intent of our curriculum every year, evaluated our strengths and weaknesses and then planned how to further improve. As our Learning Adventure curriculum is not based on the most recent Ofsted framework or DfE guidelines it does not change, so this gives consistency of focus for the school. This does not mean we do not include new ideas but we try to reduce unnecessary change.

6. We have the backing of our governing body and the parents which is really important.

7. We have tried to reduce unnecessary workload – marking, paperwork, etc. – to give staff the headspace needed to create the Learning Adventures.

8. We have recently re-emphasised the importance of rigour and that necessary knowledge provides explicit links within our curriculum so others can see how this fits within their requirements as well as providing what our children need and our community wants.

9. The known danger of putting the children first and creating a Learning Adventure curriculum is that it can be seen as children just having fun and that it is not rigorous enough or planned carefully. What has been frustrating and also painful for us as staff is that Ofsted deemed that the curriculum requires improvement. I will say that we had a secondary headteacher as the lead inspector, with no primary experience, who was implementing the current Ofsted framework which, in my opinion, is based on a very secondary curriculum model.

Takeaways

- Use all the community's experience and ideas across the school to develop your intent so it is shared and agreed together.
- Agree what implications this intent has to the teaching and learning and the type of learning sessions you want the children to experience as two sides of the same coin.
- Map out the curriculum carefully, combining learning where it is appropriate but accept that some subjects may need to be taught as standalone. With respect to the Ofsted framework, ensure knowledge is clearly identified for each Learning Adventure for each subject.
- Discuss different launch events for a Learning Adventure which would help level the playing field and what vocabulary the children will need to access the learning.
- Discuss different Learning Destinations that can bring learning together and celebrate learning with parents.
- Choose a subject to develop mini learning adventures using the stages of learning.
- Keep sharing wins with respect to adventurous learning experiences as a staff. Hunt out the good!
- It is worth it – children want to learn and teachers want to *teach*!

19 Battling the powers that be to champion Ed Tech

MATT JESSOP

School Name	Crosthwaite C of E Primary School
Age group taught within school	3–11
Location of school	South Lakes, Cumbria
Any distinguishing features	• National Support School (headteacher is NLE). • Google Reference School. • 'Outstanding' Ofsted rating (2017 and 2023). • Golden Apple School of the Year (2021). • Edufuturists School of the Year (2021).

Intent of the curriculum

Our intent is summarised by: *Enrich, inspire, achieve!* Staff, Governors and parents work ridiculously hard to provide a range of enrichment activities, resources, trips and people that inspire all learners to achieve to the very best of their ability in every lesson. Across all aspects of school we have two key strands running through our lessons, activities and all teaching and learning. These are the teaching of digital skills – the key life-skill now, along with so many aspects that are more important than huge swathes of the National Curriculum – and outdoor learning – encompassing support for mental health, entrepreneurship, outdoor learning, work on our farm and working with a variety of people, including professionals and organisations. Our statement of intent states (for these two key aspects):

Education Technology: A strand which runs across all areas of our teaching and learning is the school's groundbreaking use of Education

Technology, or Ed Tech. As a Google Reference School, children are taught a wide range of skills that enhance all areas of our teaching and learning from a young age by qualified teachers and external professionals, using Google Workspace as the basis for work. The skills and knowledge the children obtain are now essential life-skills and this is recognised by the work they do, whether when they link with schools in other countries such as Indonesia and Norway, or the work they do with Initial Teacher Training (ITT) students each year.

Outdoor Education: The school has developed an enriched curriculum focused around use of the outdoors in all subjects but also in specific, weekly timetabled sessions where children are given a wide range of opportunities to boost their confidence, reduce stress, work on short- to long-term projects and build their resilience, both on their own and in small teams and therefore improving teamwork skills and communication. Children in Key Stage 2 will link some of these sessions and opportunities to working towards their awards from the Prince's Trust, evidenced on their own work portfolios and hosted on their own websites.

Implementation

Our curriculum will be implemented with our intentions as the driving force behind our actions. By ensuring we think about *what* we learn, *who* we are when we are learning, *how* we act when we learn and *who we are* in the world, we build happy, resilient, successful and positive citizens.

In addition to learning through the National Curriculum, we promise our pupils a breadth of experiences throughout their journey at Crosthwaite C of E Primary School – these are, we believe, of greater importance than many aspects of the National Curriculum. These are our 'promises' which consistently mean all children leave us as high achieving, well-rounded, confident, independent and innovative students with a range of skills that prepare them for secondary school and life.

Examples include: providing a range of enrichment and extra-curricular activities led by specialist teachers; leading the charitable work in the school as members of various teams and committees; arranging educational visits and talks by speakers of different cultures, faith and experiences to share about their way of life; promoting and protecting emotional wellbeing and mental health; offering pupil leadership opportunities; and ensuring all children learn to work in harmony with every individual of all ages and abilities.

We empower our pupils to be engaged and creative lifelong learners who can contribute to wider society. They have presented and judged at the BETT show for the past two years, displaying maturity beyond their years and confidence to share their thoughts and opinions with others, including adults and professors while on stage! Our pupils live out our school's Vision, Ethos and Mission Statement by responding to social justice and undertaking (very effective!) local, national and international charitable work.

Our pupils develop a growth mindset approach from the earliest opportunities in school, so that they are resilient learners, who recognise that their effort is key to their success. They understand that they can improve through hard work, the use of effective strategies and help from others when needed. They are not afraid to make mistakes and learn from them – a key approach to all aspects of school life!

All pupils understand the importance of wellbeing and good mental health and its impact on our learning. They know who to speak to if they need support and that looking after their mental health is as important as looking after their physical health. These lessons are shared, by them, with family and friends and we are proud of how they embody their approach to this.

Impact

Our aim is to ensure that children will be academically and socially prepared for life in secondary school, modern Britain and the wider world – our two core strands of Digital Skills and Outdoor Learning are a huge part of this.

All children increase in confidence, independence, critical thinking and collaborative work each year and all leave us as brilliant individuals who will succeed at whatever they choose to do in life, at secondary school and beyond.

Turning vision into reality

To say the provision we now have has taken time would be an understatement! At our recent Ofsted inspection we explained – clearly and successfully – how our curriculum is never 'done' and what is in place now has taken over 10 years to produce. We constantly review and revise, enrich and enhance every single aspect of school life, working alongside the children. The challenge of doing this within the constraints of the National Curriculum, and its targets like SATs and the Progress 8, are constantly reminding us of the importance of what we do and achieve.

Attaining Google Reference School status was a huge step; a validation of our digital journey and strategy. However, it doesn't stop. The constant financial challenges we face in keeping all hardware and software up to date is huge, with new targets for the adoption of Virtual and Augmented Reality now in place, alongside the adoption of using Artificial Intelligence (AI). Partnerships we have made through networking are a huge support – whether with Google Trainers and companies, or AI companies such as Stemi, whose platform we use to teach AI, as well as our growing links with data science.

Our work with the Prince's Trust is in its fourth year at the time of writing, but being allowed to be the first primary school in the country to offer the opportunity to get an Ofqual approved diploma required a lot of persistence. It took a lot of work to get approval from both Ofqual and the Prince's Trust, was then required again when our children asked to submit digital portfolios (rather than paper hard copies), so we went back to the board and Ofqual. It's now been approved, finally!

Everything we do is a challenge that requires careful planning and a lot of work. DfE requirements, Ofsted requirements and statements by government minsters all require assessment, evaluation and then action.

Takeaways

- Network: social media can be hugely positive and the connections and links we have made and retain have been a huge help to what we do.
- Leave your comfort zone: go and see other schools, all have things to take away. Get out of your local authority and look outwards.
- There are so many brilliant role models out there. Most will chat via the phone or email, some may visit, some may welcome visitors – go and see them!
- Internationally there is so much brilliant stuff happening we can learn from: look to Estonia for technology, Finland for curriculum, etc. Take the time to read in addition to networking.
- Remember why you are here: the job is increasingly hard, often impossible, but the aim is to do your best for the pupils.

- Anything is possible – granted it is harder every year, finances become more challenging every year and time constraints increase, but things can all be done. They just have to be approached differently and may take more time than in the past!
- Don't be afraid to innovate and do things differently. Every pupil is different, which is a strength but means they need different opportunities to flourish too. We would much rather see a confident and innovative child heading to secondary school than one who has scored highly in the SPaG tests.
- Remember it's a job. It can be brilliant, it's always challenging and the powers that be almost always make it harder than it should be. Do what you think is best, but enjoy your free time too.

20 Finding natural wonder
RUTHIE COLLINS
founder of Natural Wonder

School Name	Henderson Green Primary Academy (HGPA), partnered with Natural Wonder
Age group taught within school	4–11
Location of school	Norwich, Norfolk
Any distinguishing features	• Green setting with lots of opportunities for outdoor learning, which the school makes the most of regularly to support student wellbeing and development.

Intent of the curriculum

Natural Wonder is an Arts Council England-supported cross-curricular learning framework accompanying a series of poetry and nature trails. It supports schools, educators and families in connection to nature, increasing learner engagement through ecology by taking literature, learning and the classroom outdoors, inspired by natural settings.

Developed with participating families, educators and staff from schools such as Henderson Green Primary School, it was inspired by the need to transition to learning outdoors and remotely during the Covid-19 pandemic. It's also a positive response to the climate emergency – helping to bring practical ecological action into the classroom by taking the classroom outdoors and blending curriculum aims with fun nature learning and literature.

Students engage with a broad range of nature writing and conservation topics to produce their own poems, stories and responses to the natural world, inspired by science, ecology and biodiversity, and encouraging action and awareness of biodiversity and the challenges animals face in their habitats. The students' work is then shared with a broader audience, within the school, or community, as 'public art' – creating an audience and helping to inspire practical action.

The key aims of Natural Wonder are to help improve access to literature, literacy and wellbeing through nature connection and vice versa. A science- and geography-based cross-curricular approach that recognises the wellbeing benefits of nature, as well as inequality in terms of access to nature and the growing national literacy crisis in the UK. The learning framework can be adapted for school-wide participation, integrating science and geography aims, as well as key literacy objectives within English Language and Literature.

Implementation

Natural Wonder's learning resources encourage families, schools and educators to support children and young people in connecting more closely with nature in their own communities as well as globally, and help them to see literature as a way of connecting to and changing the world around them. The framework has a hybrid approach to learning that embraces nature as an outdoor classroom, fulfilling curriculum aims by taking practical ecological action such as species surveys, pond dipping and tree planting, to support cross-curricular learning. The initial framework was piloted with the benefits of visiting conservation leaders, writers, artists and authors in mind, working closely with a school – sharing nature-inspired talks and literature and encouraging children to produce their own responses to the natural world.

Its poems, lesson plans, resources and suggested activities mean the framework can be delivered either as standalone components that can support curriculum learning, or together as a scheme of work. Using a blended approach that is tailored to the family, educator or school's own needs, the framework can be used as standalone poems that inspire, or a more structured combination or poems, with accompanying activities. Delivered with performance, poems, site visits to natural space and practical ecological action, the framework has at its heart restorative ecology – the fun and the joy of what happens when children and adults connect with the natural world. There's also scope for children to gain awards for their work, if taking part in extended learning.

While piloting the Natural Wonder framework, 29 Year 4 pupils explored a range of nature writing as a form of empowered storytelling and activism over the course of six 45-minute lessons. Taking inspiration from 'The Spell

Songs' by Rob Macfarlane and *Black Beauty* by Anna Sewell (1877), children created characters and plots using first, second and third person narrative. They also created poems inspired by biodiversity, using literary devices such as metaphors, similes and imagery inspired by the natural world. Their writing raised awareness about the challenges animals face in their natural habitats, shared with the community as an outdoor trail of magical fairy doors, with their works accessed through an online illustrated map via QR codes.

100 children were set a poetry writing challenge as part of National Poetry Day. They took part in an interactive performance of the poem 'The Last Eel on Earth' by Ruthie Collins, featuring artwork by students at Plymouth University, and used Natural Wonder's tree poetry resource to scaffold their own tree-inspired poems. Year 4 pupils also memorised and performed the poem 'Bats about Bats!' to the rest of the school. They first experienced the poem as a poetry trail outdoors, which led towards a real bat cave at Cary's Meadow nature reserve (managed by the Broads Authority). They took part in tree planting and the John Muir Award.

Natural Wonder's resources link into other successful educational frameworks, including the John Muir Award, Arts Award Discover, National Geographic Education's 'Explorer Mindset' and The Broads Curriculum as led by the Broads Authority. They also link to external global and national celebrations celebrated in the UK, including World Rivers Day, National Poetry Day and National Tree Week.

Gaining an Arts Award in nature writing and literature for their participation and learning the art of 'dendrography' (the description of trees) through poetry both helped to make literature and science more fun and accessible. Taking practical action such as tree planting and sharing nature writing as installation in public space and fun nature trails, all count towards the John Muir Award too. This is an inclusive way of raising awareness and helping people connect to nature, led by children. These activities all added to a sense of excitement and achievement for participating children and the school too.

Impact

Natural Wonder has helped educators find fun, structured ways to both take the classroom outside into nature and bring ecology into the classroom. It's helped children connect to nature, take action and find new audiences for their own creative writing – feedback shows that sharing work with public audiences increases pride and motivation. It also has broader community impact, helping to increase wellbeing, with community partners including Norwich Men's Shed also benefiting. Their members made fairy doors that were installed at Cary's Meadow, with children's nature writing shared through QR codes linked to the doors; increasing wellbeing for families from across Norfolk and beyond who visited the resulting trail and nature writing.

> *Social distancing has really changed the way members access the workshops at Norwich Men's Shed – physical making is key to our offer, but Covid regulations [made] any group projects difficult. Making the fairy doors provided the opportunity for members to be part of a community project while working individually and safely. Our members really engaged with this project and created a fantastic collection of fairy doors that reflect the skills and interests of our varied membership.*
> Roberta Wood, Co-ordinator at Norwich Men's Shed

Inspired by public poetry and sharing literature as 'text art', this kind of play-based way of experiencing poetry and literature outside as a route to learning about science, literacy and geography can easily be applied to urban environments too, with resulting nature-inspired literature shared as 'clues', or trails that the public can engage with. The impact is increased fun, excitement and access to both nature and literature. Poetry still has a reputation of being an inaccessible form of literature, so linking it to landscape, wildlife and places that people have a connection to and taking it outside can make it feel more engaging, especially for children and families.

> *The staff and I at Henderson Green Primary Academy have seen a significant improvement in children who have been learning and working with Ruthie through Natural Wonder. This has been evident in children being more attentive, more engaged, interested and self-disciplined in their attitudes to learning.*
>
> *Children's learning outdoors of science, geography and literacy has shown children being less stressed, more physically active and most of all given them a real enjoyment and understanding of how nature promotes social connection and creativity. All of these aspects of working with nature have been significant in improving learning and the love of nature.*
> Julia Henderson, Headteacher at Henderson Green Primary Academy

Sharing poetry and literature as a route into science and geography has the double time-saving benefit of fusing curriculum aims for teachers and reinforcing learning for children.

The cross-curricular approach meant we were able to cover a range of aims – from English to science, but bringing in geography, too. Getting outside and using a range of objects and biodiversity inspired realia in class and was really useful, boosting learner engagement and motivation.

Working with a real author inspired the children enormously. The children loved the trips and getting outside, which in turn has not only heightened their motivation to write and read, but also increased awareness with their families about what they're learning through their excitement, wanting to talk about their poems and stories.

Robin Pilgrim, Year 4 Teacher at Henderson Green Primary Academy

Turning vision into reality

The pandemic both acted as a huge challenge and a catalyst, with awareness of the climate emergency and concerns about safety leading many back to nature. Cary's Meadow was the perfect place to test out new ways of working, with large amounts of open green space making social distancing possible.

Norfolk is home to a quarter of the UK's rarest species of plants and animals and is a real hotbed of biodiversity. Its role in ecological education is world class, so it's great to help people learn about its natural history and heritage through getting outdoors and also learning through literature, creativity and having fun.

Nick Sanderson, Education Officer for the Broads Authority, who supported the development of Natural Wonder with expert advice, talks and hands-on practical help

It was a challenge for students to understand the differences between their local native biodiversity and that of other countries, partly because of an identified drop in awareness of geography for children in schools. This meant that the lexical range of localised vocabulary was quite low when it came to creating animal-inspired similes for their poems. However, with scaffolded support, this became an effective way of linking geography to literacy, inviting discussion on rivers, waterways, local towns, cities, regions and their biodiversity and natural habitats: 'What are the key rivers in your neighbourhood?' 'What animals might you find there?'.

Learners with lower literacy levels found the range of challenges facing animals and their habitats quite overwhelming in terms of the sheer range of issues to work with for their poems and stories. But awareness of the challenges was increased by use of games, realia, photos and videos. For example, the life cycle of eels was brilliantly brought to life using art, video and narration by Plymouth University and the Sustainable Eel Group. Kinaesthetic learning by being outside, and using objects and artefacts supplied by the Broads Authority such as bat detectors or 'eel spears' accelerated learning too. Movement, play and imagination when engaging with poems really helps.

Ecological grief and anxiety is a growing issue for young people. Linking arts and literature to curriculum aims, coupled with practical action such as advocating for biodiversity, peat restoration and tree planting, can not only really bring ecology and the curriculum to life, but also support increased wellbeing. Thanks to local authority funding, Natural Wonder was adopted by multiple schools across Norfolk, helping hundreds of children both contribute to and participate in literary public poetry trails, with significant interest in bringing similar poetry projects to schools nationwide.

Takeaways

- Take your learning outside and turn nature into your classroom using poetry trails, hunts and games.
- Explore literature as forms of empowered storytelling and activism that can change the world.
- Integrate curriculum aims across English, science and geography with practical ecological action such as tree planting.
- Make the most of curriculum-friendly national environmental awards, which can integrate literacy with science and geography aims, such as the John Muir Award.
- Take part in national events and celebrations such as National Poetry Day or National Tree Week to share your pupils' achievements.
- Apply exemplary environmental learning methodologies like National Geographic Education's 'Explorer Mindset' or the Broads Curriculum.
- Team up with environmental charities or community groups to find external expert guest speakers who can help to make nature more accessible in your communities.
- Look at fresh ways to share your pupils' literary works in public spaces as public art.

Tools and resources

Natural Wonder – Poems, trainings and trails
www.wondernatural.co.uk
Broads Curriculum
broads-authority.gov.uk

Tree Poem Writing Sheet

Tree Poem – Natural Wonder 2021

> Dear Tree,
> You are like a ……………………………………………………………..
> You make me feel……………………………………………………….
> You sound like…………………………………………………………..
> Thank you for……………………………………………………………
> You want to say to us "…………………………………….."
> Can you think of more tree words?
> For example:
> Magical Tall Calm Strong Majestic Happy Wistful Colourful Empowered Soft Peaceful Relaxed Energized Recharged Full Better Vibrant Wonderful Beautiful Incredible Bountiful Abundant Lovely Super Fun Luscious Loud Silent Flowing Intelligent Thoughtful Gnarly Tangled Curvy Homely

> www.wondernatural.co.uk / www.ruthiecollins.co.uk

Editor's reflection on Part 4: Behaviour and attitudes to learning

The five case studies in this section recommended giving educators a great deal of freedom and trusting in them as professionals to work alongside the children to make the learning adventures as fulfilling and enjoyable as possible. I can't help but think that working in these schools with such innovative approaches must be hugely enjoyable and rewarding for the teachers. Prioritising fun, joy and connection is also a highly effective way to keep teachers motivated and wanting to remain in our profession.

Christian Kitley has identified six key areas that contribute to his Outdoor Learning curriculum. The expectations are increasingly demanding as pupils progress through the school, and the skills and competencies the children learn are transferable to other contexts. Christian acknowledges it is important to have had the headteacher's support for his curriculum vision and for them to have the same positive regard towards the benefits of learning in nature and the outdoors. Christian has created a unique curriculum, drawing on a range of ideas from various sources, including social media and other activities, such as country shows, as well as ideas that come from an inspirational walk in the woods. The Outdoor Curriculum shows what is possible when the imagination is allowed to run wild and free and when one believes anything is possible.

Working with other colleagues, Joe Hallgarten and Jo Franklin came up with nine habits of mind and character that they wanted the children to develop. These transferable essential dispositions are ones that will be useful to the learner today as well as to them in the future. But as Joe and Jo recognised, ensuring there was a genuine focus on these nine behaviours required dedicated time outside of the National Curriculum. So they came up with a pragmatic solution, which was to dedicate Friday afternoons to their Explorer Curriculum. What is particularly appealing about the LETTA Explorer Curriculum is it allows children to work and learn in mixed-aged groups, collaborating on projects that, where possible, address real-world challenges. The Explorer

Curriculum is successful not only because children are practicing a range of transferable skills but they are simultaneously learning about themselves and having fun!

In the Learning Adventure Curriculum, Jonathan Le Fevre has identified ten Explorer outcomes including curiosity, collaboration, independence and integrity as well as spirituality, mastery, taking responsibility and pupils having a love of the world around them. The aim of specifying these is to develop a collective understanding across the school. A Learning Adventure starts with a launch day: a shared experience that includes the introduction of key vocabulary to support the learning focus for the Learning Adventure. Jonathan has involved parents and governors in the vision for the curriculum, which is well-mapped against National Curriculum objectives. Crucially, Jonathan says the culture in the school is one where the children are enthusiastic and want to learn and the teachers want to teach.

The opportunities that Matt Jessop's passion and leadership create for the staff and pupils in his school are truly visionary. Matt is relentless and uncompromising in his bid to ensure that what happens in his school goes well-beyond the comfort zone of a traditional curriculum model. At the heart of the curriculum are two key aspects: Education Technology and Outdoor Education. Through the curriculum the children have had a great many notable experiences including his pupils presenting at the BETT show in London, which is truly impressive!

Natural Wonder is an Arts Council England-supported cross-curricular learning framework accompanying a series of poetry and nature trails. Ruthie Collins has worked with hundreds of children to engage them in nature writing and conservation topics. The interdisciplinary project sounds absolutely enthralling: inviting pupils to respond to the natural world, and at the same time increasing their awareness of habitats, ecology and biodiversity. At the end of the project, the students' work is shared with a broader audience as public art, which then builds an audience and helps to inspire practical action.

What I love about all of these case studies are the amazing moments and positive experiences that such unique opportunities create. They are ones that send positive ripples through communities and make powerful memories that may last a lifetime.

PART 5

Behaviour and respect

Introduction

In the previous section I talked about attachment and about Milton Road being a relational school. This is a very important aspect of our school's warm, caring ethos; however, this approach needs to be reinforced with proactive and protective measures to ensure children and staff feel as secure and as safe as possible. It is important that teachers and leaders take time to put procedures in place that set 'clear routines and expectations for the behaviour of pupils across all aspects of school life, not just in the classroom' (Ofsted, 2019).

The word rule comes from the Latin word 'regula', a straight stick used for consistent and fair measurement. We also know 'rules' as the word to describe expectations and a guide for behaviour and conduct. Self-regulation and co-regulation mean to manage ourselves and to regulate in community. Schools are places that depend greatly on shared co-regulation, norms, agreements, rituals and customs.

In his international best seller, *Atomic Habits*, James Clear (2018) talks about the incremental benefit of implementing small daily actions, which cumulatively contribute to positive and significant change. Taking this idea on board, teachers at Milton Road are asked to think very specifically and carefully about every routine that governs the day-in, day-out rhythm and life of their classrooms and our school. How the children come in in the morning; where they sit, what they do; where the pencils are kept; how the children ensure their table is tidy above and below the table before going out to play; what the cloakroom is supposed to look like; how they line up for assembly – all of these simple daily routines should ideally be automatic to the children to help ensure that the school can run safely and predictably. The success of this is, of course, down to the teacher: the time they dedicate to perfecting each routine and the importance they place on practising them with the children until they are perfect – the divine is in the detail!

Behaviour management is a vital component to a successful school. It is establishing systems that ensure routines are predictable and dependable so that children know what's happening and what's going to happen next – there are no shocks and no surprises. This is beneficial not only for pupils with social, emotional or mental health needs, but for all children. Good behaviour management, in essence, minimises the opportunities for pupils and teachers to be emotionally triggered and causing their fight, flight, flock or freeze response. When children or adults are shocked, unsettled or scared, the amygdala creates dysregulation and the hippocampus cannot connect with the pre-frontal cortex. We are not able to make good decisions and our behaviours may be in conflict with the norms of the rest of the group. A blustery day, an unexpected fire alarm going off or a dog in the playground can cause chaos and be the source of much collective consternation!

Dr Bill Rogers, leading educationalist, trainer and author of bestselling behaviour management books, says 'you establish what you establish'. He recommends that teachers plan for the behaviour they want to see in the classroom and around the school and should have high expectations for this being sustained. He says that anything the teacher allows becomes permissible. If, for example, at the start of the academic year, the teacher says she expects the children to be quiet while she is teaching, but one or two children are whispering while the teacher is speaking, then the children learn that they can get away with a little bit of noise. They learn that just a little bit of whispering is okay, even though the teacher has asked for silence. Then perhaps by the end of the year, this permissiveness has been passed on throughout the class and the teacher will have a really challenging job of keeping their class quiet and in order. For this reason, Bill Rogers recommends that teachers invest time in setting up routines, discussing with the children precisely what is expected, with descriptive feedback for what is going well, along with regular reinforcement and practice.

Of course, good behaviour is not just expected or limited to the classroom. It should be everywhere in the school: the library, the dining room, the playground, in assembly. Often it is during those times, including transition times, that someone else is supervising the children. And at such times the behaviour of children can be worse than in the classroom situation under their teacher's supervision. Paul Dix has an important point to make about such times. He states, 'Teachers should pick up their own tab' (2017). By this he means that the teacher must not abdicate responsibility for the behaviour of their children to the support or senior team just because they are not with them. They should keep a regular eye on how their children are getting on, going onto the playground and eating lunch with the children from time to time.

Milton Road Primary School

At Milton Road, teachers are expected to practise all the routines that the children will experience during the day and week, making it very clear as to what other colleagues should be able to expect, i.e. expecting children to be ready, respectful and responsible. When lining up for lunch, the teacher should not assume that the children will somehow know that the expectations are to line up quietly, to say 'please' and 'thank you' to the chef, to collect their lunch and to have a calm and sociable time with their friends. This must be specifically taught. Similarly, if children are not able to behave well, out of sight of the teacher, then the teacher must put in appropriate strategies. Let's say that two particular children just love to play tag games with each other in the line when they should be standing calmly waiting in line for their lunch, then it is the teacher's responsibility to socially engineer the positioning of the children so that this daily kerfuffle is not handed along for a midday lunch-time supervisor to deal with, on a frustratingly daily basis.

At Milton Road, we say 'We are a kerfuffle-free school!'.

Inspired by headteacher Rachel Tomlinson and her inspirational leadership of Barrowford Primary School, Lancashire, (whom I met through the Whole Education network: https://wholeeducation.org) we have a Relationships and Behaviour Policy. Expectations for how children and adults should behave towards each other are predicated on the idea that there should be polite, kind and respectful relationships everywhere. But on occasion, where this does not happen, there are no punishments; only natural consequences. Natural consequences are ones where the consequence is related to what has happened: the consequence is reasonable and logical, relationships are maintained and the consequences support the pupil to make better choices in the future.

As an attachment-informed school, we never want our children to feel shamed through punishment; however, it is important that we provide clear guidance so that children learn the difference between right and wrong.

Our approach prioritises promoting pro-social relationships and community building through games, dialogue and fun activities to ensure that there is a positive intrinsic motivation for children to co-regulate with the rest of the CREW, to have a strong sense of belonging, to align with the morals of the school and recognise how they contribute to the overall success of the class.

At Milton Road, we are also fans of the good old-fashioned marble jar – collecting marbles over the half-term for good work and working towards a collective treat. Children work with the teachers to decide what group reward they would all like to work towards; this could be a film and popcorn afternoon, a class picnic, or an old-fashioned party with games such as musical statues and flip-the-kipper.

The word 'discipline' tends to have a negative connotation, however; it has the same root as the word 'disciple', meaning someone who is being taught. Without good discipline the teacher cannot teach and the pupil is not able to learn, so it is essential that the teacher pays attention to the conditions for learning, making sure they are as effective as possible.

As every educator reading this book will know, being in school is so much more than just learning concepts and facts: children are also learning how to participate positively as a microcosm of an ideal, just, pro-social society. Learning how to be kind, to listen, take turns, negotiate and get along with others is just as challenging and complex as learning how to ride a bike or the seven times table. Practice, trial, error and improvement and support is therefore just as vital for this aspect of learning as it is for practical skills or academic study.

This balance between a warm relational approach and high expectations with natural consequences is an authoritative style of educating, similar to the optimal one of the four parenting styles.

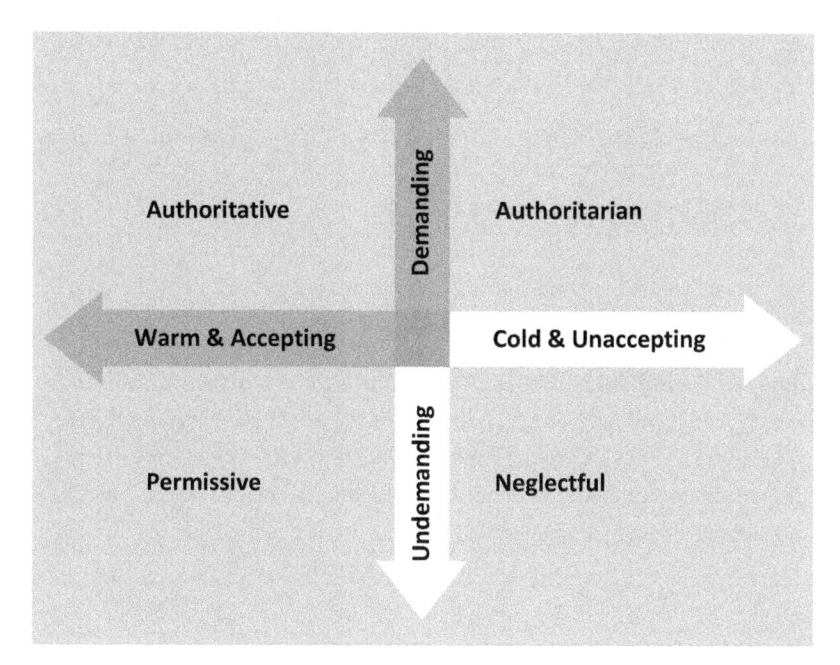

Figure 15: *The four parenting styles*

A note on the case studies

The next five case studies reflect on the growing rates of poor child mental health and the need for whole-school approaches to wellbeing. Wellness for staff and children is not seen as an add-on but is intrinsic to the curriculum design. As suggested in the upcoming 'Curriculum K – Putting health at the heart of education' case study: 'Stressed, anxious, tired, unfocused children will not learn'. Our contributors focus on the importance of raising physically and mentally healthy children who are self-confident, resilient and able to cope with the challenges of a rapidly changing, volatile, uncertain and complex world.

21 Mental health and wellbeing in the curriculum
ANDREW COWLEY

> **Andrew Cowley** supports the Carnegie Centre of Excellence for Mental Health in Schools as a coach, both on the School Mental Health Award and on the Senior Designated Mental Health Leader programme. He is an expert on wellbeing in schools and author of *The Wellbeing Toolkit* and *The Wellbeing Curriculum*.

Intent of the curriculum

Mental Health and Wellbeing (MHWB) is a subject without being a subject. It sits within PSHE and astride it. It exists in every lesson, every interaction and every moment in the school day. It is not a bolt-on, a tick box exercise or something fluffy and superfluous. MHWB is a concrete concept, a life-skill and at the forefront of our current concerns post-Covid-19 and facing a cost of living crisis.

If we have an 'intent' for anything we need to know our 'why', as readers of Simon Sinek can tell us. Not only do we need to know our 'why', we also need to share, communicate, evaluate and review it to reflect our community and our context. Context is key, as our context is different from every other school.

A starting point for your school's MHWB intent should be a definition of what you understand mental health to be. Read the World Health Organisation definition as a first step: in short, the WHO states that 'there is no health without mental health' (2024) and that there are socioeconomic, biological and environmental factors to consider. Schools need to understand that mental health and physical health must be equally recognised and that positive mental health is integral to positive wellbeing. The role of the school is not to diagnose or treat mental health, but to recognise when a level of support may be required by our young people. The school will also educate about mental health to challenge stigma, prejudice, discrimination and any form of bullying.

To return to my opening point, in recognising that MHWB is everywhere please think holistically. There should be a link to your intent and policy for safeguarding, for behaviour and for pastoral care. In addition, reference how the school intends to acknowledge how good mental health supports good learning health in the same way as positive behaviour management supports positive learning environments.

Implementation

In developing the implementation of the curriculum, consider three levels at which this may operate.

1. The universal support for all the children, which covers what all of them are taught and the support that is available for every pupil.
2. Early levels of intervention, which is the support offered within school.
3. Support for children who are experiencing or demonstrating symptoms requiring the support of a mental health professional.

Delivery of the MHWB curriculum, as for the statutory subjects, requires a combination of what is taught and what is measured and assessed. In discussing this we will begin with measurement, for reasons which will become apparent.

Measurement

When school leaders want to find out about staff wellbeing, the usual next step is to turn to a survey to establish a baseline to work from. In the same way with our young people, there are several survey tools commercially available that allow children to indicate their mood and concerns. Some of these generate suggested areas to be covered in lessons within a whole class or year group and will also indicate which children might need some additional level of intervention. A school will need to evaluate how it uses such tools, and of course more cash-strapped institutions may want to consider developing their own measurement tools. The very youngest children who don't necessarily have the communication skills may need adult support, or use of a resource requiring adult knowledge and input, but in time they will gain the skills and confidence to complete tasks independently. If the school chooses to go down this route the school must have a culture of acting on concerns, to encourage the children to be open in their responses.

Data is only as good as what is done with it, but there is another side to consider: professional judgement. We will recognise that there may be some rogue data from any survey, but that there will also be children who don't, won't or can't indicate their emotional concerns for a number of diverse reasons. We can have a culture of 'noticing' in our schools, and many places do this very well already. This culture encourages the staff to look for differences in mood and body language, which can be picked up in something as simple as the meet and greet at the gate and on entry to class. Perhaps the children use a mood board to indicate how they feel as they come to class; maybe the school uses 'zones of regulation' as a strategy. Whichever is the case, a culture of noticing generates a level of soft data, which, alongside the information our spreadsheets and graphs, can give a clear picture of levels of support and need.

Teaching

MHWB has its obvious place within PSHE but if we leave it there, are we doing enough? This is why we need to think holistically and to also consider what curriculum is. Curriculum is not simply the content the children cover in their lessons in class, but it is what they learn in assemblies; how they move along the corridor and interact with their peers and adults; how they behave on the playground; and how they deal with disagreement and disappointment. Curriculum begins as the children come through the gates and covers every moment in school and, arguably, given life online, it goes beyond school.

There is a place for MHWB across the breadth of subjects, some more obvious than others. PE can promote good physical health and fitness and here is the place to bring endorphins into the children's lexicon, as well as discuss how being outside as well as being physically active is good for mental wellbeing. In science we teach about good dietary health, the impact of exercise on the body and the importance of hydration and sleep, but we can also talk about brain health and the functions of the amygdala. The texts we choose in English, the challenges to their feelings and emotions that the characters deal with, can generate some obvious points for discussion. In teaching history and art, the mental health of significant figures such as Alan Turing, Frida Kahlo or Pablo Picasso can be another means of bringing the conversation around mental health into daily conversation, rather than stigmatising it or hiding it away.

If a school is going to find a place for MHWB in the broadest definition of the curriculum, it is essential not to make it a token or to shoehorn it in. Allow for a period of a year for curriculum leads and colleagues to consider how and where it fits their curriculum, where it can be taught about specifically and the culture of the school can be seen to support it fully. The takeaways that follow give some further suggestions.

Impact

'How do you know?' is a question that can challenge and encourage healthy debate and discussion around any topic. For MHWB, we need to recognise not only that our data, soft or hard, will show variation as issues arise, but also that taking the best practice approach means acting on it. We can assess our impact asking the following questions and evaluating change over time:

- Is there a shared language around mental health; a language used by pupils as well as staff and leaders? This language should include the use of the words 'mental health' with an emphasis on positive mental health, but also include associated vocabulary around emotions and feelings.
- Are children comfortable in discussing mental health in general and their own health? Can they talk about strategies for self-help and where to turn if they feel they need greater support? Are empathy and kindness embedded into your school values?
- Does the shared language reflect the accurate use of mental health terminology? There is a huge difference, for example, between exam and test anxiety and the anxiety that impacts the ability to function socially and emotionally.
- Is there a stigma within any part of the community around mental health and how is this challenged or embraced? This returns to the early emphasis on knowing your context, and which parts of your community have some different perspectives around mental health and how it impacts them and their families.
- Is there buy-in from all staff? This is a consideration for CPD where we need to include everyone, especially among our support staff. Please consider your midday supervisors too; they can be worth their weight in gold in identifying a concern with a young person that might be missed in the classroom.

- Are pupil, staff and parent surveys conducted regularly and consistently? Are they acted on and are these actions communicated and evaluated? Something as simple as a 'You Said, We Did' display can show all members of our community how much their input is respected and utilised.
- Do all relevant staff know what your data shows? This includes class teachers, teaching assistants, family support staff and anyone who has regular contact with children or whom children have identified as a trusted person.
- Pupil progress meetings: are they simply concerned with academic progress or is there a conversation around the emotional needs of the children? To return again to the holistic nature of MHWB, good learning is supported by good mental health and the recognition that those children with lower resilience and emotional difficulties may find learning a challenge if these needs aren't supported.
- What statistics are there about bullying around mental health in school? These might be recorded on your safeguarding tool. Crucially, is there evidence of how incidents are dealt with and what steps are taken to prevent any repetition?

Turning vision into reality

The biggest barrier to MHWB in schools is that we don't cover it in ITT and very infrequently in CPD. We often rely on the enthusiasm or reading of a few colleagues, on someone with a background in counselling or on those members of staff who take on a role as Mental Health First Aiders. This leaves many of our teaching colleagues and overstretched teaching assistants with a sense of this being something extra to do. This is the reason for establishing your 'why': to engage staff. While we cannot determine what content our ITT providers give our new trainees, the school can incorporate MHWB into its CPD programme; in the same way we have annual safeguarding training, so too should we with mental health.

Understanding why some colleagues may be opposed to incorporating mental health in the curriculum is important to recognise. It is likely that a number of colleagues have had issues with their own or their family's mental health and they may be reluctant to discuss it. Equally they may exhibit a degree of stigma or lack of understanding, which will often manifest itself in their use of language and might not match the desired shared language. There is also an understandable sense of fear of saying and doing the wrong thing, especially if a child is approaching a point of crisis. Furthermore, we might also be faced with those who seem to block change and new initiatives. This needs careful consideration of management strategies to bring everyone on board.

Likewise, we might have colleagues who readily diagnose children with conditions. This is something for leaders to be very aware of. Pathways of referral need to be very clear and adhered to. The processes employed by the SENDCo in tracking and referring children are a good starting point for sharing pathways, but it is of equal importance that colleagues know that a child with MHWB needs won't necessarily be on the SEND register too. Though the academic and pastoral teams need to work in tandem with each other, the separate levels of need have to be understood.

Success comes with a positive culture around mental health, where the terminology is used openly and in a knowledgeable way and children are able to identify their emotions and feelings. Success may also be identified through the confidence staff have in supporting young people, parents and each other and knowing where to turn to if children need that additional level of support and help. Mental health will always have a constantly changing picture as new challenges arise and our contexts change, but a culture where positive mental health thrives should be your ultimate goal.

Takeaways

- Take your statement of intent to your pupils. Ask them if it is fit for purpose and if it fits their experience. There is, after all, no more honest critic than a child. Work with your school council or other pupil representatives to present the intent statement in child-friendly language. This then effectively becomes a charter and a commitment.
- Create a mental health and wellbeing display in a communal part of the school and give children a role in its development and update. The charter could well be a focus of this, as could the five ways to wellbeing. When your school is inspected or visited, allow the children to talk about this display so they can demonstrate their knowledge, attitude and positive language around mental health.
- Look at your focus days and weeks, such as Safer Internet Day and Mental Health Week, and evaluate how they fit the culture of the school. Are the lessons from those days adding to the shared language and discussions and do they challenge barriers and problems that arise?

- Plan for one assembly each week which supports MHWB and ensure it is followed up in class in some way. Plan a programme for the year, but allow a free space every four weeks or half term to address something of immediate concern.
- The 'meet and greet' is the simplest and most affordable way to show your commitment to MHWB. It isn't there just to be polite to parents in the morning, but serves as an essential point of contact for those families with challenges and offers the chance to pass key information to a senior leader or members of the pastoral team. This also allows the culture of noticing to develop. If those children who normally bounce cheerfully through the gate in the morning or those who always arrive a little grumpy because they haven't warmed up yet enter the gate in a different mood, this may be something to be aware of.
- Take the idea of the 'meet and greet' to the classroom with an emotional check in or mood board. Placing their name next to an emoji, on a colour chart or a formal zone of regulation shows instantly where that young person is emotionally. If this is well established in the culture of the school, the adults in the classroom have the opportunity to identify and act to support the emotional needs of the young person.
- Sociograms (see Tools and resources) are an exercise for teachers to do to understand the relationship structure in their classrooms. By considering the interactions within the classroom, verbal or otherwise, it can build a picture of who speaks to others, who may be more introverted, if anyone is more dominant than others, if anyone influences others in any particular way. The arrows show the direction of interventions and the thickness and colour are a qualitative measure of the value of those interactions. This is an excellent exercise to carry out with support staff, SENDCo and Designated Mental Health Lead too. This will help enable class teachers to know their class in a way that goes beyond their academic data and to see if children are isolated, 'hidden' or 'hiding' because if they are, these are the children who may require some form of intervention as a support. If children don't have an arrow back to them, or few arrows at all, this is an indicator of the need for some concern or maybe of lack of staff knowledge about them.
- As an aside, a sociogram is also a useful tool to use for analysis of staff interactions too. Senior leaders may wish to do this to consider the balance of relationships within the workplace, especially if this has been raised as a concern by staff.

- Consider strategies around cognitive overload, for both pupil and staff wellbeing. Cognitive overload can induce stress, fatigue and frustration as an onslaught of new information or additional tasks can result in a shutdown in thinking and strains on relationships.
- For those colleagues who say they have no time for mental health in the curriculum, point out that learning interventions are also mental health interventions. Anything that gives a child confidence, a feeling of success in a topic they have found challenging and the chance to be listened to, is supportive of the emotions of the young person concerned.
- Use your surveys, observations and discussions with your young people to establish just where their concerns are right now. Keep these current, constantly updated and flexible.

Tools and resources

Tracking tools

Bounce Together – Wellbeing surveys
www.bouncetogether.co.uk
Thrive – Training and planning tool for wellbeing in schools
www.thriveapproach.com
Boxall profiles – Wellbeing measurement tools
www.boxallprofile.org
Strength and Difficulties Questionnaire (SDQ) – Freely available wellbeing measurement survey
www.corc.uk.net/outcome-experience-measures/strengths-and-difficulties-questionnaire-sdq
Sociograms
www.6seconds.org/2017/07/03/sociogram-definition

Online resources

Anna Freud Centre – Mental health resources for schools
www.annafreud.org
Molly Rose Foundation – Youth suicide prevention charity which shares resources and statistics on their social media
www.instagram.com/mollyrosefoundation

22 Curriculum K – putting health at the heart of education

BEN LEVINSON AND KAYLEIGH COWX

School Name	Kensington Primary School
Age group taught within school	3–11
Location of school	East London
Any distinguishing features	• Over 95 per cent of pupils are multilingual. • Over 100 pupils join mid-phase each year – the vast majority of pupils are from abroad.

Intent of the curriculum

Stressed, anxious, tired and unfocused children will not learn.

At Kensington, when we started to look at why children were struggling, so often the reasons were health-related. Combine this with a global health pandemic for our young people and we knew that something needed to change.

Our 'Curriculum K' (for Kensington) prioritises children's physical and emotional health. We knew that if we could improve these, children would learn more effectively and be more able to retain what they had learnt. We also knew that by focusing on these and building the foundations we would be starting them on the road to healthier, happier lives.

While health was a key driver, it wasn't the only one. Everywhere we looked and everyone we spoke to identified challenges, whether mental health, obesity, the ability to communicate or the disparities between different socioeconomic groups. This was in addition to climate change, the changing political landscape and rapid advances in technology. The world was challenging and it seemed that our children were not adequately prepared to cope.

We were really aware that the world around us was changing, and fast. Despite this, the fundamental curriculum hasn't changed since the Victorians first introduced it in schools 150 years ago. Personally, I left university just over 20 years ago, at which point I didn't have a mobile phone or an email address and I'd just been on the internet for the first time. Change continues to accelerate and schools had been preparing our children for the world as it was 20 years ago. There seemed to be a disconnect.

We had developed our new vision – a place everyone loves to be – and we wanted our curriculum to match this. We wanted our children to love being here: to be excited, inspired and enthused by their learning on a daily basis.

Curriculum K is the result of a two-year research project into what our children need from a 21st century education. Focused on the burgeoning opportunities, aware of the challenges, and determined to address some of the entrenched issues, we set out to create a curriculum that delivered for our children, community and team. The result – Curriculum K – is based around four key areas: Academic, Health, Communication and Culture.

Implementation

Our team are skilled, knowledgeable professionals. They know their children best so we give them the autonomy to tailor what they teach and when. This was a crucial element of how we implemented Curriculum K. Themes are created by teachers with support from senior leaders based on areas of interest and current issues. Teachers know the end points and are given the time, space and challenge to reflect on these. Day-to-day they have the autonomy to adapt their teaching and their timetable to deliver what their children need.

Timetables are flexible and balanced. We invest a significant amount of time in physical and emotional health as well as communication and culture. This means fewer maths and English lessons in particular, as they traditionally dominate the primary timetable. It also means morning lessons are just as likely to be physical health or culture as they are English or maths. There are only so many hours in the day so this required stripping out content that wasn't as important. With unlimited time and resources we'd teach children everything but as this isn't realistic we had to make some difficult decisions.

Our physical health curriculum focuses on just that – health. Lessons are split into 'Fitness' and 'Skills for Life'. Fitness lessons get children moving and their heart rates up. In Year 1 this might be playing 'stuck in the mud' whereas Year 6 might be using MyZone heart rate monitors to better understand when they are working hard and when they need to increase or decrease effort. Skills for Life builds flexibility, strength, agility and coordination. It's all about building the physical literacy needed for a healthy life. This means less time on sports skills. We love sport but we believe physical literacy builds the foundations our children need more effectively.

To support this, our children wear tracksuits and trainers every day. It increases time to be active and children are more active incidentally during the day as well. They also have regular active lessons using the TeachActive resources for English and maths, as well as regular active breaks to get them up and moving, which improves focus and helps them to self-regulate.

Our emotional health curriculum is a progressive curriculum that builds the skills and knowledge children need to understand and regulate their emotions. Children develop a rich emotional vocabulary, understand the importance of experiencing a wide range of emotions, build strategies for coping with strong emotions and learn about the biological and chemical processes behind their emotions. This is part of a wider ethos where behaviour is recognised as the communication that it is and children are supported in learning how to regulate this, rather than just rewarded and sanctioned.

To ensure teachers have sufficient time and energy for delivering the curriculum effectively – and because our experience shows it is the most effective way – we encourage them to focus on teaching to the need in front of them, rather than overly relying on summative data. Teachers aren't required to mark books; instead they assess learning in the moment and use marking time to reflect on it and to develop and improve learning in a lesson and over a period of time. They have the time and space needed to build deep, meaningful relationships with their children, enabling them to really understand where they are in their learning and what they need next.

Impact

Attendance in the autumn term 2021–22 was 96 per cent.
Ofsted visited in December 2021 (see full report under Tools and resources).

- Pupils are taught to be independent in managing their behaviour and learn to regulate their emotions.
- Leaders have a strong vision for the school: that it is a place where everyone loves to be. Staff and pupils are interested and excited by what is learned in class.
- Leaders and staff recognise the importance of pupils' wellbeing and the impact that it can have on pupils' learning. Pupils are encouraged to be active and to learn new skills.
- Pupils said that bullying does not happen in their school. Staff quickly deal with any unkindness between pupils and support them to restore their positive relationships.

Inclusion Quality Mark Flagship School accreditation in January 2022:

- It is an exciting and dynamic curriculum and I spoke to many members of staff who have been involved in pulling it together and are now implementing it.

What staff say (the below is mainly from surveys performing during the summer term 2021, following the Covid-19 lockdown):

- 94 per cent of staff feel the rollout of Curriculum K has been well planned and implemented.
- 80 per cent of Upper Key Stage 2 children can name at least one strategy they can use to support their learning.
- 94 per cent of pupils regularly visit the school library and are able to talk about how the library has supported them to develop a love for reading.
- 100 per cent of teaching and learning judged as effective over time.
- 92 per cent of staff say children are retaining information more effectively than a year ago.
  - *'Repetitive lessons (have really helped). Keep recapping what we have learnt as a lesson starter. Using a lot of visuals and colourful semantics has helped them retain information. Practical lessons have been very helpful with retaining information.'* – Mrs K
- 100 per cent of staff say the new assessment framework is more effective; with 75 per cent of staff regularly utilising recommended AfL strategies.

- - 'Much easier way to mark. You see quicker who is struggling or moving on quickly. Focus on skills and barriers helps focus planning/next steps.' – Mrs E
  - 'The new assessment framework is better as it is catered to the new curriculum.' – Mrs K
- 100 per cent of staff say changes to the reading structure are having a positive impact on pupils' acquisition of reading skills.
- 98 per cent of staff state the health curriculum is having a positive impact on their children's learning.
  - 'It's amazing. Look at how settled they were (when the children started) in September. Also how much the quality of work has improved both in core subjects and in areas like art. Who knew Year 1 children could paint/draw so well!' – Mrs Elhossainy
- 70 per cent of children have improved physical health term-on-term, based on internal measures.
- 85 per cent of mid-phase admission children are working on their year group's curriculum (in all subjects) within one year of joining the school.
- 100 per cent of staff feel school successfully meets the differing needs of individual pupils.
- 85 per cent of pupils present improved emotional health according to Strength and Difficulties Questionnaires (SDQs).
- 100 per cent of staff say this is a place they love to be.
  - 'I enjoy my time working with the children and I like to see the children achieve in their learning.' – Mrs P

What our children say:

- 98 per cent say they feel safe and secure at school.
- 92 per cent of children say that they are more effective learners than a year ago and can say why they think this is.
- 87 per cent of children are able to name a strategy they use to manage their emotions effectively.
- 92 per cent say they are able to play safely in the playground:
  - '(If there is a problem in the playground) I tell the teacher or the school leader.'
  - 'The teachers watch us and I feel safe.'

- *'I have friends around, playing with me.'*
- *'Teachers and leaders are there to help me.'*

What the parents say:

- 100 per cent of parents state that their child coped well with the return to school post-lockdown.
    - *'It has been brilliant.'*
    - *'Yes, everyone is approachable so that really helps.'*
    - *'Yes, we have all the support we need. My children missed school so they were happy to be back.'*
    - *'Yes we are grateful for all the support we are getting from school.'*
    - *'He always has good support and you care for all the children a lot here at school.'*
    - *'You take care of all of us and put our children first. You come to us with information first which always helps us.'*
    - *'I was surprised as Year 1 was a struggle but this year she has no problems.'*
    - *'They loved returning to school.'*

Turning vision into reality

Carrying out such fundamental change required a team who were ready to take on the challenge. We invested heavily in the wellbeing of our team so they had the capacity to be their best and deal with the challenges we faced. Our vision – a place everyone loves to be – drove our approach.

We carried out a significant research project, speaking to all the people connected to the school but also businesses, other pioneering schools, academics and many more. Communication was key throughout the process and we were very focused on bringing everyone along with us. We had clarity of vision and made sure to link the deficits of the current curriculum and the opportunities of the new one to specific challenges and opportunities that our children, parents and team could relate to. Our team in particular were involved throughout, feeding into the process and evolving curriculum.

We were really focused on making the curriculum development and rollout manageable and sustainable. We introduced one element at a time alongside extensive CPD. The rollout of the whole curriculum took two years in total. We provided significant reflection time along the way and lots of opportunities for feedback, discussion and changes.

Running the new and old curricula in tandem was certainly a challenge and one that we had to manage carefully. We also had to restructure our subject leads to our new structure that reflected the curriculum. In developing specific areas we drew extensively on external expertise – particularly for the health and communication curriculum. This was very much a partnership approach.

We had flexibility as an academy to be innovative with the curriculum but we needed to balance that with ensuring we advantaged, not disadvantaged, our children. The limited time we have in the day meant making some difficult decisions about what we taught and what we didn't teach. Due to our multilingual community and the benefits of focusing on first languages we are putting our energy here. We removed elements of the English and maths curriculum that are less developmentally appropriate or as fundamental for our children. We are tracking our children's progress into secondary school and using this feedback to reflect on and tweak our approaches where necessary.

Takeaways

- You can't do it all, so what is going to be your focus?
- What's your ethos? Does your curriculum reflect it and vice-versa?
- Re-balance your timetable to focus more on physical and emotional health: if children aren't healthy they aren't ready to learn.
- Consider what is most important for your children's physical health – sport or health and fitness?
- Consider how else you can build physical activity into the school day.
- What are the benefits of a uniform vs tracksuits and trainers?
- Trust your team and watch them flourish.
- Cut workload. We use Pareto's Law to identify what makes the biggest difference and get rid of anything that doesn't.
- Focus on AfL: this is where the real impact on learning happens.
- Invest in relationships and helping children to regulate not managing behaviour.
- Have an ethos of wellbeing or to be a place everyone loves to be.

Tools and resources

'From Project K To Curriculum K' impact report
www.kensington.newham.sch.uk/attachments/download.asp?file=
    772&type=pdf
Kensington Primary School Ofsted reports
https://files.ofsted.gov.uk/v1/file/50176503

23 Teaching mental resilience
LUCY BAILEY

> **Lucy Bailey** is the founder of Bounce Forward, a national education charity for Key Stage 2 children.

Intent of the curriculum

Psychological fitness is an umbrella term that combines mental resilience and emotional wellbeing, both key attributes needed for success in the 21st century. When it comes to mental health, prevention is better than cure. Explicitly teaching young people the skills and knowledge to develop their psychological fitness will not only prevent mental health problems, but it will also equip children with the tools and capacity to face challenges head on, and lead fulfilling and healthy adult lives.

In the context of this curriculum, resilience means having the knowledge, skills and ability to feel good and function well in everyday life and the capacity to cope, even thrive, when things get tough. It does not mean being happy all the time because real life is much messier than that. We work to create safe and supportive conditions for children to explore and develop the skills needed to navigate life and the changes that are rapidly evolving in the 21st century. Our unique model develops psychological fitness (mental resilience and emotional wellbeing) in school, in lessons that sit alongside academic subjects. This six-module series is developed from sound research and designed to engage students in learning specific skills in a fun and practical way. The idea is that they will go on a journey of discovery that will help them express themselves and be able to empathise with others.

Implementation

'Teach Mental Resilience' is designed to be taught as a modular, developmental set of learning outcomes that are delivered in sequence. Each module is intended to provide flexibility on timing and allow time for discussion. The modules provide a framework for teaching activities to allow pupils the time to engage and absorb the learning through practice, discussion and reflection. Key to building resilience is being able to communicate. The lessons encourage and praise individuals and groups as they express what they have learnt and explain how it is going to be useful in real-life situations.

Each module is structured to achieve the learning outcomes through skill introduction, skill development through practice, and skill discussion (individual, group and whole class). Students capture their learning in their 'student handbook'.

The lessons begin by creating a safe learning agreement that sets out the guidelines for how the class will work together. The agreement takes into account the school safeguarding and child protection policy and the teacher's role, and is developed with full class participation.

At the start of each lesson is a calm and focused activity to provide an opportunity to explore, practise and develop self-regulation tools and techniques. The activities include breathing exercises, expressing gratitude, mental games and visualisation.

Below is an overview of the six modules and associated learning outcomes:

Module 1: Resilience and harnessing positive emotions

- Understand that life is a journey with challenges (big and small) and it is our resilience that helps us overcome these.
- Explore emotions.
- Discover that emotions can be helpful and unhelpful, and we can learn to regulate them.
- Know that we *all* have resilience.

Module 2: Connecting the brain, emotions and thoughts

- Understand the brain and the role of emotions.
- Consider the importance of being calm to help with resilient responses.
- Discover the link between thoughts, feelings and behaviours.

Module 3: 'Gremlin Beliefs'

- Understand that resilience can help us to understand why we react the way we do.
- Identify common Gremlin Beliefs.
- Recognise that Gremlin Beliefs are not in control.

Module 4: Optimism and evidence

- Understand there is a difference between optimistic and pessimistic thinking.
- Know the importance of respect for different perspectives.
- Discover how to use evidence to create more flexible and accurate thinking.

Module 5: 'Wobble'

- Understand the importance of gratitude.
- Know how to use the Wobble skill to tame the catastrophising Gremlin Belief.
- Discover how to calm down when emotions are strong.

Module 6: Resilience planning

- Understand all the resilience skills covered in the lessons.
- Create an individual resilience plan.
- Consider how resilience skills can help children express themselves and understand others.

The learning is explored through a story about two characters as they journey through a town on a day trip. During the trip the characters encounter everyday setbacks, challenges and opportunities. This approach provides a safe way for students to explore the benefits and pitfalls of the different ways in which each of the characters deal with the situations they face.

Homework activities are set each lesson to encourage use of the skills and techniques outside of the class. These are shared and reflected on at the start of each new lesson.

Impact

At the end of each lesson pupils are required to reflect and complete the following four statements:

- Today I have learnt...
- In future this might help me to...
- A question I have is...
- The part of the lesson I enjoyed the most...

This feedback creates a record of the learning for each student and acts as a marker for what to reinforce and repeat next time. The impact on pupils has been positive, with learning such as:

- 'I didn't realise that other people think the same as I do.'
- 'I really liked the characters and seeing how they deal with things.'
- 'I can calm myself down with counting.'
- 'I can use Wobble to help me not worry so much.'
- 'It can help me in future when I am arguing with my brother.'
- 'I learnt about Gremlins and they are not in control.'
- 'Building the tower was really fun.'

Teach Mental Resilience is, through independent evaluation by the London School of Economics, proven to improve: depression symptoms, anxiety scores, attendance and behaviour. The impacts are larger for children with SEND, those entitled to free school meals and those with worse initial scores for symptoms of depression or anxiety.

An unintended outcome is the language framework that is created. Children are able to express the link between thoughts, feelings and behaviour in a formulaic and clear way. This allows for support beyond the initial learning in both spontaneous teaching moments and as part of the broader pastoral support.

Turning vision into reality

The key challenge is timetable time. The lessons deliver the best results when there is dedicated teaching time set aside. This means discrete learning time that is scheduled and valued.

Teacher training is also important. When it comes to mental resilience, it is not only what is taught that matters, but also the behaviour of the adults around children. The way the teacher models resilience offers a direct impact on pupils' resilience and the way they engage with the teaching and learning.

Takeaways

- Learn about and consider your own resilience and what messages are you giving to others about how to be resilient. Resilience is *not* keeping going no matter what. Resilience is more fluid than that. It's about knowing when to stop doing something, understanding what is 'normal' for you, being equipped to solve problems and to reach out when needed. Start with you!
- Teach pupils about flexible and realistic thinking. Encourage them to be open and curious to different perspectives. Look for examples to problem-solve and, as much as possible, be wedded to reality.
- Encourage human connection as much as possible. Reward pupils' willingness to reach out, have empathy and care for others. Teach them that knowing how to do that will increase personal happiness.
- Find practical ways to help students fail 'well'. Failure is a learning opportunity but also essential for building mental resilience. Unless children are able to face challenges and to work out how to get through them by themselves, they will not develop the mental strength and self-efficacy that they need in the 21st century.
- Talk more about emotions in an everyday way. Name emotions and focus on 'helpful' and 'unhelpful' emotions, rather than them being 'good' or 'bad'. All emotions are telling us something. The more we build vocabulary and notice emotions in an everyday way, the better children will be able to manage and deal with them.
- Encourage understanding about the role of positive emotions. Teach children how to nurture and notice positive emotions so they can use positive emotions as a tool to get through difficult times but also to be the best version of themselves.
- Use process praise to build a growth mindset. Give as much thought to how you praise as you would to how you criticise. Children respond to praise, so be detailed with your praise. Explain in detail what it is that was good so they can get better at it.

- Choose optimism. Teach students that if they have a choice, and they usually will, to take the optimistic version because that is more likely to help them move forward.

Tools and resources

Explore emotions worksheet

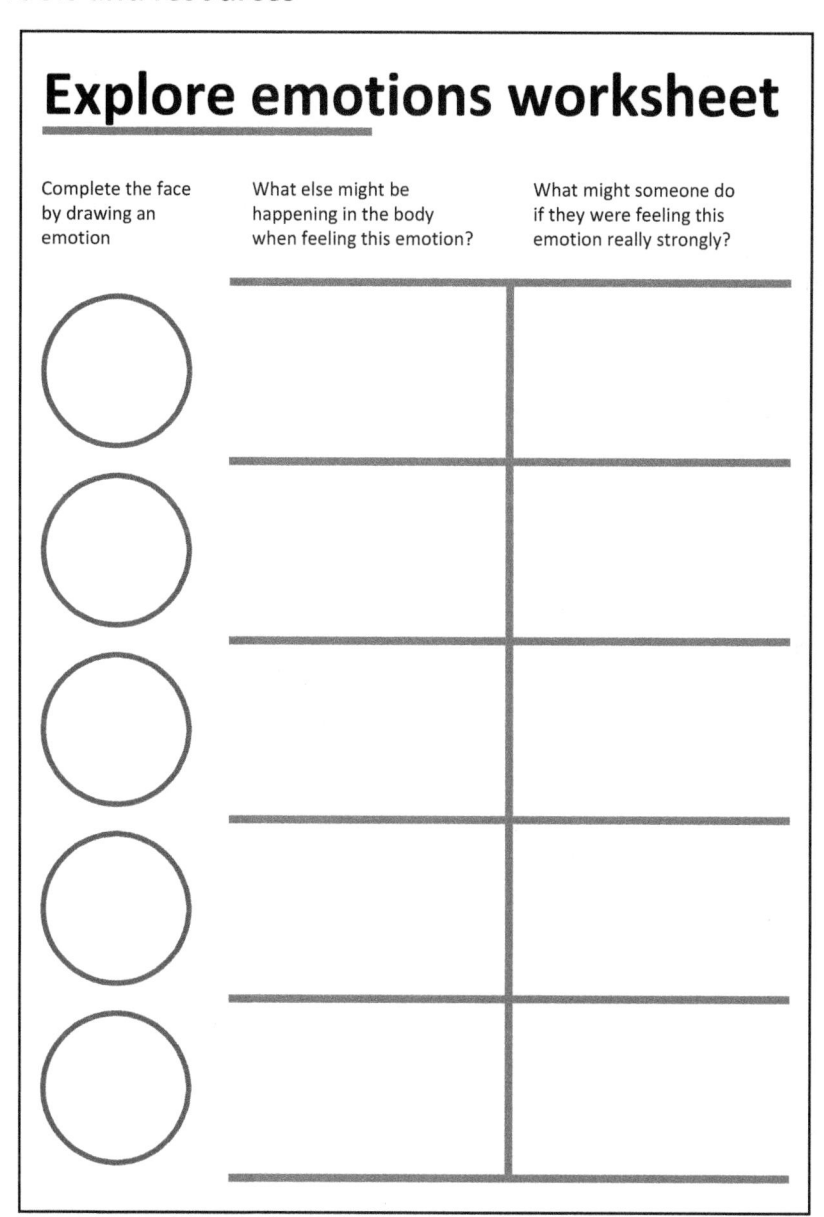

Complete the face by drawing an emotion	What else might be happening in the body when feeling this emotion?	What might someone do if they were feeling this emotion really strongly?
◯		
◯		
◯		
◯		
◯		

Figure 16: *Explore emotions worksheet*

24 Who says children must sit to learn? Can we move *and* learn?

PAULA MANSER

School Name	Birkby Infant and Nursery School
Age group taught within school	5–7
Location of school	Huddersfield, West Yorkshire
Any distinguishing features	<ul><li>466 pupils on roll.</li><li>134 pupils on free school meals.</li><li>86 per cent have EAL.</li><li>17.5 per cent have SEND.</li><li>We have classrooms of varying sizes and one indoor hall.</li><li>Outdoor space is a concrete jungle.</li></ul>

Intent of the curriculum

Schools are incredibly busy places under relentless pressures to increase standards. Meanwhile, the health and wellbeing of UK primary school children is on the decline:

- Physical activity levels among UK primary aged children are falling from as early as 7 years of age (Cooper et al, 2015).
- Increasing numbers of children in the UK are leaving school classified as obese or overweight (NHS, 2021).
- Less than 50 per cent of children achieve the daily recommendations for physical activity (Sport England, 2022).

Physical activity has always been a huge consideration for our school. Exercise for many of our children is done solely in school, due to social and economic deprivation and the low parental engagement of many of our families. As a school we recognised children's habits outside school are increasingly sedentary; how children spend their time *in* school is becoming increasingly more important. Our SLT had a vision that physical activity should not just be part of our daily exercise, reserved for our PE lessons and weekly 1km jog. Instead, it also needed to become part of our daily teaching and learning too – we wanted to consider Physically Active Learning (PAL). Why? Research has found that the PAL approach can significantly reduce sedentary periods of time. It can also:

- improve classroom behaviour and activity engagement
- offer aggregated improvement in academic performance over time.

We were fortunate as we were one of three schools who received funding from Yorkshire Sport Foundation to pilot initial PAL approaches with Move & Learn (M&L), a community interest company founded by school leaders and teachers. With a little bit of hand-holding from the team at M&L, we were ready to start our journey.

Implementation

Bringing about behaviour change can be incredibly difficult. Children are generally willing to commit to whatever you offer them; staff are not always quite so keen to adapt and change to another way of thinking, another new approach, another new initiative!

Throughout the year, through various staff training, INSET days, year group observations and meetings, we were able to continually promote the M&L messages and the importance of physical activity within learning. It plays a vital role in not only engaging children in their learning and the positive effects this has on their mental health, but also in the physical benefits it offers. The key to engaging staff was to show them how simple M&L approaches are. As the M&L team reminded us, 'It's an add-in, not an add-on.' Some teachers were initially concerned with losing control of the class, needing too many resources, not having enough space, lessons being too disruptive – only time and a different way of thinking enabled staff to see this is not the reality.

We set about creating a positive active mindset where children, parents and colleagues believe that activity is a central value of the school. We asked staff questions about the following.

The classroom environment

1. What space is there for children to move around? Could you change the layout of your classroom and learning areas so children have to move around it more?
2. Do the children always need to sit at the tables? Can they work on the floor, stand, write on the wall, etc.?
3. Does everyone need a chair? Are there other alternatives that the children could use to encourage greater movement?

Our teachers started to create classrooms that aided active learning, not prevented it. By decluttering our classroom spaces, we created room to be more active around the existing furniture. Some teachers went further by removing some chairs and tables and replacing them with large bean bags and balance balls.

Learning

1. Do your lessons create opportunities for the children to move? Are the children expected to sit and listen while you deliver?
2. Where are the resources the children need? Do you have the resources ready so the children never need to collect them themselves or can you place them so the children can independently access what they need?

Staff were asked to consider what they did on a daily basis and reflect on this when planning subsequent work. Staff considered ways to incorporate short active bursts of activity along with lessons that require moderate and vigorous activity.

Assessment for learning

1. Where can you build in assessment opportunities? How can you review regularly and recap prior learning?

2. Do children answer with their hands up? Or do you use questioning as the easiest way to incorporate activity? Could children respond to a question or prompt by moving instead of just speaking? If they know the answer, they could:

   - stand on one leg
   - stretch their hands up as high as they can up over their head
   - stand up and touch their toes/knees
   - do yoga moves – also great for multiple choice answers.

3. How can children show you their understanding? Can you swap traffic light colours for different body moves? For example: red = curl up in a ball, amber = star shape, green = hands up and on tiptoes. It really doesn't have to be a thumbs up/thumbs down. Be creative!

Impact

M&L approaches have been embraced by the children and staff in school. This is not running around the classroom, it's about appropriate and meaningful movement. As the M&L team reminds us, 'it's as much about the learning as it is about the movement.'

Staff feedback shows that lessons are more interactive, the children are more active and engaged in their learning and are increasingly willing to participate and share their ideas. Staff are enjoying the freedom that M&L has enabled them to have in their delivery of lessons. The initial concerns regarding loss of control, disruptions to learning and learning environments not being suitable have been overcome. Instead of seeing the difficulties, staff are now considering how to incorporate ways to be active throughout each area of the curriculum.

M&L is great because it gets the children up and moving; this is crucial for their physical and mental wellbeing. Also, I can clearly see it benefits the children's learning as they actively learn to read, write, discuss or solve problems at various stages throughout a lesson. We previously found that many children sit throughout lessons in a passive manner; by introducing M&L, children are now learning by doing.

Class teacher

Year 2 children feedback that they love sitting on the bean bags and working on the exercise balls: 'It helps me to concentrate while I am working – sometimes I find it difficult to sit still.' Others independently take their work to the floor: 'I enjoy writing [while I'm] on the floor; I find it easier to write my letters on the line when I lie down.' These may sound like a recipe for disaster but they really do work – our children respect the freedom to move that M&L has given them.

By using an active approach to learning, children are increasingly able to make their own choices. They are able to move between groups, activities and tables in a manner that makes them increasingly responsible for their own actions, while learning in an environment that supports them to be increasingly active. Concentration levels have improved as children are more engaged in their learning due to the active nature and approach. Some of the things they enjoy include working on the carpet, 'writing on the walls', 'spotting the crimes' in punctuation and 'speed bouncing' their spellings.

Our journey is by no means over; we will continue to enhance our teaching through M&L approaches as the children in our society rely more and more on the provision that school provides.

Turning vision into reality

We considered the existing barriers that could impact negatively a whole-school approach to M&L.

Common responses included:

- *'My class will mess around.'*
- *'It will waste valuable teaching and learning time.'*
- *'How will I get the children to listen?'*
- *'Will I be able to get their learning back on track?'*
- *'Will they understand the activity?'*
- *'I've not got enough space.'*

We knew why we needed children to reduce sedentary time. We then needed to look at how we could do this appropriately and purposefully. According to M&L, we can reduce sedentary time through either 'Activators' or 'Energisers'.

Activators are where movement is directly integrated into a part of the learning process. The five approaches reflect Rosenshine's Principles of Instruction (2012): Retrieval, Collection, Modelling, Connection and Creation.

Energisers are where movement is used as a break in learning to energise children. By reducing sedentary time, we allow them to refocus and increase time on task. It also breaks up complex learning into mini lessons.

In terms of successes, for children we saw that M&L:

- improves engagement levels
- increases attention and focus
- allows children opportunities to transfer skills
- maximises learning time
- allows children to learn subconsciously
- increases enjoyment and motivation.

For teachers we saw that M&L:

- helps (re)discover a love of teaching
- provides instant and ongoing assessment.

Our vision to be a wholly active school is continually evolving. Being involved with the M&L team has driven change and will continue to do so. Ensuring the benefits of physical activity and developing good habits early on is a crucial part of our school vision.

Takeaways

- Link M&L into the school ethos and include everyone in the school community.
- Plan a consistent CPD pathway or programme for all staff in relation to M&L. This will support staff's ongoing confidence in their capabilities, motivations and opportunities. Developing whole-school change is an ongoing process that requires you to be patient, prudent and willing to change.
- Share good practice – teachers need to see it in action.
- Give staff opportunities and forums to regularly share successes and strategies to overcome barriers linked to M&L, including:
  - dedicated time to share ideas
  - feedback from whole-school observations

- guidance on linking M&L to all curriculum areas.
- With the support of the SLT, facilitate discussions on any changes needed to the indoor and outdoor environments and resources. Consider:
  - the classroom organisation – declutter if needed
  - the position of resources, especially no/low cost ones
  - ways to utilise space (e.g. corridors, the hall and displays).
- Use the research into M&L to inspire colleagues and highlight connections to whole-school targets such as:
  - improved focus
  - academic performance
  - health benefits.
- Remind colleagues to:
  - look for simple changes you can make
  - drip feed new ideas to pupils
  - take small steps, as they make a big and lasting change
  - be prepared to fail.

Tools and resources

TEDx Talk with Dr Andy Daly Smith & Bryn Llewellyn on the benefits of physically active learning
www.youtube.com/watch?v=tARSCzHLF5g
Creative Active Schools Framework video on improving whole-school outcomes with physical activity
www.creatingactiveschools.org/#video
Move & Learn CIC – Many of the ideas we have developed at our school are now incorporated into the Move & Learn portal
https://moveandlearn.co.uk
Move & Learn's book *How to Move and Learn* (2022)
https://moveandlearn.co.uk/the-book

25 A learning framework to put wellbeing at the heart of school
RACHEL MUSSON

> **Rachel Musson** is the Founding Director of ThoughtBox Education, a social enterprise supporting schools to co-create a culture of care for people and planet. It is a community interest company supporting, enabling and allowing schools with a toolkit, training and curriculum to create learning resources and learning cultures in their own schools.

Intent of the curriculum

How the next generation thinks and feels will determine what the world becomes. The way we design our lessons, cultivate our classrooms and support young people with knowledge, skills and practices for the future are all opportunities for us to shape the sort of world we wish to live in. This invites us to think about the sort of culture we need in our schools to enable a healthier future to blossom and the foundational values, mindsets and beliefs we need to support a thriving future for people and planet.

We are living in a volatile, uncertain, complex and ambiguous (VUCA) world and our schools need to help strengthen and nurture core competencies and capacities to meet the challenges and opportunities of this. Much like a muscle, these foundational skills, values and habits need to be practised regularly in order to strengthen and become an embedded part of our natural behaviours.

A successful school doesn't focus on its outputs, it focuses on its culture; if you create a healthy culture, everything has the best chance of flourishing. Just like nurturing a healthy garden, nurturing a healthy school invites the process of cultivating the conditions for healthy growth, and tending to all those growing within the 'soil'.

ThoughtBox Education has spent the past decade learning from neuroscience and nature's wisdom, and building on key learning frameworks from UNESCO, the Organisation for Economic Co-operation and Development (OECD) Learning Compass, the Times Education Commission and the UN's Transforming Education Agenda. We have been researching and connecting with teachers from across the world to support healthier school cultures by embedding competencies to strengthen healthier futures for people and planet.

Bringing together three core skills with three core practices, the Triple Wellbeing framework is built around nine core competencies for healthy relationships with ourselves, each other and the rest of the natural world. Triple Wellbeing is an approach to deepen and strengthen personal, social and environmental wellbeing through the simple practices of 'Self-care', 'People-care' and 'Earth-care'.

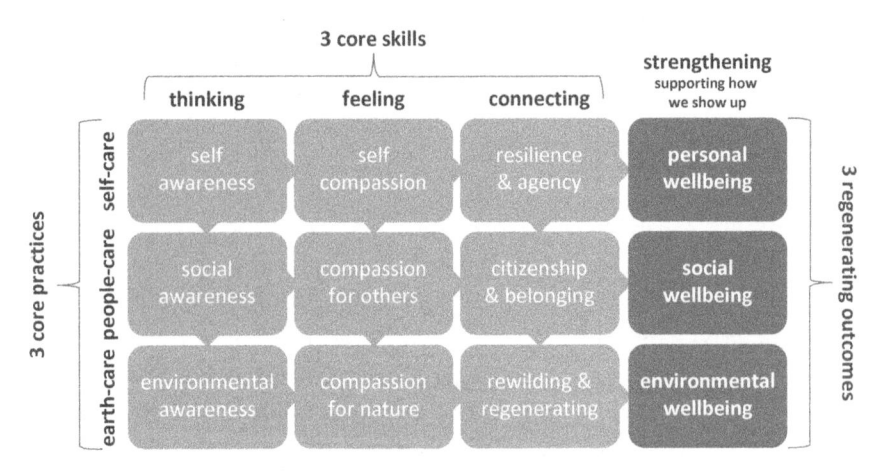

The **Triple Wellbeing®** Framework

Figure 17: *The Triple Wellbeing ® Framework*

Implementation

Since 2015 we have been designing learning resources, curricula and training courses with this framework as the foundational design. We also now also share the framework itself as a tool to enable practitioners in any school context or community to create their own resources and culture of Triple Wellbeing.

The framework contains three core skills, three core practices and three regenerating outcomes, which can be used to shape and create resources and learning cultures.

Core skills

The core abilities being developed:

- **Thinking:** being reflective, thinking critically and widening our awareness.
- **Feeling:** sensing into our emotions, nurturing empathy and strengthening compassion.
- **Connecting:** finding connections and developing active relationships.

Core practices

The practical application of these core skills:

- **Self-care:** deepening how we think and feel about ourselves by learning to tend to our needs and support our inner development.
- **People-care:** nurturing our relationships with the wider world and feeling valued in and by our communities by tending to the needs of others.
- **Earth-care:** learning how to bring our lives back into balance with all natural living ecosystems and tending to the needs of the natural world.

Regenerating outcomes

The process and continued outcome of these practices:

- **Personal wellbeing:** strengthening a sense of wellness in our own lives.
- **Social wellbeing:** strengthening a sense of wellness in our communities.
- **Environmental wellbeing:** strengthening a sense of wellness in the rest of the natural world.

Pedagogy

The theory and practice underpinning our learning resources:

- **Facilitated lessons:** Encouraging exploratory learning, encouraging active participation by the educator, welcoming shared responsibility and co-creation of the learning space.
- **Discussion-led learning:** Enabling student-voice and helping to develop opinions, strengthen values, listen actively, think critically about ideas, deepen levels of awareness and become more reflective.
- **Whole-person learning:** Creating spaces for engagement with the mind, heart, body, spirit and soul.
- **Sharing global-perspectives:** Helping explore diverse ideas, widen perspectives and mindsets, engage with alternative viewpoints, deepen empathy and engage with core values.
- **A spiral approach to learning:** Allowing maturation at each level by returning to similar content and topics at different age levels across a student's journey through school.
- **Connecting global to local:** Learning from and with others in our global communities to inspire student autonomy through local action and engagement.

Design principles

These help to shape our learning resources, recognising that it is the *process* of exploration that is the learning. Each curriculum topic developed using the Triple Wellbeing framework contains four interconnected lessons to enable and allow students to:

1. **Immerse:** Dive into a topic or issue affecting our lives on a local and global scale.
2. **Understand**: Learn and deepen awareness of the issues, causes and effects.
3. **Explore:** Engage with a range of global perspectives and alternative viewpoints.
4. **Empower**: Bring global learning into local action in our lives and communities.

We offer a whole-school curriculum for 5–18 years and all lessons designed using these competencies and principles. Alongside this we are now offering practitioner training for educators to engage more fully with the framework and embed practices for Triple Wellbeing across their learning community.

Impact

Raising a healthy child means nurturing their whole self: learning to live in balance, deepen their sense of connection and strengthening innate skills and capacities to feel activated and empowered. It means educating minds, bodies, spirits *and* emotions and recognising that *how* we educate is as important – perhaps much more so – as the 'what': the process of learning *is* the learning.

People *do* well when they *feel* well. This is as true for adults as it is for children. So how do we want our classrooms, our school, our learning communities to make people feel? And how can we tend to the relationships within our community to help people feel well and feel cared for? Renowned educator Sir Ken Robinson recognised the importance of helping young people to feel well in order to learn well, inviting us all in his final public speech to help educate the whole child by focusing on creating healthier cultures in schools.

Schools can co-create a culture of Triple Wellbeing by strengthening practices to support wellbeing in ourselves (personal wellbeing), in our communities (social wellbeing) and in the rest of the natural world (environmental wellbeing). Recognising that our own wellness is bound up in the wellness of others and the planet helps to give value to the importance of each part of our school community, and the importance of tending to the relationships that bind them all together as a whole.

The ThoughtBox learning resources are currently being used by over 5,000 educators across 76 countries. We gather a wide range of stories as our case studies, and consistently receive feedback that children love the feeling of the lessons, teachers love the shaping of the lessons and classes enjoy the connections and explorations that the lessons enable and allow.

The regenerating outcomes of our resources and the mindset of Triple Wellbeing helps to support feelings of wellness in ourselves, in our communities and in the rest of nature. While the framework can be used just to design lessons, we welcome using it as a way of supporting a much wider culture of care. We actively support schools to be using these competencies in how lessons or meetings are crafted, how communities are supported and how networks are tended to – whether that's with parents, governors, staff, pupils or the wider community. It all comes down to tending the relationships in our schools.

Healthy learning environments recognise the value of each part of the school's ecosystem – from individual teachers, pupils, administration staff and cleaners, to parents, governors, the local community and the wider natural environment – and work to support the health and wellbeing of each part that makes up the whole. Most significantly, it is the 'connection spaces' between each part that need tending to: the relationships between the different stakeholders in our school communities. How do pupils connect to other pupils? Where are opportunities for staff to connect together on a personal level, as well as professional? What about the parents – how do we welcome them into the community?

The invitation as we work to transform learning towards healthier horizons is to focus our attention on nurturing and strengthening these foundational relationships.

Turning vision into reality

The journey to synthesise this sort of learning has been a long one. It began with one teacher's journey into making education more humane. As a secondary English teacher, I spent over a decade in the classroom, connecting and exploring the world with young people. In 2012, I left mainstream teaching and embarked on a decade-long journey of action-research with educators and leaders worldwide, living and working in many countries in the Global North and South, and learning from and with teachers and communities to better understand the competencies we need for healthier classrooms, communities and futures for our children.

Triple Wellbeing and our work at ThoughtBox draws from a diverse field of study – from neuroscience and psychology to creative pedagogy, systems theory, transformative learning, indigenous wisdom and far beyond. The research has also drawn on learning from global models for education – from UNESCO and the UN to the OECD, WHO and Times Education Commission. Most importantly, however, is learning from the 3.8 billion years of life experience in healthy system dynamics to be found in the rest of the natural world. Our work builds on what is innate in children (and in all of us former children) to help enable and allow these natural qualities of curiosity, compassion and connection to flourish in schools.

Welcoming this into school isn't easy, for where is the space, time, permission for this sort of learning to take root? Yet it is foundational, for it supports a mindset of wellbeing and works to address the root causes of so many of the symptoms our teachers are currently having to support.

While schools are doing their absolute best to support, nurture and inspire the lives of young people, the mainstream system in its current form is not able to fully support or nurture these qualities. This is why we welcome the innovation of individual teachers, educators, leaders and schools themselves to lead the way in their culture setting and mindset shift, and inspire others along the way.

The challenges – and opportunities of the world we're growing into welcome us to help strengthen the innate qualities of curiosity, creativity, compassion and connection in young people. While challenges abound, opportunities are springing up everywhere and work is happening right across the world to support a healthier future of learning in our schools.

Takeaways

Creating a culture of care sits at the heart of the Triple Wellbeing approach, and allows the work to be welcomed in at any level – personally, professionally, organisationally and systemically. There is nothing stopping any of us from welcoming the practices and principles of Triple Wellbeing into our own lives to help create a healthier culture of learning. These practices are free, we've all got the capacity to strengthen them and can action them whenever we choose. We just need to give ourselves the permission to do so.

Tools and resources

Explore the Triple Wellbeing framework
www.thoughtboxeducation.com/triple-wellbeing
Read the research that sits behind this framework
www.thoughtboxeducation.com/ebook
Become an accredited Triple Wellbeing Practitioner
www.thoughtboxeducation.com/triple-wellbeing-cpd
Practise some of the activities at the end of each chapter in the ebook
www.thoughtboxeducation.com/ebook
Free ideas to try out the curriculum to bring these ideas into the classroom
www.thoughtboxeducation.com/free-resources

Editor's reflection on Part 5: Behaviour and respect

The case studies in this section are written by educators who really care about children's wellbeing. There is an emphasis on educating sustainably, to give young people the compassion, competencies and character that will be needed to bring about positive change in the world.

In recent years, even before the Covid-19 pandemic, good pastoral care with an eye on positive mental health has been a key element in school practice and pedagogy. As Andrew Cowley, author of *The Wellbeing Toolkit* (2019) and *The Wellbeing Curriculum* (2021), both published by Bloomsbury, explains in his case study: 'Good mental health supports good learning health in the same way as positive behaviour management supports positive learning environments.'

Poor mental health can have a detrimental impact on pupil behaviour and educators increasingly recognise poor behaviour as a form of communication. To that end, it is important that rather than being continually reprimanded, children are supported and taught how to co- and self-regulate so that they can be more successful in class, develop positive relationships and achieve better academically.

As Andrew Cowley explains, the 'meet and greet' is one of the simplest ways to show a commitment to mental health and wellbeing. Acknowledging the child in the morning and making them feel seen, valued and appreciated for the unique person they are, instantly strengthens connection and builds a strong sense of belonging. Children, says Andrew, need to be given the tools to talk about their feelings as well as learn a number of strategies to manage their emotions including stress. All of this happens most effectively when there is buy-in from all the educators in the school and where there is a culture of empathy and kindness.

The effectiveness of mental health policies and practices can be measured in a number of ways, including through pupil, staff, and parent surveys and questionnaires. These need to be undertaken regularly and seen as a tool to improve the school experience for the child and to improve the curriculum as a whole.

Ben Levinson and Kayleigh Cowx say that stressed, anxious, tired, unfocused children will not learn, so teaching mental and physical health must not be a bolt-on, it must be a priority! The school's Curriculum K is based around four key areas: Academic, Health, Communication and Culture. Health as a priority is embedded throughout the culture of the school; this is further evidence in the school's choice of tracksuits and trainers as the daily dress code!

Bounce Forward is a six-week module designed by Lucy Bailey to teach psychological fitness, mental resilience and emotional wellbeing in school. I know that educators would find this resource very useful as it would equip teachers and pupils with a shared set of language and terminology for emotions, as well as the resources and approaches to manage them. Lucy says research shows that teaching mental resilience helps to improve rates of depression, anxiety, attendance and behaviour.

The next case study featured in this section emphasises the importance of good physical health, asking the critical question 'Can we move *and* learn?'. It is clear from Paula Manser's contribution that physical activity levels are in worrying decline. With the prevalence of tablets being used to pacify ever-younger children, including toddlers, causing them to be docile content consumers, it will take a lot to reverse this concerning trend! To increase opportunities for more Physically Active Learning (PAL) in schools, Paula advocates for whole-school mindset shifts and culture changes, with the key to engaging staff being to show them that simple movement and learning opportunities in the curriculum are an 'an add-in, not an add-on.'

Rachel Musson says that successful schools are ones that focus on culture. Using the analogue of a garden she says 'nurturing a healthy school invites the process of cultivating the conditions for healthy growth, and tending to all those growing within the "soil"'. The Triple Wellbeing framework encourages individuals and schools to recognise that they are part of a wider eco-system. It's a beautiful and thoughtful curriculum design leading to 'regenerating outcomes'.

Since the pandemic, more and more schools have integrated wellbeing programmes and approaches into their curricula. The World Health Organization says wellbeing is when 'the individual realizes his or her own abilities, can cope with the normal stresses of life, can work productively and fruitfully, and is able to make a contribution to his or her community' (2001).

When children and adults experience a positive sense of wellbeing, they have better relationships with others, they make good choices, they are able to appreciate the world around them and enjoy the experiences available to them, they can cope better with the stresses and strains of life, they have fewer health problems and they live longer.

With all of this in mind, schools not only have a pragmatic reason to promote wellbeing but arguably a moral duty to ensure that it is prioritised!

PART 6

Personal development

Introduction

Children starting in the EYFS in September 2024 will be eligible for retirement in approximately the 2090s. What a sobering thought. What will the world look like then? What will jobs, transport, media and the weather look like, six decades into the future? In our current VUCA (volatile, uncertain, chaotic and ambiguous) world, will there even be much of a planet for our children to inherit? These are questions to consider when thinking about curriculum design.

What is sure to my mind is that having a good memory, a good recall of facts, being able to revise effectively and pass national tests is not sufficient to prepare our children for the world of work of the future. The proliferation of artificial intelligence, augmented reality, robotics, automation, 3D printing, virtual reality and the Internet of Things means that some of the tasks currently done by humans will someday be done by machines. This will include harvesting information into content, creating digital artwork or architecture and remotely assisting in complex surgery.

We cannot completely predict what the future holds, but what is clear when looking at the technological advancements that have taken place in the last ten years, never mind the last 40 years since I was in primary school, is that our curriculum needs to be broad, well-rounded, innovative, and preparing pupils for every eventuality. Indeed, we need to equip our children with the skills, attitudes and aptitudes that they need to be prepared for a world of work that we cannot yet possibly imagine.

In 2023 the World Economic Forum listed the top 10 skills required in the workplace. These are:

1. Analytical thinking.
2. Creative thinking.
3. Resilience, flexibility and agility.
4. Motivation and self-awareness.
5. Curiosity and lifelong learning.
6. Technological literacy.
7. Dependability and attention to detail.
8. Empathy and active listening.
9. Leadership and social influence.
10. Quality control.

Given what we know about the rate of technical and societal advancement, for our children to be successful in the future these are the types of skills our pupils need to be acquiring through the curriculum today.

Milton Road Primary School

Our curriculum at Milton Road is designed to be as future-proof as possible. The north aspect of our curriculum is designed to give children voice, choice and agency so that they can participate critically and creatively in the transformation of their world. Our aim is that we want our children to be happy and healthy today, fulfilled in the future and able to make their world an even better place.

To realise this aim we incorporate a range of existing programmes into our design. These include the brilliant No Outsiders programme by school leader Andrew Moffatt, Picture News and free resources found on BBC Bitesize. BBC Bitesize, for example, has a small but excellent suite of videos that can be used to teach citizenship. It includes videos on health and safety in the community, reducing risks, helping others, learning about diversity and discrimination, rights and responsibility, and democracy. These programmes also help us to deliver on our statutory responsibilities to teach about the nine protected characteristics, diversity, equality and inclusion, and Fundamental British Values.

Learning how to be a good citizen is a key part of our curriculum offer. We aim to achieve this by ensuring that children engage at least once a term in acts of service, volunteering, supporting a charity or campaigning. This activity is loosely planned at the start of the term as it is the children who will decide on what pro-social action to undertake.

Seb Chapleau, former Executive Headteacher of Gesher School, was the person who first talked to me about Citizens UK. Citizens UK is the 'home of community organising' and the organisation behind incredible campaigns such as the Living Wage Campaign. Milton Road is one of the founding institutions in the Cambridge chapter of Citizens UK. Through our membership of this organisation I was able to attend intensive leadership training, which introduced me to the tools and methodology for effective community organising, including the Five Steps to Social Change model.

At Milton Road we have a Youth Citizens Crew comprising one pupil from each of the 14 classes. These representatives listen to all the ideas that the children have for campaigns that they would like the school community to work on together. These ideas are brought back to the Youth Citizens Committee and that group decides collectively which one of the many ideas to focus on for their next whole-school campaign.

Using this methodology, the Youth Citizens decided to prioritise improving traffic safety around the school. They planned a campaign that included making a stop motion animation showing the dangerous spots that children were experiencing on their way to and from school; gathering data on the different ways that children travelled to school; enlisting the rest of the community to create hundreds of posters which were displayed on the school gates to raise awareness to road users of the issues the children were facing; holding a whole-school Road Peace day where everyone wore purple; and preparing a special assembly to which local councillors and decision makers were invited.

At the end of the assembly the children met the councillors to discuss and negotiate what changes would be needed. The children were successful in their campaign. The councillors took on board the children's concerns and are looking to improve the traffic by installing additional signage, offering alternative parking further away at a local church and building the case for our school to be part of the School Streets initiative.

```
    5.              1.
Negotiate       Organise


  4.              2.
  Act            Listen


          3.
         Plan
```

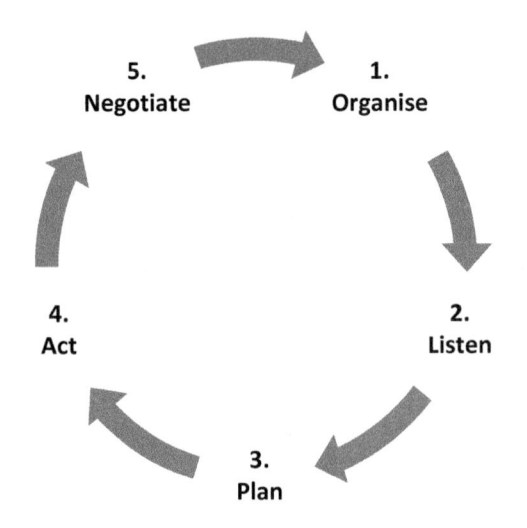

Figure 18: *The Five Steps to Social Change model*

Through this campaign, the children not only learned how to organise and plan a campaign, but they understood how to be leaders in their community themselves.

There are various terms used to describe the skills it is thought our young people will need in the future. Sometimes they are called 21st-century skills, sometimes transferable skills or even soft skills. Michael Fullan has a helpful list of these skills that he calls 'Deep Learning Competencies' or the 'six Cs'. These are creativity, communication, critical thinking, character, collaboration and citizenship.

At Milton Road, we call these essential skills. This is how they are referred to in the 'Skills Builder' framework which we also use.

Skills Builder consists of eight areas of learning: listening, speaking, problem-solving, creativity, staying positive, aiming high, leadership and teamwork. Skills Builder not only offers a way to assess children's progress through these essential skills, but also provides lesson plans with exciting projects through which the children can demonstrate their skills.

In the last couple of years, we have introduced Expert Showcases in place of assemblies, as ways for children to not only present their academic learning but also to demonstrate their competencies in these essential skills.

The very first Expert Showcase that we trialled at Milton Road was organised by the Year 2 teachers and children. The hall was arranged with tables all around the sides on which writing books, models and artwork were displayed. Our little six-year-olds stood proudly behind the tables, sharing their learning with their parents and answering questions about what they had been doing that term. In the middle of the hall, PE benches and mats were placed so that an energetic gymnastic display could take place (under the watchful eye of the teacher). At one point a group of these Year 2 infants called out to the assembled audience, 'We are about to give our presentation on Climate Change, if anyone would like to come through!'. I along with a handful of parents went through to the adjacent hall. The children had set out benches and chairs in rows, with a bench for themselves at the front. We dutifully sat in our places and then the speeches began. Each of the children took it in turns to read out an impassioned speech that they had put together, and which included ecological facts, figures and recommendations for what the adults needed to do to further reduce the devastation of our climate emergency. The presentations were followed by questions, which the children answered with suitable expertise, confidence and aplomb. It was clear through these presentations that, although the teachers had supported the children with the information, the words they had spoken and the calls to action were authentic, powerful and from the heart.

Expert Showcases have been a very effective replacement for assemblies. Teachers have been able to work with the children to design them and this has reduced their workload, instead of them feeling that they have to put together a polished performance. Unlike assemblies, the children are able to talk at length about their work, rather than simply reading off one or two lines from a strip of paper. In addition, the Expert Showcase serves as a culmination and celebration of a process with the ideas and ownership coming from the child and not from the teacher.

Twice a year we hold 'Tiny Ted Talks'. These are not affiliated with TED or TedX (as we learned that TedX events can only have a maximum of 100 audience members) but the event has a similar feel to a TedX event, in that three people give a talk about the work they do to an audience of children and adults. The last one we had was very successful and featured a cancer researcher, a doctor who researches brain patterns and an Arctic scientist.

Through our personal development curriculum we hope to ensure our children understand how they can contribute to the wider world beyond the school gates and that they have voice, choice and agency, so they can be successful civic leaders in the future.

A note on the case studies

The following five case studies focus on developing learner autonomy with particular regard to teaching metacognitive skills. Problem-solving, self-regulation, social and emotional intelligence and appreciating the joy of not knowing are ways to support the child to be lifelong intrinsically motivated learners.

26 The metacognitive curriculum
ANOARA MUGHAL

School Name	George Mitchell School and Willow Brook Primary Academy
Age group taught within school	Year 5 at George Mitchell and Year 6 at Willow Brook
Location of schools	East London

Any distinguishing features	• Waltham Forest is one of the most diverse and disadvantaged boroughs in the country. (The Metacognitive Curriculum, discussed in this section, was first implemented in Year 6 in one school and school-wide in two other schools in Waltham Forest).
	• Approximately 53 per cent of the population who reside in Waltham Forest are from a minority ethnic background.
	• In recent years there has been improvement in the area's ranking in the Index of Multiple Deprivation:
	  ○ 2019: 82nd
	  ○ 2015: 35th
	  ○ 2010: 15th.

Intent of the curriculum

We believe that all pupils are entitled to an ambitious and creative curriculum which will inspire them to become lifelong learners and will help pupils to succeed, thrive and realise their potential.

By building knowledge, developing skills, experiences and understanding through a broad and balanced curriculum, we challenge social justice issues. Each subject describes the knowledge and skills pupils will remember which will be embedded by wider subject-related experiences, underpinned by the National Curriculum. As a result, pupils acquire knowledge from experiences that build wider cultural capital.

High-quality texts, research and best practice across oracy, literacy, numeracy and cognitive science form the basis of our ambitious curriculum. Our curriculum acts as a progression model and by enriching it with memorable experiences, we make knowledge memorable, develop transferrable skills and create independent learners who can go on to be successful beyond Year 6.

We have carefully considered the knowledge, skills and attributes we want our pupils to acquire so that they confidently develop their voice and reach their potential. Our curriculum is sequenced by our subject leaders so that each phase builds on what has come before and prepares for what comes after. Understanding what they learn, how they learn it and the importance of the order of learning provides pupils with a rich learning experience.

Our curriculum approach builds independence by giving pupils ownership of their learning. It gives pupils an insight into how they learn and helps them to recognise underlying reasons for strengths, areas to develop and to diagnose problems when faced with difficulties.

We understand metacognition as an awareness and understanding of one's own thought processes. Our metacognitive approach also builds habits of self-regulation in learning, such as valuing mistakes, resilience, persistence and adaptability, which are valuable to the learning process and have been proven to generate equally significant classroom benefits. It reinforces and extends their range of learning strategies, transferring their learning to new situations and helping them to develop more efficient and thorough approaches to their work, which lead to deeper learning.

Our learners develop metacognitive skills and strategies to enhance, deepen and improve their learning. Pupils develop their understanding of what is required to succeed and take greater responsibility for their learning.

Implementation

Our curriculum develops understanding of concepts through knowledge, skills and experiences, and through making connections to prior learning. The progression model allows vocabulary to be deliberately linked throughout the curriculum within and across subjects, year groups and topics. By applying prior learning in different ways and in different contexts, it becomes transferable knowledge.

Teachers encourage pupils to become more independent and give learners more responsibility over time to plan, connect, track and review their learning. Our curriculum also moves pupils' attitudes from fixed mindsets towards growth mindsets. It addresses how learners get to grips with subject content as they reflect on their growing understanding of concepts and incorporate new material into their mental schemata.

We focus on motivating learners as they start to own their learning journey and understand processes involved in building and reinforcing understanding. Once pupils have grasped fundamental concepts, they have more time to apply learning in new contexts and in real-life situations, leading to deeper learning.

Building pupils' metacognitive faculties involves these reflective routines:

- signalling when to step back and pause when they are considering an activity
- encouraging them to ask themselves questions to unpick and navigate their learning journey.

Performances and end of term celebrations are closely linked to learning, as they involve parents and celebrate learning. Each term, a year group will showcase the children's achievements in a whole-phase event as well as year group events. Educational visits are also integral to the curriculum to provide our children with new opportunities and experience linking to their learning.

Impact

This curriculum design ensures that the needs of individual and small groups of children can be met within the environment of high-quality teaching and supported by targeted, proven interventions where appropriate. In this way it impacts children's outcomes in very positive ways. Enjoyment of the curriculum promotes good behaviour, confidence and achievement to the fullest.

Due to our metacognitive approach which develops skills of self-regulation and gives pupils ownership of their learning, our pupils are able to transfer their learning to new situations. They feel motivated and safe to try new things, enabling them to develop and discover their interests and talents. Children have opportunities to share their learning with each other, their parents and carers and other learners through school-based and external exhibitions, performances, competitions and events involving other schools. Developing their independence and motivation as learners and their sense of responsibility as future citizens is at the heart of all our teaching and learning.

Turning vision into reality

At our school one of the issues was that pupils' working memories seemed to be poor as they struggled to remember learning from one year to the next. Just as we started to consider changing our current curriculum to create a more metacognitive curriculum to help develop metacognitive skills and memory, two articles were published. The first was Claire Sealey's blog post (2017) on 'The 3D Curriculum that Promotes Remembering'. Shortly after, the Education Endowment Fund (EEF) published its report on 'Metacognition and Self-Regulated Learning' (2018), stating that teaching metacognition explicitly improves pupil progress and attainment by seven months. With this research, we knew it was time to change our curriculum.

In order to change our curriculum, we started off by auditing the curriculum through two lenses: the subject knowledge lens and the metacognitive lens. These highlighted the cognitive and metacognitive gaps and provided us with the next steps for curriculum development.

We then carefully considered different types of curriculum model and, in particular, the ones that would promote metacognitive thinking. There was not one model without disadvantages, so we decided to utilise a variety of models. The four curriculum models we chose were the Product Model, the Process Model, the Thematic Model and the Spiral Model. Let us look at the four models we considered in our curriculum design below.

Product model (Bloom, 1956) – adapted

The product model is based on focusing on the end result by setting goals to reach and evaluating whether you have been successful based on a comparison. It is a highly motivational model for pupils due to its behaviourist approach. Pupils know what the end goal is and have clear direction, along with rewards (internal or otherwise) if they reach the goal. This model lends itself well for the development of metacognitive thinking and in particular at developing self-efficacy.

However, one of the disadvantages is that it hinders creativity. Being aware of this, we adapted the curriculum so half of the curriculum time would be spent on the product model and the other half on developing creativity. The decision was made to use this model to teach and assess subjects such as art and design.

Process models (Stenhouse, 1975)

With this model, it is the process that is identified as being successful and not the outcome. Being successful at something and being acknowledged for it is one of the pillars of metacognition. Although this model is excellent for engaging creative skills and getting pupils thinking, there are some disadvantages. Usually there is pressure to complete work and your performance is judged on what the end product is in real life.

This curriculum model is evaluation-based and not dependent on the subject, skill or ability. Although this curriculum model can develop metacognitive skills, evaluating a process without a goal can lead to inaccuracy of judgments and can affect pupils' levels of self-efficacy.

Thematic model (Holt and Krall, 1976)

The thematic model can be used effectively to engage pupils as they will enjoy a theme they are interested in and can become engrossed in it. However, there are some disadvantages to only using this model. If pupils are not interested in the theme, they can lose focus and engagement. In addition to this, specific skills may be missed and not be taught. Thematic models can be used in tasks such as website development but this is something that is largely left up to teachers to decide.

Spiral curriculum (Bruner 1960)

With the spiral curriculum topics are revisited on different occasions, building incrementally on previous learning and deepening learning. Existing knowledge is reinforced each time a topic is revisited and repeatedly covered in greater depth. The challenges within the curriculum help develop the metacognitive skills of reflection and evaluation. Both the product and process models can be utilised for assessment purposes. However, some disadvantages are that with the spiral curriculum there is an assumption that all learning is linear and we all know that it is not. The spiral curriculum is better suited to subjects such as maths, computing and science, which are more fact-based than other subjects.

A spiral curriculum model does not lend itself to make links with ideas within a subject. One way of supporting the development of mental models is by associating two concepts which are inverse but at the same time symbiotic, such as multiplication and division.

Adapting the curriculum models

Sometimes misconceptions can arise when pupils are taught concepts which are not age-appropriate, as they are not cognitively able to understand the concept in full, and learning therefore becomes superficial. When the topic is revisited at a later time misconceptions may need to be unlearned. In order to address this, we structured the maths curriculum so that misconceptions could be addressed prior to new learning. Another disadvantage was that gaps in knowledge could sometimes present themselves if the spacing of topics was too large. For example, if fractions (a complex conceptual topic) was taught once per year, pupils would forget what they had been taught the year before. As a result of this, we decided to teach fractions three times per year, building on what was taught in the term before. For complex conceptual topics, there needs to be a spiral within the spiral curriculum.

Another feature of the spiral curriculum is that it is taught in blocks usually over a two- or three-week period. Pupils carry out the same processes over and over again and are not required to think about other types of problems. This limits their progress and conceptual understanding of maths. Research has shown that interleaving, the sequencing of topics in an interspersed and repeated order (rather than linear blocks), improves mathematical understanding. As a school, we decided to interleave other topics with the current topic studied.

The spiral curriculum does not lend itself naturally to forming connections and links. However, deliberate links can be made for example when multiplication and division are taught as one topic; such as highlighting commutativity, which is crucial to developing fluency and the use and application of maths knowledge, skills and understanding.

Teachers were given autonomy on the cognitive curriculum: making decisions on topics to teach, connections between topics, vocabulary and texts to teach from. Teachers were also given autonomy on which metacognitive strategy to teach and when.

Training on metacognition included:

- dialogic teaching
- effective questioning
- teacher modelling

- using analogies
- using the planning, connecting, monitoring and evaluating cycle
- spaced and interleaved practice
- taking risks in learning and building resilience
- growth mindset
- transferring learning to new situations
- developing more efficient and more thorough approaches to their work, leading to deeper learning.

One of the issues was that assumptions were made about teachers' understanding of what metacognition was. When we carried out a survey, most teachers thought that they knew what metacognition was and that they were teaching metacognition explicitly, but this was not the case. In addition to this, some teachers assumed that every lesson should be taught by direct instruction. However, guidance tells us that metacognitive strategies should be taught both through direct instruction and the inquiry approach. The challenge was to develop teachers' understanding of what metacognition is, how to teach it and to observe what the explicit teaching of metacognition would look like in the curriculum.

Once the curriculum models were decided and methods put into place about how subjects/topics would be structured, teachers felt empowered and confident to develop connections within the cognitive curriculum. Having the autonomy to make decisions about the knowledge to teach, how to connect the knowledge and how to teach metacognition gave teachers the ownership and excitement that was missing from the curriculum, and this filtered through into the classroom.

We also noticed a marked improvement in pupils' spoken vocabulary and articulation of thoughts. Over time pupil behaviour and confidence improved and more pupils started securing and achieving a deeper level of learning.

Takeaways

- Conduct an audit of your current curriculum through cognitive and metacognitive lenses.
- Assess staff subject knowledge and metacognitive knowledge.
- Challenge assumptions about what teaching metacognition explicitly looks like in the classroom and how it could be incorporated.

- Develop staff members' metacognitive thinking before developing pupil metacognitive thinking.
- Use a range of curriculum models to structure different subjects.
- Reiterate the significance of sequencing content and topics in the curriculum in order to secure concepts by the end of Year 6.
- Revisit topics *progressively* in terms of knowledge, vocabulary and tasks.
- Increase levels of difficulty and make explicit links between old and new learning.
- Provide CPD on metacognitive strategies with ongoing support.

27 I am a problem solver... How about you?
DR ANITA DEVI

> As founder and CEO of not-for-profit organisation TeamADL, **Dr Anita Devi** has been involved in raising the quality of education in a variety of settings.

Intent of the curriculum

If I were a headteacher, my curriculum intent would be simple: to develop problem-solvers. This intent is positioned around the *identity* learners would adopt, not just the skills they would acquire. This would ensure they have agency, confidence and authority to use the skill across different circumstances and in different future vocations.

'Isn't this a bit simplistic?' I hear you say.

Not at all. Learning in the classroom is a continuum of time: we use what we know from the past by teaching in the present to build a better future – a better future not just for the learner, but the community, wider nation and the world. Progression is based not just on hope, but also confident contributions by all.

Looking into the past, we want learners in the present to be curious. It starts with the basics: what could be better? Or in metacognitive language, as some schools use: even better if? Curiosity emerges from a gap in either knowledge or learning, as well as heightened interest. Think about why you use a search engine, i.e. what kinds of things you search for. Most classrooms comprise of a combination of motivations around curiosity. Curiosity helps to frame the problem of pertinent interest to the learner, thereby combining personalised learning with high-quality teaching delivery.

Thinking to the future, every vocation involves an element of problem-solving. So, the core subjects (language, numerical competency, science and basic technology skills) all aid this deeper inner process of finding solutions.

From a humanitarian perspective, what if the learners chose to solve problems that positively impacted the world and, through this, harnessed new innovations for a better tomorrow? This is agile intelligence (AQ) using traditional intelligence (IQ), emotional intelligence (EQ) and spiritual intelligence (SQ) in a collaborative manner. This is the core social, moral, spiritual and cultural (SMSC) education element of the curriculum.

Implementation

Every lesson would need to include some element of problem-solving.

Problem-solving allows for learning to be undertaken individually and in groups, or even as a whole class. Processes and information can be chunked, thus enabling those with learning difficulties to operate from a place of strength and contribution, not deficit. There is no single way to solve a problem.

Let's deconstruct the process with the following five steps:

1. Firstly, define the area of interest. This flexibility allows for different problems to be explored simultaneously.
2. Articulate the exact problem. The problem should not be too big. It has to sit within the learner's sphere of influence. This involves an element of elimination and choice.
3. To solve the problem, the learner has to first find out what is known and unknown, as well as compare different possible known solutions. This would involve connecting with others in the classroom and outside the school. Communities are strengthened through shared dialogue.
4. Having weighed up all the options, the learner has to again make a choice and put forward their best solution at the time, with clarity around the why. This is a deeper level of reasoning.
5. The learner needs to persuade others to adopt their solution to the problem. This level of persuasion embraces high-level thinking and emotional and social skills.

Any lesson or subject could embrace all these steps or parts of it.

Senior leadership teams would be able to visibly see the process in action and the curriculum intent would be cross-curricular, going beyond content knowledge to shaping the individual as a person.

Case study

I once asked my eight-year-old learners: What 'local' problem do you want to solve? After much deliberation, they decided on litter in the neighbourhood. The motivation wasn't to do with helping the environment. In fact, on the way home from school, they had seen a snail crawl into an empty dumped drink can. The can was then squashed by a passer-by. That was the problem they wanted to solve – how to stop snails being squashed! They started asking people about the litter, they made graphs, calculated costs and looked at options. They designed solutions. They wrote to the local Member of Parliament, and he wrote back. They designed a programme for change. At the end of the problem-solving, they knew they could identify a problem and solve it. They had agency and, in terms of their identity, they could call themselves 'problem-solvers'. This lesson was taught long before Charles Leadbeater wrote his book *The Problem Solvers* (2016).

Let's consider secondary and a scenario if I were a headteacher and am opening a school from scratch. What if classes were organised in mixed abilities (as the research shows are more effective) and then grouped by interest for problem-solving? I know in other parts of the world (e.g. Germany), one day a week is dedicated to this level of collaborative problem-solving. The structure of the school day remains, but there is fluidity in pace and direction of learning within a framework. The schools boast not only some amazing ideas that have changed communities, but also highly effective adult alumni who attribute their success to problem-solving opportunities.

Impact

A problem-solving approach shifts the curriculum from being static and content-driven to being about dynamic learning. In my experience when I have used this:

- Learners are keen to get to school to work on 'their problem'. They form better relationships too.

- Staff, especially subject specialists, value the innovative element of stretching thinking around their own specialism.
- We see enhanced inclusion, as it no longer about who is the best, but what each child can offer and bring to the table.
- I have seen many learners use problem-solving out of school; in some cases, teaching their parents and siblings, thereby shifting family situations. Surely this is a better way for levelling up and driving social mobility.
- For many learners the big problems of the world seem too far away, so we start with local issues that affect the community. Problem-solving is not about fundraising. Resources are only one dimension to problem-solving and, in fact, much can be done without extra resources, just doing things differently.

Turning vision into reality

It starts with vision and values. Imagine a classroom that has positioned problem-solving at the core of the curriculum. What would that look like in terms of:

- class structure
- seating
- content
- visual aids and resources
- learner dynamics and classroom flow
- boundaries
- structure
- determinants of success?

To be clear, a problem-solving focus is not the same as an investigative learning or a discovery learning approach. Problem-solving starts with focusing in on an issue, defining the problem and then framing it as a question that can be answered or addressed through curriculum learning. There needs to be defined structure and scaffolded supports.

The internet and technology, without a doubt, would be used for some of the research. This is possibly where distraction can set in, and why a framework is necessary. We've all been there – start searching for one thing, see something, click another link and another. Before we know it, we are stratospheres away from the original problem. The process, if structured well, could aid learners to use discernment online use. Instead of just accepting anything they read online, they would need to verify from other sources. This vital lesson between real news and fake media is a significant problem that would be partially addressed by developing curious thinking and a problem-solving curriculum.

From a staff development perspective, teachers would need to learn more about cognition, thinking skills and the power of curiosity. Teacher training would have to shift from didactic delivery to facilitating 'learning conversations'. Progression could be defined through both complexity of issues and complexity of problems. For example, a 'how' problem requires less imaginative thought than a 'what if' scenario which starts to shape discovery and alternative possibilities.

Developing problem-solvers at the heart of the curriculum naturally lends itself to metacognition and talking about the thought processes. Research by the EEF has shown metacognition to have high impact on accelerating learning. A core element of metacognition is having a shared language.

Takeaways

A few pointers to move towards a problem-solving curriculum in a school that is not a new-build:

- Start by evaluating how much problem-solving is currently the focus of your curriculum. How is this delivered? Is it prescriptive or is there scope for learners to define the problems they want to solve? Possibly a mix?
- Undertake a learning walk. How much problem-solving can you see in the teaching? Not just the traditional problems in maths or science, but problems with open-ended solutions. The process needs a defined framework, not just the question. How much conversation around the problem is being generated and by whom?
- Consult widely to define a vision. Be explicit: What it look like? How would you know when you are there?
- Adopt a problem-solving approach to the change process.
- Test it out, initially on a small scale.
- Learn from the trial and expand to the whole school.

- Continually train staff in curiosity, cognition and problem-solving.
- As with any change process, the planning, communication and feedback loop are vital.

Imagine a world of problem-solvers not afraid to tackle the challenges that we do not even know exist. Imagine adults of tomorrow (your learners of today) faced with a problem and knowing how to adopt a systematic, non-reactive response because you taught them. Imagine your students of today solving the generational challenges of poverty, cancer, energy shortage, war etc., through innovation because they care and know how to channel their compassion into global solutions that benefit everyone.

That's the dream (for now). Now make it happen! Are you ready to nurture future problem-solvers?

Tools and resources

Yates, J. (2021). *Fractured: Why our societies are coming apart and how we put them back together again.* HarperNorth: Manchester.

Catalyst 2030 – 'Pathways to Transforming Education' Report (2022)

https://catalyst2030.net/resources/pathways-to-transforming-education-proven-solutions-from-social-entrepreneurs

Catalyst 2030 – 'Pathways to Transforming Education' Toolkit (2023)

https://catalyst2030.net/resources/pathways-to-transforming-education-toolkit

Ashoka U

www.ashoka.org/en-gb/programme/ashoka-u

Skill Builder Partnership

www.skillsbuilder.org

Teach A Man To Fish

www.teachamantofish.org.uk

School Enterprise Challenge

www.schoolenterprisechallenge.org

28 The joy of not knowing – a curriculum for lifelong learners
DR MARCELO STARICOFF

> Dr Marcelo Staricoff is a Lecturer in Education at the University of Sussex.

Intent of the curriculum

I find it fascinating to think of the curriculum as a potter thinks of their clay. If we imagine that at the start of the year every child is provided with a block of clay (curriculum content) then it is really interesting to postulate that the intent for us all in education is to enable every child to use the 'potter's wheel' (school infrastructure and philosophy of education) to then shape, personalise and give meaning to the clay during the course of the year. By the end, every child has acquired all the tools, skills and dispositions needed to allow them to produce, describe and celebrate their unique work of art.

The exciting challenge for schools then lies in being able to establish the conditions with which to deliver the curriculum intent so that all children feel intrinsically motivated to *want* to engage with, explore, shape and give meaning to their block of clay.

From a teaching and learning perspective, this vision of curriculum intent places educators in a very interesting position. In wanting to encourage every child to engage, shape and give meaning to their block of clay during the course of the year, we begin to establish an intent that is ambitious and transformational for children's life chances. It introduces them to the principal characteristic of effective lifelong learners from a very early age: the realisation that the acquisition of knowledge, often perceived as the end goal in education, is merely the first step in the process of learning. Acquisition of knowledge is of limited value unless it is accompanied by the ability to give *meaning* and *understanding* to what has been learnt. When coupled with *wisdom*, this enables learners to apply this new knowledge for the good of themselves and society.

Using the analogy of the potter and the potter's wheel enables us to convey a curriculum intent that not only shapes the end product (summative assessment). It also shapes the person that has created the end product in a way that allows them to thrive now and in a future full of uncertainties as effective and successful members of their family, school and local, national and global communities.

Implementation

The vision that underpins this curriculum intent also helped to shape the philosophy of education and school leadership that is now known as The Joy of Not Knowing™ or the JONK™ approach (Staricoff, 2021). Interestingly, when thinking back to the early days as a newly qualified teacher, when the ideas that now constitute the JONK™ approach began to form and emerge, it seems that I was subconsciously using a version of the analogy of the potter. I was viewing myself, the teacher, as the potter who, through the implementation of an exciting and inspiring curriculum, could shape, grow, evolve and celebrate the uniqueness of every child during the course of the year. It seems that I was envisaging the children as my 'mouldable' blocks of clay. Later, as a headteacher, this same belief in the expertise and potential of every member of staff enabled the JONK™ philosophy to incorporate a leadership, as well as a pedagogical, perspective where we all worked towards creating a motivational school culture. This meant that all staff felt inspired to inspire the children in all aspects of the curriculum.

In terms of implementation of the curriculum, one of the key principles of the JONK™ approach is the emphasis on ensuring that all children are equipped with all they need to succeed in all aspects of the curriculum *before* the learning is presented to them. The proposal here is that schools devote the first week of the academic year to what is now known in our school as the JONK™ Learning to Learn week. There is nothing more exciting than schools planning for this week and including all the aspects that make every school so unique and special. In other words, the idea of Learning to Learn in schools is the same, but the week will look completely different in every school and, possibly, in every class of the same school. The JONK™ Learning to Learn week is nominally divided into five distinct areas that are introduced to the children on each day of the week. These are:

- models and cultures of learning
- strategies for creative thinking
- visible thinking and learning techniques
- philosophy and a philosophical approach to the curriculum
- the lifelong learning dispositions.

The idea of using the first day of this week to introduce children to how brilliant it is to *not* know supports their emotional wellbeing for the rest of the year. This is accompanied by them each developing and annotating their own model of learning to describe how learning feels for them, which is displayed in the class from day one. This creates a learning environment where children feel equally valued as individuals and as learners. These models are fantastic as during the year the teacher uses the language of each model to have personalised feedback conversations with each child. The week also helps the teacher to get know every child extremely well and, for the child to feel that the teacher has got to know them as individuals, as learners and thinkers, is very special indeed.

The Learning to Learn week equips children with all they need to be able to succeed as learners and enables the teachers and children to co-create a classroom culture from the outset which is a values-led, children rights-driven, dialogue-rich community of inquiry and places. When implementing the curriculum, importance is given when to *how* we teach and *how* children learn as well as to *what* we teach and *what* children learn. The week also ensures that all children are comfortable with being in a position of *not* knowing, rather than this making them feel anxious or worried. They realise that to learn something new, we *must* not know it first. This really transforms the way they feel about school, learning and the year ahead.

How we teach the curriculum then becomes very exciting indeed. The JONK™ approach places great emphasis on the teacher being a partner and on incorporating the multicultural and multilingual richness which every child brings with them into the everyday teaching and learning process. For example, the day launches with a motivational, open-ended thinking skills starter designed so that all learners can succeed. The learning objective is always previewed so that the children have had a chance to engage with the learning, discuss it at home, formulate their questions, develop their curiosity, and ascertain what they know and what they know they don't know, all before the lesson starts.

As the lesson starts, the presentation of the learning is often framed using a philosophical question to induce whole-class dialogue. The engagement in tasks tends to be framed along a thought-provoking and 'intellectually playful' approach, using the pedagogical principles that underpin EYFS but across all year groups and phases of education. Lessons are enriched with challenge that encourages the children to use what they have learnt in a different context. They conclude with the opportunity for reflecting metacognitively and looking forward to what comes next.

Impact

The JONK™ approach was first established as a whole-school philosophy of education and school leadership at Hertford Infants and Nursery School in Brighton. The impact was illustrated not just by the school being graded 'Outstanding' for the first time in its history, but more importantly by the significant rise in standards, pupil motivation, family engagement and attendance.

It is very moving to meet alumni of the school from the time, who are now leading such successful and fulfilling lives. In a school that was in the 10th percentile in terms of disadvantage nationally at the time, the approach and culture became very aspirational. In the space of four years behavioural incidents decreased substantially and quite incredibly the school, despite competition from other successful schools nearby, launched an academic year with all 60 families choosing the school as their first preference for the first time ever.

The sense of community that arose at the school during this time was incredibly special indeed. School events were always full, family learning mornings became a wonderful way of nurturing the child-school-family relationship and 'Community Sundays', where the community would come together on a weekend to build something for the school, was very special and included building vegetable beds, outside classrooms and improvements to the playground.

It is a great privilege to be working now with so many schools across the country who are using the JONK™ philosophy to create a bespoke vision and philosophy of education for their schools and who are reporting similar findings, both in terms of the impact on pupils, but also on staff:

We've had the most amazing Learning to Learn week. The children have come up with some wonderful ideas about how they see their learning; all talk about being in the pit when struggling in lessons [has gone]; homework books have been replaced with family home learning journals; we have been using De Bono's hats; are planning maths calculation videos (the children love these!) for the website; and in form time this afternoon every group is having a philosophy session. Staff have been telling me how much they have enjoyed the week and how it has reminded them why we do this job in the first place.

Headteacher in Norfolk

It is also interesting to reflect on the voice of pupils who having been immersed in this approach to the curriculum and the teaching and learning process; expressing sentiments that are at the heart of everything I believe is fabulous about education. The wonderful thing about these quotes is how the children associate and equate the JONK™ approach with a sense of fun and of academic *and* emotional wellbeing.

- 'The Thinking Skills Starters are fun and make me feel happy and ready for the rest of the day.'
- 'The Thinking Skills Starters wake me up like an alarm clock. They make me feel wonderful – a magical start to the day.'
- 'The Thinking Skills Starters help me a lot with my learning – I love the way they are so challenging.'
- 'The Thinking Skills Starters rev me up for the day. I want to skip time to get to the next one. We are allowed to bring our own ones in!'
- 'The Thinking Skills Starters make me feel welcome and confident to create a new piece of knowledge. If I created a Mind Map of the Starters, it would be huge!'
- 'Philosophy helps me to think and it is very thinkable!'
- 'Philosophy teaches me how to disagree with my friends.'
- 'Philosophy is relaxing.'
- 'In Philosophy you can express yourself without feeling embarrassed.'
- 'It's great to do Philosophy in all the subjects.'
- 'In Philosophy we talk to each other rather than through the teacher.'
- 'Philosophy helps me to become a critical thinker.'
- 'Because of doing Philosophy we will know so much when we are older.'
- 'In Philosophy people actually change their views during a lesson!'
- 'Through Philosophy we learn to respect each other.'

The most striking impact, however, that I have always experienced and continue to experience with the JONK™ approach, is the way that it promotes a real sense of intrinsic motivation to *want* to engage and to learn. The approach frees children up from the constraints that usually lead to barriers in their learning, which are very often associated with feeling worried and anxious when finding things difficult or not knowing how to launch into the learning. Instead, as children often say, they love to learn as they are equipped with all they need to know *how* to know what they *want* to know that they know they *don't* know!

Turning vision into reality

It has been fascinating how over the past 25 years or so, the vision first turned into reality within my own classroom, then as a headteacher, as part of a whole-school approach to education and to leadership. Now as a lecturer at the University of Sussex on the Initial Teacher Training Course, the vision is becoming a reality in the hands of the next generation of teachers.

I remember my first few years of teaching so clearly, when I was coming across all these really exciting initiatives in primary education. The headteachers at the two schools, where so much of the JONK™ developed, gave me the freedom to *experiment* in the classroom. Having just moved into teaching from a career as a research scientist, I embraced this opportunity wholeheartedly and used it to establish a culture of learning which was rooted, as research scientists have to be, in being comfortable with not knowing and with uncertainty. I was amazed at how quickly this way of being inspired all children with a wonderful enthusiasm and thirst for *wanting* to know.

As a headteacher, I then set out to emulate this philosophy with all members of staff. Despite the usual pressures, I wanted all staff to feel that they were the experts in whichever role they had in the school and, as such, had a great degree of professional freedom with which to keep developing this expertise as part of their everyday practice and professional development. Every term, the teachers and support staff could choose an area that they valued as the source of their inquiry and then share their findings with the school at the end of each term. This was fabulous in terms of enabling the school to adopt strategies that were found to be successful within our own setting and context.

For every member of staff to feel equally valued as an expert, I developed the concept of multi-professional teams where every member of staff, including all clerical, administrative, caretaking and support staff, picked a 'team' to join at the start of the year, with each team then collaborating and using everyone's ideas to move each of the school's development plan priorities forward. This later expanded to the concept of having children as learning leaders, who would also become members of these teams and use the information gathered by working with the staff to write a children's version of the school development plan.

This way of being, where every child, family and member of staff felt that their voice was integral to the way the school was moving forward, relied on spending the first two years or so using everyone's thoughts and ideas alongside a democratic voting process to derive a framework, one aspect at a time, that would give everyone at the school a common vision. This started with deriving a whole-school set of values (e.g. care, thoughtfulness, respect), then introducing a set of children's rights (e.g. right to an education, to play, to be listened to) and then developing and introducing a set of lifelong learning dispositions (e.g. creative, curious, resilient). The key is to give the school a lot of time and to establish each new initiative by building on the previous one. This is what is known as the 'Onion Model' (Staricoff, 2021).

The most exciting but most difficult challenge is in the ability to translate the curriculum statements, aims and objectives into a motivational culture of learning on a daily basis and across all areas of the curriculum.

For this, there are two main opportunities that are fabulous to experiment with. One is the idea of presenting the learning objective to the children using a philosophical question rather than a statement. For example, replacing 'To be able to learn about the properties of 2D shapes' with 'Do 2D shapes exist?'.

The other opportunity is based on the idea of trying to nurture children's natural curiosity by emulating the pedagogy of the EYFS across all year groups. For this, the JONK™ approach introduces the concept of 'dis-metacognition,' which describes the idea that children's learning is at its best when they don't realise that they are learning! In practice this means trying as much as possible to give children the opportunity to engage in the curriculum through investigative approaches and open-ended challenges. For example, when studying the properties of sound, the children are challenged to develop a way of measuring the speed of sound in the playground. In planning for this, they will be incorporating a very wide set of knowledge and skills from a variety of subjects, but without being consciously aware that that is what they are doing!

The opportunities that arise from developing this culture across the school are endless and form part of a continuous circle of ideas and, very importantly, ideas that are contributed by all. Prioritising these opportunities and placing them on a strategic timeline is the key to their successful implementation into the school's vision, philosophy and strategic development for a JONK™ curriculum for life.

Takeaways

I have taken one idea from each of the chapters of *The Joy of Not Knowing* (2021) as a Takeaway:

- Introduce the children to how brilliant it is to *not* know from a very early age.
- Introduce a whole-school set of values on children's rights and lifelong learning dispositions.
- Introduce the concept of multi-professional teams to include all staff and children (as learning leaders) in the strategic development of the school.
- Introduce the concept of metacognition as well as dis-metacognition, to immerse children in learning opportunities during which they don't realise that they are learning.
- Launch the academic year with a Learning to Learn week bespoke to your school and inspire every child to create their own model of learning at the start of the year.
- Welcome the children every day with a Thinking Skills Starter in the playground for families to engage with as they are waiting for school to start, and in the classroom accompanied by music and the register in a language other than that of instruction.
- Introduce the children to the wonders of thinking philosophically and philosophical learning objectives.
- Introduce children to the lifelong learning dispositions. Link each one to an animal (the resilient tortoise, for example) and integrate these as part of the daily teaching and learning process.
- Introduce an open-ended thinking skills approach to home learning tasks which incorporates learning at home and with their families.
- Experiment with enabling the children to use all the cultural and linguistic richness that they possess as part of a diverse 'culture for learning'; using their preferred language to engage rather than only using the language of instruction as a means of accessing the curriculum.

Tools and resources

Books

- Staricoff, M. (2021) *The Joy of Not Knowing*. Oxon: Routledge.
- Staricoff, M. and Rees, A. (2005) *Start Thinking*. Birmingham: Imaginative Minds.

Podcasts, videos and other media

- ThinkLab talk – 'The Joy of Not Knowing: How to Unlock your Learning Potential'

    www.youtube.com/watch?v=BkODqvabGzM

- Recess Duty podcast – 'Episode 034 with Marcelo Staricoff'

    https://open.spotify.com/episode/2R4YXVCbq89kpdDASwJ7rP

- Talking Their Language with Helen Bodell podcast – 'The JONK Approach with Marcelo Staricoff'

    www.twinkl.co.uk/resource/talking-their-language-with-helen-bodell-episode-twenty-three-the-jonk-approach-with-marcelo-staricoff-t-eal-1683100194

- CERIP University of Cambridge – "The Joy of Not Knowing" – Seminar and Q&A with Marcelo Staricoff

    www.youtube.com/watch?v=3qL3HgUSl08

- Edlink. – Image the Week - with Dr Marcelo Staricoff

    www.youtube.com/watch?v=OtmkhkkbtbE

29 Big picture learning – the student is the curriculum
PROFESSOR SCOTT BOLDT

> **Scott Boldt** is a Professor of Practice at the University of Cumbria and the National University of Wales. He writes extensively on the initiatives, principles and practices of Big Picture Learning, a glocal school network.

Intent of the curriculum

In conventional schools, students are often limited in, if not deprived of, learning opportunities because of a well- or over-organised programme established by educators, where students have few or no decisions to make on a day-to-day basis. The problem is that when people are told what, when, where, with whom, and how to do something, they may learn some content and gain a level of competency (mostly through memorisation and repetition) but this is nothing compared to a learner making these decisions, especially if it is connected with their interests and happening with others who share that interest and demonstrate their skills while allowing the learner to practise them. What turns information into knowledge that sticks is where there is agency, allowing students to pursue and practise their interests with others.

The curriculum of Big Picture Learning (BPL) schools is designed for learning simply because the student is the curriculum and humans are designed for learning. People do not learn primarily or best by sitting quietly at a desk – we learn when we are engaging in and pursuing our interests, interacting, making mistakes and figuring out how to correct them. We learn when all our senses are engaged in school and out of school; with our friends, through our interests, in relationships and when we are practising and applying our knowledge to real-world problems.

BPL schools work on the basis that the three elements of interests, relationships and practice are interwoven and mutually supportive of learning. Interests are fostered and developed through relationships and experiences. They are deepened, tested, refined, and expanded through practice. Relationships are often formed and normally develop around shared interests, and they are strengthened when people practise in a community, working together to finish a task, complete a project or enhance their skills. The interweaving of interests, relationships and practice provides for pupils' agency (guided by an educator) and provides the context for successful and sustained learning.

Implementation

Big Picture Learning has grown considerably over the years into an international network of schools and learning environments. They serve approximately 12,000 students in 30 US states and an additional 75 schools and learning centres in 13 countries, with upwards of 35,000 students across all phases. The approach of BPL is to operate flexibly and in response to the needs of each learner and the community in which they are situated. In a BPL school, each student is part of an advisory (a learning community) led by a supportive advisor (teacher) who guides students to identify their interests, passions, and learning needs. With the students and their families, learning plans and goals are developed which make learning personal, engaging and relevant with the participation of mentors and other supportive adults.

Out-of-school activities involving interest exploration, engagement with the community and student-curated projects are central to the BPL approach. Mentorship in a real-world setting offers students access to skilled adults and therefore to deep learning and skill development in fields they are interested in. All students are challenged to pursue their interests and are supported by a community of educators, professionals and family members. Learning is assessed through regular exhibitions and presentations of students' work with reference to their learning goals and targets.

Positive student interests, whatever they may be, are the context for their learning. As mentioned above, the student is the curriculum and the entire community (their town, their city) is the school. Education is everyone's business, not the preserve of or limited to educationalists. A student-driven curriculum is developed around real-world experiences and standards. As distinct from conventional schooling with the focus on a prescribed curriculum and academic testing, BPL involves interest-driven explorations and internships that establish the context for learning where the disciplines are integrated with student interests.

BPL schools have an advisory structure where the advisor (teacher) knows the students and their families well. The schools are purposely not large because in schools where there are 1,500 or 5,000 students, young people are not known and they don't know everybody. The BPL motto is 'One-Student-at-a-Time-in-a-Community', which recognises that every student brings their unique abilities, interests, needs, circumstances and context into school and into their learning.

BPL schools support the concept of 'leaving to learn' because that enables the powerful learning that occurs when students leave their school to expand and deepen their learning; to get exposure to new practices, ideas, people and opportunities; and to learn through their interests in the best places where those interests are happening.

Schools are organised around a culture of collaboration and communication. They are not bound by the structures of buildings, schedules, bells or calendars. There is an interdependence between school and community. Leadership is shared and spread between a strong, visionary principal, a dedicated, responsible team of advisors and other staff and students.

With few exceptions, BPL schools are all publicly funded and recognised by the educational systems of which they are a part. The cost of schooling is comparable to any other state-funded school. In general, BPL schools serve young people who are furthest from opportunity, in diverse and often marginalised communities.

Impact

The principles, activities, practices and lessons of BPL have paved the way for its long-term success with learners and the spread of its design for schooling at every level, as well as in innovative initiatives, which have resulted in an extensive international network. Even more significant is the success and life-transforming activities of its students. In the findings of longitudinal research by Arnold and Mihut (2020) on 'Post-secondary Outcomes of Innovative High Schools', BPL graduates in the USA were equally likely to enrol in university no matter their race, gender or parents' level of education. This finding is unprecedented and no other network of schools in the US can make this claim.

Knowing that school transformation requires change to the way learning is assessed and credentialed, BPL has developed new measures in the form of the International Big Picture Learning Credential (IBPLC). The IBPLC offers to *all* students, particularly those overlooked and undervalued by their educational systems, access to an equitable and educationally sound mode of assessment. 'The IBPLC is a sophisticated tool representing a comprehensive certificate of achievement for students who are on pathways to college, employment, further training or apprenticeships.'

Families are delighted with the IBPLC experience and how it has positively impacted on their children's educational progress, university and employment potential, mental health, and self-esteem (Johnston and Milligan, 2020). The findings from the research and appraisal of the IBPLC attest to its functionality, usefulness and scalability, stating that, 'The IBPLC provides a reliable, accurate and rigorous measurement of the distinctive and valuable learning attainments of BPL graduates. It has the precision required for use in selection and recruitment of graduates into further study or work.'

The IBPLC offers a unique and innovative form of assessment that can be scaled and which contains huge potential for cultivating, recognising and credentialing the relevant necessary academic, vocational, creative, and sociocultural competencies. The IBPLC allows learning taking place beyond the walls of the school to be counted and credited. It is currently accepted for admissions consideration by half of Australia's universities and has been accepted by universities in the USA, the Netherlands, Italy and the Caribbean.

Turning vision into reality

BPL was established in 1995 by Dennis Littky and Elliot Washor in the inner city of Providence, Rhode Island, USA as part of a school transformation movement built on innovative educational principles with a primary focus on learning, in and out of school. The BPL network of schools can now be found from India to Italy, Barbados to Belize, Kenya to Canada, the Netherlands to New Zealand and from Australia to the UK. Some Big Picture schools exist in gleaming new buildings, while some can be found in retrofitted structures that haven't been in use for some time. Some are standalone schools, others are schools-within-schools; there are BPL schools that were new start-ups and many that have transitioned from being conventional schools. In short, Big Picture schools (like the students they serve) often look dramatically different from each another. Each is its own unique environment where students can flourish as individuals within a community of learners. However, there are many elements within the learning design that are less common and distinct, which pull our network together and distinguish them from most other schools.

The entire learning experience is personal to each student's interests, talents and needs. This arrangement expands beyond mere academic work and involves looking at every student holistically. An advisory structure is necessary and is the core organisational and relational structure of a BPL school: its heart and soul, often described as a 'second family' by students. Regular advisor professional development is conducted at each school by principals, other school staff and BPL staff and coaches. A BPL school is a community of lifelong learners who embrace continuous improvement.

Parents are welcomed and valued members of the school community who play a proactive role in their children's learning, collaborating in the planning and assessment of student work. They use their assets to support the work of the school, and often play an integral role in building relationships with potential mentors. In BPL schools, there is palpable trust, respect and equality between and among students and adults. Students take leadership roles in the school and teamwork defines the staff culture. Student voice is valued in the school's decision-making process.

Although most BPL students across the globe will sit local or national examinations, students are assessed in school by public displays of learning that track growth and progress in the student's area of interest. Assessment criteria are unique to the student and apply real-world standards of any project work they have been involved in. Students present multiple exhibitions each year and discuss their learning growth with staff, parents, peers and mentors.

BPL school leaders have to navigate people, places and communities as well as the complexities of power relations within existing social, political, and institutional arrangements. Furthermore, school leaders have to interrupt what they already know about curriculum and pedagogy as schools are reorganised with BPL around student interests. This generates new kinds of work for everyone and is disruptive. Active learning, sharing, and reflecting on practice, and recognising, admitting to, and learning from mistakes becomes part of the new culture of the school.

Takeaways

- Educational change requires new ways, forms and measures.
- A focus on school or curriculum reform will *not* result in any significant and sustained improvements; what is needed are *new* forms not *re*forms.
- The curriculum needs to be designed *with* the students, and focused on their interests and needs.

- The curriculum should *not* be designed for teaching but for learning; teaching is important but is most successful when it facilitates and becomes secondary to learning.
- Real curriculum change involves and requires cultural change.
- Curriculum change comes about and happens best from collaborative work: communities of practitioners learning from each other and with the support of coaches who show and model how to engage learners.
- Schools and curriculum designers should focus on one-student-at-a-time if the goal is to enhance education.
- Curriculum change is difficult work requiring leadership, collaboration, vision, patience and openness to making mistakes and learning.
- The reality is that curriculum change cannot happen without changing assessment.

Tools and resources

Big Picture Leaning – 'Our Approach'
www.bigpicture.org/approach
BPL - 'All in' video
www.youtube.com/watch?v=CmR4B1cm-nw
'Meet a BPL School – Kenya Big Picture Learning' video
www.youtube.com/watch?v=1-VYEGm2Vz4&t=4s
Big Picture Doncaster – The UK's first BPL learning provision
www.bigpicturedoncaster.org

30 Evolving education
LUCY STEPHENS

School Name	The New School
Age group taught within school	4–14 (currently, as we're a new school; we will be soon be up to 16)
Location of school	South London
Any distinguishing features	• Democratic school ethos. • Non fee-paying private school. • Using research, impact and financial modelling to understand how a new model of education could include all young people and support their mental health and life satisfaction.

Intent of the curriculum

Our ultimate aim is that young people leave our school with a strong sense of personal agency. We define this as having a sense of purpose and goals, and the skills and competencies needed to action those goals, which include cognitive, physical, social and emotional skills. By creating an educational environment that supports learner agency and self-determination we are able to engage all our learners in an inclusive provision, allowing all current achievement levels to develop knowledge, skills and understanding. The underpinning values of The New School are rooted in the belief that developing intrinsic motivation in all aspects of learning and behaviour is key to self-determination, which creates the foundation for psychological health and wellbeing. We focus on building young people's academic competencies, connection, autonomy and attachment with other young people and staff. As a result, we hope to promote equity and enable young people to thrive in their future lives.

The curriculum for most subjects is based on the National Curriculum, but for social sciences in the primary years we use a concept-based curriculum, allowing key skills and concepts to be built and developed across the social sciences: history, geography, economics and citizenship, with topics determined by the teacher and class. Our focus is on engagement in learning. Learners own their learning journey and start-points through the use of 'I can' statements.

Our curriculum supports young people to gain depth of knowledge and critical thinking skills in nine key areas: literacy, maths, social sciences, media/ICT, science, art, physical movement, PSHE and religious education. The rest of the curriculum is focused on creating the time and space for the development of personal interest areas such as: optional workshops (cooking, weaving, gardening, origami, DT, woodwork), either run by teachers or other young people; optional subjects (Forest School, music, DT, Spanish, choice of sports); and self-directed time (which includes play, work on personal learning goals, or engaging in personal projects). The curriculum is underpinned by a relational model and an environment that does not use rewards or punishments, instead focusing on transformative justice, building intrinsically motivated principles of care, acceptance of difference and the skills needed for relationships, social and emotional learning and wellness.

Implementation

Our approach to the implementation and development of our curriculum is co-created through a governance structure of sociocracy, which draws on the unique competences of our staff team. We have shared principles that underpin our teaching, learning and relational culture that we believe are the foundation for satisfaction in life and success in future lives:

- Belief in equity of access and inclusion for all learners in the classroom; and developing the skills needed for self-direction and executive function.
- Creation of the conditions and relational autonomy needed to support intrinsic motivation, self-regulation and self-direction for learning in the classroom.
- Belief that learning includes cognitive, social and emotional skills and competences, and that the development of how we think about and reflect on learning, alongside the skills to learn with others, is key to engagement in and mastery of successful learning practices.

- Professional autonomy in teaching practice, coupled with a focus on learning inquiry and dialogue, develops the approaches that work best to create quality learning in the classroom and the key skills of learning for young people.
- Belief that embracing diversity of thought and a healthy level of challenge from staff and young people is key to creativity and innovation.

Developing learning competence

Teachers aim to make the language of learning explicit in order to develop learners' self-talk; build the cognitive, social and emotional learning skills needed to engage in curriculum content; and to develop personal agency in learning. The teacher's role is to model and grow young people's understanding of learning habits; to develop and make learning visible; to develop young people's learning capacity; and to provide learning content that is delivered in a way that provides scaffold and stretch.

How teaching delivery looks is determined by teacher skill and professionalism to choose the appropriate pedagogy for the outcomes planned. Planned reflection time enables mistakes and misconceptions to be identified and celebrated as learning tools, and these are used as feedback to stretch and challenge in the next learning cycle, building self-efficacy and learning skills. Content is planned in combination with the learning skills needed for young people to engage in and 'own' their learning.

We see teachers as learners too, and we actively develop a culture of asking for peer observations and team-teaching to develop aspects of practice. Specialist teachers (science, art and media/ICT) teach across the school from 4 to 16, enabling greater depth of subject knowledge, supporting cross-curricular learning and freeing up time for class teachers to collaborate and plan.

Teachers use ongoing formative assessment as a means of progressing learning and to identify gaps in knowledge. The purpose of assessment for learning is to provide learners with evidence of their own learning. Teachers ask questions and give feedback to grow understanding: supporting young people to clarify their thinking, and to enable them to make progress against self- or teacher-identified goals. Summative assessments are done annually. Teachers may use mini action research cycles to develop ideas within the classroom that support learning, and time is given for reflection as a teaching team to grow understanding and develop best practice. Teachers design processes to capture learner feedback and include young people in the development of their learning.

Our systems for assessment help learners embed and use knowledge fluently, check understanding and inform teaching.

Developing autonomy

Young people build skills of self-regulation, executive function and collaboration within the classroom. Gradually they take ownership of aspects of their learning and assessment, increasing the accuracy of their learning judgements and perceived next steps. Our aim is for learner-centred classrooms where young people can own their starting points in their learning journey, building self-direction, depth and engagement in learning. We support this through our pedagogy, providing content that builds and requires retrieval of prior knowledge. We offer different means of representing and recording information (visual, verbal, written) that supports the development of connections between different knowledge and skills. We share 'I can' statements with young people so they know their start points in a topic or lesson. Within each subject area, there is also a range of ways in which students can develop their own learning to allow them to challenge themselves and gain deeper levels of knowledge and understanding. For example:

- Self-directed learning challenges to extend and challenge, and to scaffold and practise prior knowledge.
- We use some of the school day as self-directed learning time where young people can follow their own interests, choose optional subjects, play, and develop personal projects.
- 'My learning plans' help young people set goals for personal projects and also to develop areas to work on in specific subjects.
- Continuous provision environments are being developed to enable young people to engage in learning outside of key subject lessons. Subject-specific content can be organised in a number of ways in the classroom to allow young people to gain deeper levels of knowledge and understanding.

Developing relational practice

Developing a relational culture in the classroom, including between teachers and young people, is key so that young people can engage in and share responsibility for learning, as well as to support each other's development. Modelling clear, consistent, respectful boundaries is key to a learner-centred environment and successful relationships in the classroom. Negotiated boundaries build agency and ownership as teaching without the use of rewards and punishments requires a different approach to support young people's engagement in learning.

We work in multi-age class groups, which enables inclusion and offers support to those at different current achievement levels, but it also allows for stretch. Young people with additional needs are supported within lessons as well as through support from additional adults. Team teaching enables splitting of classes for different topics. Young people may also have small group or one-to-one sessions to support learning and social and emotional development. Groupings are flexible and dynamic to fit the changing needs of our young people and we avoid any kind of streaming. A young person usually stays with a teacher for a number of years so this allows for strong relational practice and depth of knowledge of the learner, as well as offering a rolling curriculum so content is revisited regularly.

The application of our principles of sociocracy allows for learner voice to be heard and develops oracy skills that supplement and reinforce the young people's ability to reflect on their learning and to identify areas of interest and areas to develop. Play is fundamental to learning, and time and space is made for this in the school day both outside and inside classrooms.

Impact

We believe that learning is an activity of co-construction involving the whole staff team and is always driven by our ultimate outcome of young people's developing agency. Monitoring and review of our approaches and strategies are central to our work and allowing us to continually learn and iterate within our context.

Internal data

We use internal data from teacher and student questionnaires to bring quantitative understanding across a range of measures, which also include questions about a learner's approach to the curriculum, their beliefs about their learning ability and their feeling of the level of support they receive at home and at school. All these outcomes are combined with teacher professional judgements to create a picture of a young person as a learner and the progress they are making. Termly progress meetings are then held with the whole teaching and pastoral team to identify individuals who are not making progress, either academically or in social and emotional aspects of their learning. This enables the team to put support in place in the form of interventions, additional adult support, or a needs plan to be addressed across the whole teaching team. It also enables discussion and action at an individual child-, class-, and/or a whole-school-level depending on what emerges from the analysis. As a whole school we measure young people's self-esteem, self-efficacy, educational engagement and life satisfaction as key outcomes that form the foundation for future wellbeing, equity in outcomes and personal agency.

Young people are supported to run their own termly reflections (equivalent of a parent's evening) on personal learning goals, in collaboration with their teacher and their parent or carer. This plan helps them to reflect on their learning, their strengths and weaknesses, and to identify three goals to work on throughout the term (areas of goals include: communication, problem-solving, setting and achieving goals, emotional literacy, self-esteem, self-knowledge, and executive functioning).

External data

We engage with research organisations such as the University of Nottingham and University College London to understand the strengths and weaknesses of our model against our intent and theory of change. We use this data to draw out the mechanisms of change within the school, enabling us to further develop the activities and practice and refine the model to enable young people to learn and thrive.

Professional development

Professional development is co-planned and designed by a wide range of staff members through our governance structure of sociocracy. We are developing a training cycle across all areas of our practice. This will further develop our inquiry approach to practice, answering questions such as:

- How do we communicate our approach to learning and development in a way that engages parents and other stakeholders?
- Does our practice really develop the attributes of successful learners and what are the key activities we undertake that are crucial for this?

- How do we translate professional ideas, models and best practice into learning experiences in the classroom?
- How do we monitor and detect inclusive learner-centred practice and its impact on learner outcomes that is broader than academic attainment?

Turning vision into reality

Processes and challenges

- Finding time within the school day (specifically, timetabled) for self-directed learning time can be difficult with a wide range of subjects to fit in. Balancing autonomy with content delivery isn't easy and pedagogical decisions have to be made, which impact one or the other. Consider making some subjects optional and allowing young people to choose aspects of their timetable, as well as focusing on learning as the outcome, not just knowledge acquisition.
- Understanding the skills and scaffolding needed for young people to engage in self-directed learning can take time. Consider the classroom environment, the skills, the scaffolding and the teacher values and attitudes to enable young people to follow their interests and to play – it won't always look like typical school-based 'learning'.
- Developing learner-centred classrooms that enable agency is time consuming, iterative and needs continuous reflection and development. Consider a strong continuous provision practice, typical of an Early Years classroom, as a useful model.
- Finding the sweet spot between the consistency of pedagogical practice alongside professional autonomy. This is a work in progress, one that grows with time to build strong professional development practice using inquiry learning.
- Without the use of rewards and punishments in learning, executive function challenges become more evident. This can be more challenging personally and professionally, and requires a strong inclusion lens and an adaptation of pedagogy to engage, scaffold and explicitly teach learning skills.

Pitfalls and setbacks

- When starting something new there are those who engage immediately, those who are unsure and watch and wait, and those who don't want to change for anything. Creating vertical 'slice teams' (or circles in sociocracy) that develop practice in a group which includes a cross-section of the teaching team and leadership, with a consent-based approach to decision making, can ensure you have a wider range of staff to support the embedding of practice.

- Change can sometimes look messy and confusing and there may be a lot of emotional offloading. This can feel very stressful and can be an anxious time. As leaders, when we simply don't know the answer, be cautious of falling back on a top-down control-based approach – it doesn't work if innovation is the end goal. Listening, getting consent to try one small step at a time, or taking a step back and not doing too much at once seems to work better.

- If young people are used to a more controlled environment, too much freedom too soon can be chaotic. Negotiated autonomy is a better place to aim, building the skills required to act autonomously. Young people are often very good at voicing ideas, but implementing those ideas can be harder. When supporting young people to take ownership of aspects of learning, projects or ideas within school, the project management skills are often the place where support and scaffolding are needed.

Successes and opportunities

- Building a strong culture of trust and professionalisation with a model of sociocracy develops a culture that enables us to take risks, to try things out, to innovate and to make change in education. This is the reason why many of us came into teaching and a culture that stifles this is often the reason we leave.

- Focusing on learning, inclusion and wellbeing creates the conditions in which young people flourish and gives the time and space needed to just be children. To play, to have fun, to learn, to grow, to form strong relationships with young people and adults, to take risks, and to work in partnership with people of different ages is crucial for optimal child development and mental wellness.

- If we focus on different educational outcomes and a different approach to the structures within educational settings, we have the opportunity to broaden the concept of education, to demonstrate a different impact and to evolve the educational narrative and, hopefully, policy. This would enable more schools to take innovative approaches to support young people's development and ultimately to effect positive social change.

Takeaways

- Build self-directed learning skills and executive function development into the school day.
- Focus on relational practice and pedagogical approaches that build intrinsic motivation for learning without the use of rewards and punishments.
- Ensure social, emotional and pastoral practice is embedded alongside learning as an underpinning foundation.
- Consider a flattened hierarchical structure, with the teaching team taking ownership of pedagogy and practice, rather than a top-down approach.
- Consider developing a theory of change and outcomes which are broader than just academic attainment to enable professionals to widen their scope of practice and focus on more than content delivery.
- Consider engaging with external research organisations to understand the activities and practice within the school that lead to outcomes, as well as the strengths and weaknesses of your approach.

Editor's reflection on Part 6: Personal development

The last five of our case studies take a philosophical approach to curriculum design; the focus is much less about what knowledge a child will acquire (although this is important) and much more about what sort of a person and learner they will become. There is an emphasis on learning for the joy of learning as an end in itself, rather than just to pass exams. Taking this perspective requires the educator to constantly reflect and revise their approach, working alongside young people as mentors and co-creators in order to develop learner agency.

In recent years, research, including in education and neuroscience, has played a role in the teacher's toolkit and has helped educators to understand how to approach their classroom practice to ensure new knowledge sticks and that learning is memorable.

Developing metacognition, the process of thinking about one's own thinking and about how one learns best, is an important skill. It helps to build positive habits of self-regulation including: valuing mistakes, resilience, persistence and adaptability. Anoara Mughal, author of *Think!: Metacognition-Powered Primary Teaching* (2021), helpfully lists a number of effective strategies for teachers to incorporate into their practice to develop metacognition, including using the planning, connecting, monitoring and evaluating cycle. To be effective throughout the school, Anoara says that all staff must be trained explicitly in metacognition and appreciate the benefits of metacognition in their own practice before it can be applied successfully in the classroom. In addition, teaching young people how to be open minded, resilient problem-solvers is also critical to effective pedagogy.

Dr Anita Devi, author of *Grow Analytical Mindset* (2023), believes one of the most important things that schools can do is to train young people to be problem-solvers. This would ensure they have agency, confidence and authority to apply problem-solving across a range of circumstances and in different future vocations. To develop this skill, Anita suggests that every lesson would need to include an element of problem-solving. She says a problem-solving approach shifts the curriculum from being static and content-driven to being about dynamic learning. She lists a number of positive outcomes where schools have taken this approach including better pupil engagement, attendance and relationships and enhanced inclusion.

Being originally from the Potteries, a stone's throw from where The Great Pottery Throw Down is filmed, I must say that I love Dr Marcelo Staricoff's opening sentence, 'It is fascinating to think of the curriculum as a potter thinks of their clay'. Marcelo is the author of *The Joy of Not Knowing* (2021). The JONK™ philosophy promotes intrinsic motivation where children *want* to engage and to learn as well as placing great emphasis on the teacher being a partner in the learning process, appreciating the multicultural and multilingual richness that every child brings as part of the everyday teaching and learning process.

With Big Picture Learning, Professor Scott Boldt makes the compelling case that the student is the curriculum. He says: 'People do not learn primarily or best by sitting quietly at a desk…We learn when all our senses are engaged in school and out of school, with our friends, through our interests, in relationships and when we are practising and applying our knowledge to real-world problems.' This is an inspiring proposition and the Big Picture Learning network reaches into many countries across the world, including the UK. While many of the case studies emphasise the importance of parental and community engagement, parents in BPL schools play a proactive role in their children's learning, collaborating in the planning and assessment of student work.

As Lucy Stephens explains, The New School curriculum is designed to support young people to acquire the knowledge and critical thinking skills in nine key areas: literacy, maths, social sciences, media/ICT, science, art, physical movement, PSHE and religious education. What sets The New School's curriculum apart from others, however, is the time and space given for pupils to develop their personal interests through optional workshops or optional subjects, as well as self-directed time to work on personal learning goals, or engage in personal projects. Through this approach, young people learn how to develop the skills for self-direction and executive function. The time and space given for young people to direct their own learning also creates the conditions for relational autonomy, intrinsic motivation and self-regulation. The school organisation allows for multi-age class groups, which support inclusion, stretch and challenge. Team-teaching enables classes to be split for different topics. Groupings are flexible and dynamic to fit the changing needs of the young people. At The New School, teachers are seen as learners too. Professional autonomy is coupled with a focus on learning inquiry and dialogue.

Like many, if not all, the case studies in this book, it is clear that the school curriculum at The New School is designed with children at the heart of everything the school does. With an emphasis on professional and pupil agency, a balance between subject specific knowledge, essential future-proof skills, equity, inclusion and diversity and wellbeing, the conditions are created which will ensure all young people are given the time and space needed to be just children.

Final thoughts

I am so grateful to the 30 contributors who have shared their amazing pieces with me for this book. Each educator has written with passion, creativity and a commitment to designing an inspiring and effective curriculum based on their own values, vision, research, experience and expertise. No two case studies are alike.

It is my hope that in among all these case studies there will be a nugget of something to try in your own setting, an idea of interest to develop further in your practice or something that will prompt you to explore a new way of doing things in your own classroom or setting. And if this happens, please do let me know.

The curricula in our schools should keep evolving. From day to day, week to week, year to year, the young people and the needs of our young people vary and new possibilities and opportunities emerge. As educators, we should therefore remain responsive, ready to adapt and prepared to keep questioning, to keep searching, in order to secure the most optimal outcomes for the young learners in our care.

As with my previous book, *The Headteacher's Handbook* (2021), I will conclude with a poem by Rudyard Kipling. The poem is about the natural curiosity and sense of wonder that children have. As educators I believe we too should hang on to that innate sense of enquiry; we should stay open-minded and open-hearted to new ideas, inventions and innovations, and we should not allow ourselves to become static or cynical or stuck.

Instead, we should keep questioning and we should keep being curious, allowing that curiosity to inspire powerful and purposeful curricula that open new doors for our children, curricula which will ensure they realise their potential and learn how wonderful the world can be!

I Keep six honest serving-men
  (They taught me all I knew);
Their names are What and Why and When
  And How and Where and Who.
I send them over land and sea,
  I send them east and west;
But after they have worked for me,

> *I give them all a rest.*
> *I let them rest from nine till five,*
>   *For I am busy then,*
> *As well as breakfast, lunch, and tea,*
>   *For they are hungry men.*
> *But different folk have different views;*
>   *I know a person small—*
> *She keeps ten million serving-men,*
>   *Who get no rest at all!*
> *She sends 'em abroad on her own affairs,*
>   *From the second she opens her eyes—*
> *One million Hows, two million Wheres,*
>   *And seven million Whys!*

Rudyard Kipling, 'The Elephant's Child', 1902.

Contributor biographies

David Aston is the headteacher at Wilburton C of E Primary School, Cambridgeshire.

Lucy Bailey is the founder of Bounce Forward, a national charity. Lucy's passion is to drive a movement to influence policy to form a positive system of change for children. Lucy has trained thousands of teachers and parents, directed national research projects, and has a BSc in Social Policy and Criminology, an MSc in Practice-Based Research and a PGCE.

James Biddulph started his career following a PGCE at the Faculty of Education, University of Cambridge. In 2002, his creative approach to teaching gained him Advanced Skills Teachers (AST) status in Music and in 2003 he was awarded Outstanding New Teacher of the Year for London. Having transformed two failing schools in East London as Deputy Headteacher, he was the inaugural headteacher of a new Hindu-based primary school. He is now the first headteacher of the University of Cambridge Primary School, the first primary University Training School in the UK, which was graded as 'Outstanding' by Ofsted. He has completed his PhD which focused on creative learning in ethnic minority immigrant children's homes.

Scott Boldt is a Professor of Practice at the University of Cumbria and the National University of Wales. He resides in Belfast and writes extensively on the initiatives, principles and practices of Big Picture Learning. His most recent book (co-authored with Elliot Washor) is *Learning to Leave: How Real-World Learning Transforms Education* (Word Wise, 2023).

Craig Chaplin is an assistant head at Fortuna Primary School, a special school in Lincolnshire. He has over 15 years' experience working with pupils with SEMH needs. Craig is a member of the Attachment Lead Network and has an MEd in School Leadership and Management.

Ruthie Collins is a writer, socially engaged artist, poet and educator who specialises in access to art and literature. In 2021, she was commissioned by restorative ecology social enterprise RAIN Umbrella to write a series of resources supporting UK schools, young people in Brazil and Indigenous communities to bring nature learning into the classroom with a cross-curricula approach. Her first series of poems, *Natural Wonder* (2022) contains both nature trails and poetry with an accompanying cross-curricula learning framework for educators developed with support from participating schools such as Henderson Green Primary Academy. Her public poetry is installed as public art in Great Yarmouth, UK.

Andrew Cowley is an experienced primary school teacher and leader with nearly 30 years in the classroom, many years on SLT and eight as Deputy Headteacher. He now supports the Carnegie Centre of Excellence for Mental Health in Schools as a coach, both on the School Mental Health Award and on the Senior Designated Mental Health Leader programme. Andrew serves as a Local Academy Councillor (Governor) in a primary school in his community, most recently as Chair. Andrew speaks about mental health and wellbeing and is a twice-published author: *The Wellbeing Toolkit* (2019) and *The Wellbeing Curriculum* (2021), both published by Bloomsbury Education.

As Assistant Headteacher, **Kayleigh Cowx** has been instrumental in the research, planning, coordinating and implementation of Kensington Primary School's innovative and groundbreaking curriculum, Curriculum K. Kayleigh was a driving force behind disrupting the status quo at the school and was an integral part of reshaping the curriculum to meet the needs of its pupils and the wider community. As a result, Kensington Primary School's Curriculum K has generated huge interest from other schools.

Bob Cox is an educational consultant and award-winning author whose *Opening Doors* series of books (Crown House) has stimulated ambitious and exciting English which all learners can access. Bob was a teacher for 23 years and has presented at regional, national and international conferences. Bob facilitates a huge UK network of schools developing rich English pathways, a community learning how to open doors to opportunity via equity and excellence. Find out more at www.searchingforexcellence.co.uk.

Dr Anita Devi has taught across phases, from Early Years to postgraduate, in the UK and around the globe. As Founder and CEO of TeamADL, she has been involved in raising the quality of education in a variety of settings. Whilst Anita's strength lies in strategic change management, her heart is focused on 'the joy of learning', which for her is more than just light bulb moments. Anita is a writer, speaker and researcher and her PhD added a unique model to the body of knowledge on career development for those who lead on special educational needs, disability and inclusion.

Rosina Dorelli is the co-founder and Director at Biophilic Education Alliance (BE All) and co-creator of the Da Vinci Life-Skills Curriculum. She has a background in art and design technology and 20 years' experience teaching creativity to learners of all ages. She is a serial entrepreneur and project manager who has initiated and run numerous creative projects around the world.

Ben Erskine is the Executive Principal for the Four Cs Multi-Academy Trust and Principal at Fulbridge Academy, an 'Outstanding' four form-entry primary school in Peterborough. He has been working in education since 2002, with experience of being a teaching assistant; working in a Pupil Referral Unit; leading on maths and assessment; and being a maths advisor, team leader, assistant principal, vice principal and now principal.

Alex Fairlamb is a senior leader in charge of T&L, CPD and literacy based in Newcastle. She is an SLE and an ELE. Alex is a member of the Historical Association Secondary Committee and the Schools North East Steering Board. Alex is a History teacher and former Lead Practitioner, with a strong commitment to ensuring that curricula are diverse. She is co-editor of the bestselling *What is History Teaching, Now?* (2023) and a contributing author to OUP's (2023) *Fight for Rights* textbook. Alex tweets as @lamb_heart_tea.

Jo Franklin has been the Chief Executive Officer of the LETTA Trust since it was established in 2017. Prior to this, Jo had 15 years' experience in headship in inner city primary schools. In these settings the primary goal was to tackle disadvantage and level the playing field through exceptional teaching, a rich, innovative curriculum and unwavering high expectations.

Joe Hallgarten is Chief Executive at the Centre for Education and Youth, a think-and-action tank. Following teaching for five years in urban primary schools, Joe has over 20 years' experience leading and influencing change as a programme leader, researcher and policy analyst. In 2020–21 Joe had a part time role on the leadership team at LETTA Trust, working on curriculum strategy.

Christopher Harrison is a co-headteacher and curriculum lead. He has worked in a range of challenging, diverse schools and this has fostered his passion to champion the unique child. Following a background in Early Years, Christopher worked in all primary school age groups. He is currently based in Year 6 where he balances classroom teaching with whole-school leadership as a co-headteacher alongside his friend and mentor, Chris Parkhouse.

Matt Jessop is the headteacher of a small, rural school in the Lake District. He has been in education for over 20 years and enjoys developing and facilitating innovative approaches to education in his school.

Christian Kitley is Head of Outdoor Learning at a large preparatory school in Hertfordshire. He holds an MA in Education and a BA (Hons) in Primary Education. He has a background in Outdoor Education and has combined this with his teaching for the past ten years.

Jonathan Le Fevre is an independent curriculum consultant and leadership coach for Adventurous Life, Learning and Leadership (www.allandl.co.uk). Jon was previously a primary headteacher for 17 years. He has always had a passion and determination to make learning an adventure for all.

As Head Teacher, **Ben Levinson** has led Kensington Primary School to its current status of a flagship school in a manner of areas, from inclusion to wellbeing. Under Ben's guidance Kensington Primary School has launched an innovative new curriculum, specifically developed to provide the best outcomes for children and prepare them for life in the 21st century. As a result, the school was Primary School of the Year and Mental Health and Wellbeing School of the Year in 2020 and Ben was awarded an OBE in the 2021 Queen's Birthday Honours List for his service to education. Ben has advised the Department for Education on workload and wellbeing and he was part of the Expert Advisory Group responsible for the Education Staff Wellbeing Charter. He is a board member of Well Schools and an ambassador for the Youth Sport Trust, the British Council, and TeachActive.

Heather MacNeil has been teaching in schools for over 16 years in primary education, across both key stages. She has always had a keen interest in PE and sport and her priority is for all children, irrespective of their level or prior experience, to have a positive experience in PE.

Paula Manser is Assistant Head Teacher and a full-time teacher in a large infant/nursery school in Huddersfield. Following a pilot with Move & Learn and time spent considering research, Paula has helped colleagues transform their teaching and learning. Her school has moved from traditional sedentary lessons, to lessons which involve purposeful movement, allowing their children to flourish. Paula now inspires others via conferences and workshops across the north of the country.

Dr Jen McGaley is a researcher based at the Crop Science Centre, University of Cambridge, who uses molecular and microscopy techniques to investigate mycorrhizal symbiosis. Alongside laboratory work, she uses her microscope images to try and spread public awareness and engagement with plants and fungi.

Anoara Mughal is a former assistant headteacher, with 15 years' experience in primary schools in London. She is the author of *Think! Metacognition-powered Primary Teaching* (2021). Over the last two years she has been working with schools delivering staff CPD on metacognition. She has also worked in the world of business, developing staff growth mindset training. You can follower her @anoara_a and @TFLearn.

Rachel Musson is a teacher, trainer and thought leader on regenerative education and Triple Wellbeing in schools. A former English teacher with 20 years' experience in education, Rachel is the Founding Director of ThoughtBox Education, a social enterprise supporting schools to co-create a culture of care for people and planet.

Nicole Ponsford, FRSA is the co-founder and CEO of the Global Equality Collective, whose mission is to give organisations and schools all they need to break their own new ground in diversity, equality and inclusion. Previously an Advanced Skills Teacher, award-winning teacher and Harvard University Press author (*TechnoTeaching*, 2014), she is now an educational and technology thought leader.

Zachary Reznichek is the author of *The Teacher-Gamer Handbook* and a teacher trainer with a focus on SEL, adult readiness and life-skills.

Ian Roberts is a local authority school improvement consultant in Cambridgeshire and a National Strategic Adviser for PE. He believes that well-taught PE and school sport makes children's lives better and our young people have never needed it more.

Philippa Rollins has worked alongside children with SEMH needs for 20 years. Philippa is an assistant headteacher at Fortuna Primary School, a special school in Lincolnshire. She has had experience in both primary and secondary SEMH settings. Philippa is a member of the Attachment Lead Network.

Luke Rolls is the Associate Headteacher and founding member of the University of Cambridge Primary School. His main areas of interest are in developing primary curriculum, pedagogy and assessment through high-quality professional development as an entitlement for all teachers. Luke has previously taught in a variety of schools in London, Japan, China and Ghana. Luke has co-edited the Routledge books *Re-imagining Professional Development in Schools* (2021) and *Unleashing Children's Voices in Democratic Primary Education* (2023). Luke is a Speicalist Leader of Education, member of the primary contact group at the Royal Society for the Advisory Committee on Mathematics Education and strategy group member for the U.K. Japanese Lesson Study Collaborative Lesson Research group.

Dr Marcelo Staricoff is the author of *The Joy of Not Knowing* (2021), published by Routledge, and a Lecturer in Education at the University of Sussex. Marcelo is an former primary headteacher and research scientist. Marcelo is a member of the All Party Parliamentary Group on Education and a Founding Fellow of the Chartered College of Teaching.

Lucy Stephens is Founder and Director of The New School, an innovative educational charity seeking to evolve the educational narrative in the UK through the development of a model which puts young people at the heart of an inclusive learning community and gives every student a powerful sense of agency. The New School is an action research model of education collaborating with research insitutions, education and health systems, to understand the impact and potential scalability of an evolved model of education on young people's health, wellbeing and life chances.

Kyrstie Stubbs has worked across primary schools for over 20 years with over 10 years' experience in executive and leadership positions, and is now Deputy CEO. Her experience ranges from successful leadership within industry to successfully leading different schools in challenging circumstances, improving them significantly through transformational leadership. She currently also works as a school improvement partner supporting a range of schools in developing practices and leadership capacity. She has worked extensively with schools both locally and nationally to support them in championing wellbeing and diversity and also supports leaders as an executive coach. She has been on the LGBTQ inclusion board at Leeds Beckett University.

Allen Tsui is the subject leader for computing at Willow Brook Primary School Academy in East London. Passionate about primary STEM education,

Allen is undertaking a MA in STEM Education at King's College London on a Teacher Scholarship. He is also taking part in the Ogden Trust Senior Teacher Fellowship.

Sally Todd is a visual artist, with an MA in Sculpture from the Chelsea College of Art, and theatre practitioner. She makes objects and installations and also devises theatre for children and adults, seeking out the theatrical potential of materials and the narrative possibilities within the everyday.

Tom Turnham is the headteacher of Lyndhurst Primary School, part of the Charter Schools Educational Trust. He has been teaching in inner-city London schools for over a decade and is passionate about curriculum. Having not benefited from a broad curriculum himself, he is determined that future generations have their full entitlement.

Nancy Wayman is a deputy headteacher in London. She worked as a musician before becoming a teacher. In 2015 she moved to a new school in Peckham to establish a musical, creative culture. She has worked with a number of other organisations to support schools to establish a culture of music and creativity.

Caroline Wendling is a multidisciplinary socially engaged artist. She creates site-specific artworks addressing environmental issues with performance, sound, film and printmaking. Her teaching and her art research are concerned with ways of being and connecting to land, offering meaningful understanding to place and ideas of belonging.

Lucy Wheeler is a freelance ceramicist, creative producer and facilitator. Passionate about the environment and the intrinsic benefits of nature for our health and wellbeing, she is motivated by the transformative power of interdisciplinary arts programming.

Sarah Wordlaw is a headteacher working in an inner-city south London primary school and author of *Time to Shake Up the Primary Curriculum* (2023). She is restlessly passionate about how educators can use the curriculum to make the next generation better than us! She has led various subjects and areas of the school over her educational career and worked in many different capacities in a wide range of educational establishments. She identifies as a queer woman of mixed heritage and often felt unseen in taught subjects, both as a child and as an adult, which has fuelled her interest in diversity and inclusion.

Editor biography

Rae qualified as a teacher in 1994 and has been a headteacher since 2007. Formerly at The Spinney Primary School, Cambridge and at Milton Road since January 2020, Rae describes being a headteacher as the best job in the world!

Interested in policy and passionate (some might say obsessed) about education, Rae was a member of the Primary Headteachers' Reference Group at the Department of Education for 9 years. Rae was a system leader for a number of years, leading the Kite Teaching School Alliance and working as a Local and National Leader of Education.

Rae is passionate about the transformative power of the arts and creativity. With anchor institutions in the City, she co-founded the local cultural education partnership called My Cambridge which precipitated the Cambridgeshire and Peterborough Region of Learning project, through which young people can gain a range of skills and experiences as well as secure digital credentials.

Rae's school Milton Road Primary is one of the founding institutions of the Cambridge Chapter of Citizen's UK. Rae is a judge for the Smiley Foundation's Charity Film Awards, and a Founding Fellow of the Chartered College of Teaching (FFCT). In October 2021, Rae was delighted to receive an Honorary Fellowship from The University of Suffolk and in February 2024 was thrilled to receive the Inaugural Award at the Cambridge Arts Network for her 'Outstanding commitment to the Arts'.

Rae is an occasional conference speaker and trainer and talks about the joys, trials and tribulations of school leadership as well as how to stay in the profession and keep smiling! Rae is particularly keen to support new and aspiring headteachers on their leadership journey.

Rae has contributed to several books on education. Rae wrote her first book *The Headteacher's Handbook* which was published by Bloomsbury in August 2021. *The Curriculum Compendium* is her second book, and continuing with the alliterative theme she is exploring the idea of writing a third (and final) book to be called *Powerful Pedagogies*. The idea of this book would be to take a more global perspective of education and to hopefully include case studies from Bali, Singapore, Spain, Italy, Greece, Wales, Ireland, Columbia and the USA.

Rae met her wonderful husband Guy over 40 years ago. He works as a counsellor at the University of Cambridge, and he also took the photographs for the hugely successful book, *101 Places You Should Not Miss in Cambridge*, published by Emons Verlag. Rae and Guy are the very proud parents of two brilliant and talented children, Charlie and Jupiter.

In her spare time Rae enjoys the company of her fabulous family and wonderful friends and likes to take long walks with her lovely Scottie/Cairn cross terrier, Bramble.

References

Alexander, R.J. et al (eds.). (2010). *The Cambridge Primary Review Research Surveys*. London: Routledge.

Arnold, K., & Mihut, G. (2020). Postsecondary Outcomes of Innovative High Schools: The Big Picture Longitudinal Study. *Teachers College Record*, 122(8), 1–42.

Arnold, M. (1869). *Culture and anarchy: An essay in political and social criticism*. London, UK: Smith, Elder & Co.

Bishop R. (1990). Mirrors, windows, and sliding glass doors. *Perspectives: Choosing and using books for the classroom*. 6(3). Ohio State University.

Bloom, B. S. (1956). *Taxonomy of educational objectives: the classification of educational goals; Handbook I: Cognitive domain*. In M. D. Engelhart, E. J. Furst, W. H. Hill, & D. R. Krathwohl (eds.), *Taxonomy of educational objectives: the classification of educational goals; Handbook I: Cognitive domain*. New York: David McKay.

Boswell, J. *The life of Samuel Johnson*. London: printed by Henry Baldwin, for Charles Dilly. Available at: http://name.umdl.umich.edu/004839390.0001.001. (Accessed: 29 January 2024).

Bruner, J. (1960). *The Process of Education*. Cambridge, MA: The President and Fellows of Harvard College.

Callaghan, J. (1976). [speech] Towards a national debate. Ruskin College, Oxford. Reprinted in *The Guardian*, 2001. Available at: www.theguardian.com/education/thegreatdebate/story/0,,574645,00.html (Accessed: 12 January 2024).

Clear, J. (2018). *Atomic Habits*. London: Penguin Random House.

Computing at School. (n.d.). Available at www.computingatschool.org.uk. (Accessed: 29 January 2024).

Cooper et al. (2015). Objectively measured physical activity and sedentary time in youth: the International children's accelerometry database (ICAD). *International Journal of Behavioral Nutrition and Physical Activity*, 12(113).

Cox, B., Crawford, L., Jenkins, A. and Sargent, J. (2023). *Opening Doors to Ambitious Primary English*. London: Crown House.

Dana, D. (2020). *Polyvagal Exercises for Safety and Connection*. London: Norton.

Davies, W. H. (1911). 'Leisure'. Available at: www.poetrybyheart.org.uk/poems/leisure. (Accessed: 29 January 2024).

Davis, J. (2020). *The Trust Revolution in Schools*. London: Routledge.

Department for Education. (2014). The national curriculum in England: key stages 1 to 4 framework document. Available at: https://assets.publishing.service.gov.uk/media/5a81a9abe5274a2e8ab55319/PRIMARY_national_curriculum.pdf. (Accessed: 29 January 2024).

Department for Education. (2020, revised 2023). Development Matters. Available at: https://assets.publishing.service.gov.uk/media/64e6002a20ae890014f26cbc/DfE_Development_Matters_Report_Sep2023.pdf. (Accessed: 29 January 2024).

Department for Education. (2021). The Education Staff Wellbeing Charter. Available at: https://assets.publishing.service.gov.uk/media/6194eb37d3bf7f0551f2d1a5/DfE_Education_Workforce_Welbeing_Charter_Nov21.pdf. (Accessed: 29 January 2024).

Department for Education. (2021). *The Importance of Teaching*. Available at: https://assets.publishing.service.gov.uk/media/5a7b4029ed915d3ed9063285/CM-7980.pdf. (Accessed: 29 January 2024).

Department for Education. (2023). The reading framework. Available at: https://assets.publishing.service.gov.uk/media/65830c10ed3c34000d3bfcad/The_reading_framework.pdf. (Accessed: 29 January 2024).

Devi, A. (2023). *Grow Analytical Mindset*.

Dix, P. (2017). *When the Adults Change, Everything Changes*. London: Independent Thinking Press.

Education Endowment Foundation. (2017). Metacognition and Self-Regulated Learning. Available at: https://educationendowmentfoundation.org.uk/education-evidence/guidance-reports/metacognition. (Accessed: 29 January 2024).

Education Endowment Foundation. (2019). Putting Evidence to Work: A School's Guide to Implementation. Available at: https://d2tic4wvo1iusb.cloudfront.net/production/eef-guidance-reports/implementation/EEF_Implementation_Guidance_Report_2019.pdf?v=1704939421. (Accessed: 29 January 2024).

EL Education. (n.d.). We Are Crew: A Teamwork Approach to School Culture Videos. Available at: https://eleducation.org/resources/we-are-crew-a-teamwork-approach-to-school-culture-videos. (Accessed: 29 January 2024).

Fielding, M. (2007). 'Jean Ruddock (1937-2007) 'Carving a new order of experience': a preliminary appreciation of the work of Jean Ruddock in the field of student voice'. *Educational Action Research*, 15(3) pp. 323–336.

Flecha, R. (2015) *Successful educational actions for inclusion and social cohesion in Europe*. Cham: Springer.

Flutter, J. and Rudduck, J. (2004). *Consulting Pupils: What's In It For Schools?*. London: Routledge.

Fullan, M., Quinn, J. and McEachen, J. (2017). *Deep Learning: Engage the World Change the World*. New Pegagogies for Deep Learning.

Garvey, P. (2017). *Talk for Teaching: Rethinking Professional Development in Schools*. London: John Catt Educational Ltd.

Hill, M., (2020). Curating the Imagined Past: World Building in the History Curriculum. *Teaching History 180*. Historical Association.

Holt, L. and Krall, F. (1976). Thematic Approach to Curriculum Development. *The Clearing House*, 50(4) 1976, pp. 140–43.

Kagan, M. (2015). *Kagan Cooperative Learning (Revised Edition)*. San Clemente, CA: Kagan Publishing.

Kidd, D. and Roberts, H. (2018). *Uncharted Territories*. London: Independent Thinking Press.

Kipling, R. (1902). 'The Elephant's Child'. Available here: https://americanliterature.com/author/rudyard-kipling/poem/the-elephants-child-poem. (Accessed: 29 January 2024).

Leadbeater, C. (2016). *The Problem Solvers*. London: Pearson.

Llenas, A. (2015). *The Colour Monster Pop-Up*. London: Templar Publishing.

McNeill, P. (1991). The Core Curriculum. *Society Today 2*. Palgrave, London.

Milligan, S. K., Luo, R., Hassim, E., & Johnston, J. (2020). *Future-proofing students: What they need to know and how to assess and credential them*. Melbourne Graduate School of Education, the University of Melbourne.

Milton Road Primary School. (2023). Acceptable Use Policy & Agreement. Available at: https://primarysite-prod-sorted.s3.amazonaws.com/milton-road-primary-school/UploadedDocument/0801a860-31a0-4d4c-86af-37206e9252d5/acceptable-use-policy.pdf. (Accessed: 29 January 2024).

Milton Road Primary School. (2023). Lone working Policy. Available at: https://primarysite-prod-sorted.s3.amazonaws.com/milton-road-primary-school/UploadedDocument/4fa602ac-f9f8-4eec-b201-2e8769b0d63a/lone-working-policy.pdf. (Accessed: 29 January 2024).

Milton Road Primary School. (2023). Missing Child and Child Exiting the School Policy. Available at: https://primarysite-prod-sorted.s3.amazonaws.com/milton-road-primary-school/UploadedDocument/9381a436-6990-425a-b01a-60cf2246c018/exiting-school-premises-and-missing-child-policy.pdf. (Accessed: 29 January 2024).

Milton Road Primary School. (2023). Whistleblowing Policy and Procedure. Available at: https://primarysite-prod-sorted.s3.amazonaws.com/milton-road-primary-school/UploadedDocument/5eb258cd-ecf1-464f-a67a-22b535403d3d/whistleblowing-procedure.pdf. (Accessed: 29 January 2024).

MindUP. (n.d.). Available at: https://mindup.org. (Accessed: 29 January 2024).

Mortenson, G. and Relin, D. O. (2006). *Three Cups of Tea*. London: Viking.

Mughal, A. (2021) *Think!: Metacognition-Powered Primary Teaching*. London: Sage.

Myatt, M. (n.d.). Curriculum pace. Available at: www.marymyatt.com/blog/curriculum-pace-slow-philosophy. (Accessed: 29 January 2024).

NHS. (2021). Significant increase in obesity rates among primary-aged children. Available at: https://digital.nhs.uk/news/2021/significant-increase-in-obesity-rates-among-primary-aged-children-latest-statistics-show. (Accessed 29 January 2024).

Ofsted (2019, updated 2023). Education Inspection Framework. Available here:www.gov.uk/government/publications/education-inspection-framework/education-inspection-framework-for-september-2023. (Accessed: 12 January 2024).

Ofsted. (2019). School Inspection Handbook. Available at: www.gov.uk/government/publications/school-inspection-handbook-eif/school-inspection-handbook-for-september-2023. (Accessed: 12 January 2024).

Paton, G. (2010). 'Michael Gove unveils education reforms'. *The Telegraph*, 24 November 2010. Available at: www.telegraph.co.uk/education/educationnews/8156116/Michael-Gove-unveils-education-reforms.html. (Accessed 29 January 2024).

Putnam, Robert D. (2000). *Bowling Alone: The Collapse and Revival of American Community*. New York: Simon & Schuster.

ReflectED. (n.d.). About ReflectED. Available at: www.reflectedlearning.org.uk/about-reflected. (Accessed 29 January 2024).

Robinson, K. (2021. [speech] Creating a New Normal. Available at: www.youtube.com/watch?v=lUvNTt6crFM. (Accessed 29 January 2024).

Rosenshine, B. (2012) Principles of Instruction: Research-Based Strategies That All Teachers Should Know. *American Educator*, 36(1).

Ruskin, J. (1859) 'Lecture II. The Unity of Art', *The Two Paths*, 14 March. Available at: www.public-library.uk/ebooks/06/35.pdf. (Accessed 5 February 2024).

Sealey, C. (2017). The 3D Curriculum that Promotes Remembering. Available at:https://primarytimery.com/2017/10/28/the-3d-curriculum-that-promotes-remembering. (Accessed 29 January 2024).

Shaull, R. (1970). 'Foreword'. In Freire, P. *Pedagogy of the oppressed* (pp. 29–34). New York, NY: Herder and Herder.

Sherrington, T. and Cavigloli, O. (2020). *Teaching Walkthrus – Five step guides to instructional coaching*. London: John Catt Educational Ltd.

Sinek, S. (2011). *Start With Why*. London: Penguin.

Snape, R. (n.d.). A Learning Community – Welcome from the Headteacher. Milton Road Primary School. Available at: https://miltonroadschool.org.uk/a-learning-community-welcome-from-the-headlearner. (Accessed 29 January 2024).

Spielman, A. and Ofsted (2018). 'HMCI commentary: curriculum and the new education inspection framework.' Available at: www.gov.uk/government/consultations/education-inspection-framework-2019-inspecting-the-substance-of-education. (Accessed: 18 January 2024).

Sport England. (2022). Children's activity levels recover to pre-pandemic levels. Available at: www.sportengland.org/news/childrens-activity-levels-recover-pre-pandemic-levels. (Accessed 29 January 2024).

Staricoff, M. (2021). *The Joy of Not Knowing*. Oxon: Routledge.

Staricoff, M. and Rees, A. (2005). *Start Thinking*. Birmingham: Imaginative Minds.

Stenhouse, L. (1975). *An Introduction to Curriculum Research and Development*. London: Heinemann.

Stonewall. (2019, updated 2022). Creating An LGBTQ+ Inclusive Primary Curriculum. Available at: www.stonewall.org.uk/system/files/stw_pearson_creating_an_inclusive_primary_curriculum_2022_1_-_march.pdf. (Accessed 29 January 2024).

Style, E. (1998). 'Curriculum As Window and Mirror.' *Listening for All Voices*. Availale at: https://nationalseedproject.org/Key-SEED-Texts/curriculum-as-window-and-mirror. (Accessed 29 January 2024).

Sweller, J., Ayres, P. and Kalyuga, S. (2011). Cognitive load theory. *Springer Science & Business Media*.

Takahashi, Akihiko. (2021). *Teaching Mathematics Through Problem-Solving: A Pedagogical Approach from Japan*. London: Routledge.

Teach Computing. (n.d.). Available at: https://teachcomputing.org. (Accessed 29 January 2024).

The Children's Society. (2023). The Good Childhood Report. Available at: www.childrenssociety.org.uk/information/professionals/resources/good-childhood-report-2023. (Accessed: 29 January 2024).

The Key. (n.d.). The Key Support. Available at: https://thekeysupport.com. (Accessed 29 January 2024).

Thoughtbox. (n.d.). Resources. Available at: www.thoughtboxeducation.com/resources. (Accessed 29 January 2024).

Thoughtbox. (n.d.). Training. Available at: www.thoughtboxeducation.com/training. (Accessed 29 January 2024).

Thrive. (n.d.). What is Thrive?. Available at: www.thriveapproach.com. (Accessed: 18 January 2024). (Accessed 29 January 2024).

UNICEF. (2015). UNICEF and the Sustainable Development Goals. Available at: www.unicef.org/sustainable-development-goals. (Accessed 29 January 2024).

Uttley, J. and Tomsett, J. (2020). *Putting Staff First: A blueprint for revitalising our schools*. London: Hachette.

Whitemore, J. (1992). *Coaching for Performance*. Boston, MA: Nicolas Brealey/Hachette.

William, D. (2011). *Embedded Formative Assessment*. Bloomington, IN: South Tree Press.

William, D. (2013). *Redesigning Schooling – 3 Principled curriculum design*. London: SSAT. Available at: webcontent.ssatuk.co.uk/wp-content/uploads/2020/03/20105155/Redesigning-Schooling-3-Principled-curriculum-design-Dylan-Wiliam.pdf. (Accessed 29 January 2024).

Willingham D. T. (2009) *Why Don't Students Like School?* San Francisco, CA: Jossey-Bass.

World Health Organization. (2001). The World health report: 2001: Mental health: new understanding, new hope. Available at: https://iris.who.int/handle/10665/42390. (Accessed 5 February 2024).

World Health Organization. (2024). Promoting mental health. Available at: www.who.int/westernpacific/activities/promoting-mental-health. (Accessed 29 January 2024).

Index

academic rigour 3
Active Heart 21, 27
Active Identity 21, 26
Active Mind 21, 26
Active Voice 22, 27
AfL 123, 197, 200
agile intelligence (AQ) 240
ambitious curriculum 29
art, and school culture 130-5
Artscaping 13-14
assembly, for mental health and wellbeing 192
assessments 25, 32-3, 108, 259, 262
Aston, David 16
Atomic Habits (Clear) 181-2
auditing 86, 121, 237
autonomy 50, 236-7, 263
awareness raising, among parents 16

balanced curriculum 28
barriers, identification and analysis of 42
BE Hub, curriculum of
   design iteration 49
   enterprise pathway 46
   feedback and evaluation 47-9
   food pathway 46
   impact 47-9
   implementation 45-7
   intent 44-5
   multiverse games pathway 46
   personal exploration pathway 46
   production pathway 46
   role-playing game (RPG) 46
   takeaways 50-51
   turning vision into reality 49-50
Belham Primary School, curriculum of
   Artsmark Award process 132
   Glittering Curriculum 130
   impact 131-2
   implementation 131
   intent 130-1
   takeaways 134-5
   turning vision into reality 132-4
Bennett, Emma 99
Berger, Ron 4
Big Picture Learning (BPL) schools, curriculum of
   impact 256-7
   implementation 255-6
   intent 254-5
   and interests 255
   International Big Picture Learning Credential (IBPLC) 256-7
   leadership 256
   'leaving to learn' concept 256
   mentorship 255
   out-of-school activities 255
   parents' role in 258
   practice 255
   relationships 255
   takeaways 258-9
   tools and resources 259
   turning vision into reality 257-8
Biophilic Education Alliance (BE All) 43, 44
Birkby Infant and Nursery School, curriculum of
   barriers 212
   classroom environment 210
   energisers 213
   impact 211-12
   implementation 209-11
   intent 208-9
   learning 210
      assessment for 211
   Move & Learn (M&L) 209
   takeaways 213-14
   tools and resources 214
   turning vision into reality 212-13

Bishop, Rudine Sims 70
Boothroyd Primary Academy,
    curriculum of
    cohesion 38, 40–41
    community 38, 39–40
    creativity 37, 37
    cultural capital 38, 40
    extended curriculum 39, 41
    floor books 40–41
    impact 41–2
    implementation 39–41
    intent 37–8
    takeaways 43
    turning vision into reality 42–3
Bounce Forward 223
brave, being 42, 135, 149
British Computer Society (BSC) 111
broad curriculum 28, 134

Cambridge Connected Curriculum 3–5
Cambridge Curiosity and Imagination
    (CCI) 13, 17
Cambridge University Primary School 157
Cary's Meadow 176
celebrating together 17, 18
challenges and possibilities 171
Chartered Institute for IT 111
Chatmore British International School,
    Bermuda 47
children voice, in curriculum planning 34
citizenship 3
Citizens UK 227
clarity 28, 34, 42, 94
co-construction 264
cognitive overload 193
cognitive skill 261
cohesive curriculum 37, 39–40
collaboration 45, 50, 256, 259
communities 17, 28, 37, 38–9, 45, 177, 248
    experience and ideas of 166
    and school, relationship between 256
competences 261, 262–3
Computer Science Teachers Association
    (CSTA) 111
computing 109–13

Computing at School 112, 114
concept, repetition of 121
concerts 135
connections 217
connectivity 13, 15
context-oriented curriculum 36–42
continuous provision environments
    263
co-regulation 181
core practices 217
core skills 217
Cowley, Andrew 222
CPD 28, 68, 107, 133, 190, 200, 213, 238
creativity 36, 38, 67
CREW 4, 141, 142
Crops Science Centre 17
Crosthwaite C of E Primary School,
    curriculum of
    and Educational Technology 168–9
    Google Reference School 168, 169
    impact 169
    implementation 168–9
    intent 167–8
    outdoor education 169
    takeaways 170–1
    turning vision into reality 169–70
cultural capital 37, 39, 42
culture 215–16, 259
    for learning 252
    significance of 79
curiosity 13, 239, 243, 273
curriculum continuity 101–8
curriculum progression planning 35
curriculum statements 66

Da Vinci, Leonardo 44
Da Vinci Life-Skills Curriculum
    (DVLS) 43–50
Deep Learning Competencies 228
DEI (Diversity, Equity and Inclusion) 79–80
design iteration 48
discussion-led learning 166, 218
dis-metacognition 251, 252
diversity 84–5, 262
dynamic learning 241–2

earth-care 217
ecology 177
ecosystem 220
Ede, Jim and Helen 139–40
Educational Technology (Ed Tech) 168–71
Education Inspection Framework (EIF) 97–8
EL Education 141
emotional practice, 268
emotional skill 261
emotional wellbeing 247
emotions 206
Empathy Middle School (EMS), Bali 46
encouragement 18
English, curriculum for
 flight paths 117–18
 impact 119–21
 implementation 117–18
 intent 116–17
 'opening doors' strategies 118
 planning 117
 support 117–18
 takeaways 121
 taster drafts 118
 text 118
 tools and resources 121
 turning vision into reality 118–19
 whole text reading 118
enterprise pathway 45
environmental charities 177
environmental wellbeing 217
equity of access 261
essential skills 3
evaluation 25
exemplary environmental learning methodologies 177
exhibitions 135
experimentation 50
Expert Showcases 228–9
explanations 24
exploration 50, 170
explorer curriculum 150–9
extended curriculum 38
external research organisations, engaging with 268

facilitated lessons 218
failure, and resilience 206
feeling 217
flattened hierarchical structure 268
flexible and realistic thinking 206
floor books 39–40
focus 13, 15
focus days and weeks 191
food pathway 45
formative assessment 32–3, 262
Fortuna Primary, curriculum of
 immersive classrooms 73
 impact 74–5
 implementation 72–4
 intent 71–2
 interconnectedness o subjects 73
 play curriculum 74
 purpose 72–3
 sparkles, inclusion of 72, 75
 staff wellbeing 75
 takeaways 76
 tools and resources 76
 turning vision into reality 75–6
forward planning 17–18
free time 171
Fulbridge Academy, curriculum of
 Active Learning framework 21–2, 26, 27
 impact 26–8
 implementation 22–5
 intent 20–2
 making learning memorable 22–6
 PREPARE framework 23–5
 takeaways 29
 turning vision into reality 28–9

George Mitchell School and Willow Brook Primary Academy, curriculum of
 curriculum models, adapting 236–7
 impact 233–4
 implementation 232–3
 intent 231–2
 process models 235
 product model 234–5
 spiral curriculum 235–6
 takeaways 237–8

turning vision into reality 234–7
glimmers 143
Glittering Curriculum 130
global, connecting to local 218
Global Equality Collective, curriculum
    DEI (Diversity, Equity and Inclusion) 79–80, 81
    impact 80–1
    implementation 79–80
    inclusive approach 78
    intent 78–9
    Plan Do Review Assess Repeat cycle 80
    redesigning 82
    takeaways 82–3
    tools and resources 83
    turning vision into reality 81–2
global-perspectives, sharing 218
goals, significance of 149
good practice, sharing 213
Google Reference School 168, 169
'got it grid' approach 38
Grove Road Community Primary School, curriculum of
    creativity and fun 67
    'Fabulous Finish' 67
    impact 67–9
    implementation 66–7
    intent 59–65
    key documents and formats 66
    PRIDE characteristics 60, 61, 62, 66, 67, 69–70
    PRIME areas 60, 61, 62, 63–5
    'Stunning Start' 67
    subject specialisms 60, 61
    takeaways 70
    turning vision into reality 69–70
GROW coaching model 80
growth mindset 169, 206, 233

Hanifan, L. J. 10
Hannon, Valerie 2
Henderson Green Primary Academy (HGPA), and Natural Wonder *see* Natural Wonder

HR policies 54
human connection 206

inclusive curriculum 29, 78–83, 85–6, 261
ink making, from berries 19
innovative, being 171
innovative curriculum 29
inspirations 149
integrated curriculum 177
'intelligent client' approach 114
interest-driven explorations 255
International Big Picture Learning Credential (IBPLC) 256–7
International Society for Technology in Education (ISTE) 111
internet and technology 242–3
intrinsic motivation 260, 268

joint professional development 54
Joy of Not Knowing™ (JONK™) approach 246
    academic and emotional wellbeing 249
    dis-metacognition 251
    impact 248–50
    Learning to Learn week 246–7, 252
    sense of fun 249
    takeaways 252
    teaching approach 247–8
    Thinking Skills Starter 252
    turning vision into reality 250–2

Kensington Primary School, curriculum of (Curriculum K)
    and communication 199
    emotional health 196
    fitness lessons 196
    impact 196–9
    implementation 195–6
    intent 194–5
    physical health 196
    skills for life lessons 196
    takeaways 200
    tools and resources 201
    turning vision into reality 199–200

kinaesthetic learning 177
Kingsfield Primary School, curriculum of
   assessment 123, 128
   content 124, 128
   curriculum map 124–6
   extending 125, 128
   impact 126–7
   implementation 123–6
   intent 122–3
   pedagogy 123, 128
   specific 123, 128
   successes 127–8
   takeaways 128
   tools and resources 128–9
   turning vision into reality 127
Kings Priory School, curriculum of
   Curriculum Continuity programme 102–3, 107
   impact 106–8
   implementation 103–6
   intent 101–3
   progression model 103–4, 106
   schemes of learning (SoL) 103, 105, 106
   turning vision into reality 103–6
   world building 105
knowledge development 15
knowledge sharing 149

language, significance of 252
law to identify (Pareto) 200
leadership 53–5
learner-centred classrooms 263, 266
learners teaching each other 50
Learning Adventure 160–6
learning competence 262–3
learning leaders, children as 251
learning walk 243
lifelong learners, curriculum for
   community activity 248
   impact 248–50
   implementation 246–8
   intent 245–6
   JONK™ *see* Joy of Not Knowing™ (JONK™) approach
   takeaways 252
   tools and resources 253
   turning vision into reality 250–2
literature, as forms of empowered storytelling and activism 177
Littky, Dennis 257
local environment, and art curriculum 135
local researchers, reaching out to 18
London East Teacher Training Alliance (LETTA) schools, curriculum of
   and behaviours 152–4
   Explorer Curriculum 154, 158
   and destinations 156–7
   gap between 151–2
   impact 158
   implementation 155–7
   intent 150–5
   and National Curriculum 150–1
   objectives 155
   pedagogy 157
   precision 152–3
   space 153–4
   and structure 155–6
   takeaways 158–9
   turning vision into reality 158
   turning into behaviours 152–3
   vision 152
long-term overviews 66
long-term view 108
low-stakes opportunities 135
Lyndhurst Primary School, curriculum of
   impact 93
   implementation 91–3
   intent 91
   interim period 92
   middle leaders, powers of 93
   progression maps 93
   'quality first' teaching 92
   takeaways 94
   turning vision into reality 93–4

Manor Lodge School, curriculum of
   Art 144, 146
   Bushcraft 144, 146
   impact 146–7
   implementation 145–6

intent 144–5
Natural World 144, 146
Outdoor Cooking 144, 146
takeaways 149
tools and resources 149
Traditional Crafts 144, 146
turning vision into reality 147–9
Wellbeing 144, 146
mapping out of curriculum 161–2, 166
Maslow's hierarchy of needs 61
McGaley, Jen 14
medium-term planning templates 66
meet and greet 192
Mental Health and Wellbeing (MHWB) curriculum
impact 189–90
implementation 187–9
intent 186–7
measurement 187–8
takeaways 191–3
teaching 188–9
tools and resources 193
turning vision into reality 190–1
zones of regulation 188
mental health and wellness 222–3, 267
mental resilience curriculum
explore emotions worksheet 207
Gremlin Beliefs 204
homework activities 204
impact 205
implementation 203–4
intent 202
modules connecting the brain, emotions and thoughts 203
optimism and evidence 204
resilience and harnessing positive emotions 203
resilience planning 204
takeaways 206–7
Teach Mental Resilience 203, 205
teacher training 206
timetable time 205
tools and resources 207
turning vision into reality 205–6
Wobble skill 204

metacognition 231–8, 252
Milton Road Primary School 1–3
attachment approach 140
behaviour and attitudes to learning 139–43
Cambridge Connected Curriculum 3–5
CREW 3–4, 141, 142
curriculum design at
Expert Showcases 228–9
governors 55
impact 5–6
mental health approaches 142
personality development 226–9
pod area 142
principles 8–9
processes 9–10
protective ethos 56
quality of education 98–9
routines 182, 183–4
safeguarding 56
Skills Builder framework 228
staff 55–7
'Take Care' agreements 142
Tiny Ted Talks 229
trustees 55
mindset, significance of 117
MindUp™ programme 142
Mini Learning Adventures 162–4
mistakes, handling 50
Move & Learn (M&L) 209–12
multi-professional teams 250–1, 252
multiverse games pathway 45

National Centre for Computing Education 111, 112–13
National Curriculum for Physical Education 123
national events and celebrations 177
National STEM Learning Centre 110–11
Natural Wonder, curriculum of
impact 174–6
implementation 173–4
intent of 172–3
takeaways 177

tools and resources 178
tree poetry resource 174
turning vision into reality 176–7
nature-connectedness 14
network, significance of 170
new forms of curriculum, need for 258
New School, The, curriculum of
   autonomy, development of 263, 266, 267
   external data 265
   impact 264–6
   implementation 261–4
   intent of 260–1
   internal data 264–5
   learning competence, development of 262–3
   pitfalls and setbacks 267
   processes and challenges 266
   professional development 265–6
   relational practice, development of 263–4
   sociocracy 261, 264, 267
   successes and opportunities 267–8
   takeaways 268
   turning vision into reality 266–8
non-contact time 110
No Outsiders programme 226
Norwich Men's Shed 175

Ofqual 170
one-student-at-a-time approach 256, 259
Onion Model 251
open-ended thinking skills 252
'opening doors' strategies 118
optimism 207
outcomes, regenerating 217, 219
outdoor activities, preparation for 18
outdoor learning 144–9, 169, 177

parental engagement 27, 115
parenting styles 185
pastoral practice, 268
peer support 149
people-care 217
personal development 2–3

personal exploration pathway 45
personal professional development (PPD) 68
personal wellbeing 217
philosophical thinking and learning 252
physical activity 208–14
physical education 122–9
physical health 222–3
Picture News 226–7
Pilgrims' Cross C of E Aided Primary School, curriculum of
   Great Guiding 164
   impact 164–5
   implementation 161–4
   intent 160–1
   mapping out of 161–2, 166
   Mini Learning Adventures 162–4
   takeaways 166
   turning vision into reality 164–5
planned sequences of learning 34
planning 24, 27
planning, preparation and assessment (PPA) provision 110, 133
play, significance of 264
poetry 173–5
Polyvagal Exercises for Safety and Connection (Dana) 143
pop-up exhibition 18
positive emotions 206
positive engagement, with parents 16
practice 25
praise 206
PREPARE framework 23
   assessment 25
   evaluation 25
   explaining 24
   planning 24
   practise 25
   retrieval 24
   review 25
PRIDE characteristics 60, 61, 62, 66, 67, 69–70
primary colleagues 107, 108
PRIME areas 60, 61, 62, 63–5
Prince's Trust 170

Principles of Instruction (Rosenshine) 212
problem-solving approach, curriculum for
   case study 241
   impact 241–2
   implementation 240–1
   intent 239–40
   takeaways 243–4
   tools and resources 244
   turning vision into reality 242–3
process models 235
production pathway 45
product model 234–5
professional autonomy 262, 263, 266, 267
professional development 34
professional judgement 188
progression model 232, 243
psychological fitness 202
public education 2–3
pupils' literary works, sharing 177
pupils' voice 191, 249
'Putting Evidence to Work' 54–5

Raspberry Pi Foundation 111
reading 66, 120, 121
reading aloud 121
real world applications 49–50
'Redesigning Schooling – Principled Curriculum Design' 2
refining, the curriculum 42
ReflectED 67
relational practice 263–4, 268
relationships 17
research, allotting time for 28
resistance, planning for 94
resourced curriculum 34
resources, being creative with 149
retrieval 24
review 25
risk-taking 13
Robinson, Sir Ken 219
Rogers, Bill 182
role models 170
role-playing game (RPG) 45
routines 182, 183–4

safeguarding 56
saving and sharing work 115
scaffolding 18, 114–15, 267
School Streets initiative 227
secondary colleagues 108
self-awareness 88
self-care 217
self-directed learning 263, 266, 268
self-regulation 181
sequences of learning 35
sequencing content and topics, significance of 238
simple, inexpensive materials 18
Skills Builder framework 228
slowliness 14
Social Change model 228
social media 114, 170
social practice, 268
social skill 261
social wellbeing 217
sociocracy 261, 264, 267
Sociograms 192
SPACE framework
   assessment 123, 128
   content 124, 128
   extending 125, 128
   pedagogy 123, 128
   specific 123, 128
specialist support 135
spiral approach to learning 218
spiral curriculum 235–6
spirituality 13
staff
   development of 28
   significance of 54, 159
   training 55
Start With Why (Sinek) 97
Streatham Wells Primary School, curriculum of
   and audits 86
   diverse 84–5
   impact 87–8
   implementation 85–7
   intent 84–5
   purpose of 87

takeaways 89
tools and resources 90
turning vision into reality 89
student-driven curriculum 255, 258
students, significance of 50
subject flowcharts 66
subject knowledge, of staff 28, 237
subject leaders 94
subject-specific CPD 107
summative assessments 33, 262
support network 28
SWOT analysis 76

'Take Care' agreements 142
Talk for Teaching (Garvey) 67–8
taster drafts 118
Teach Computing 114
teaching and learning 259
text-rich curriculum 34
theory of change 268
thinking 217
Thinking Skills Starter 252
ThoughtBox Education 216, 219, 220
THRIVE model 2, 67, 68
Tiny Ted Talks 229
Todd, Sally 14
topic webs 67
training on metacognition 236–7
transition gap 101
Triple Wellbeing 216–17, 219, 220, 221
Trust Revolution in Schools, The (Davis) 54

University of Cambridge Primary School, curriculum of
  critical thinking nature 31
  impact 32–3
  implementation of 31–3
  intent 30–31
  principles 30–31
  takeaways 35–6
  turning vision into reality 34–5
Uttley, Jonny 57

values-led curriculum 34

Washor, Elliot 257
wellbeing 13, 15
Wellbeing Charter 57–8
wellbeing policy 54
wellbeing prioritizing curriculum
  core practices 217
  core skills 217
  design principles 218–19
  impact 219–20
  implementation 216–19
  intent 215–16
  pedagogy 218
  regenerating outcomes 217
  takeaways 221
  tools and resources 221
  turning vision into reality 220–1
Wendling, Caroline 14
whole-person learning 218
whole text reading 118
Wilburton C of E Primary School, curriculum of
  collaborative design 14–15
  impact 15–16
  implementation 13–14
  intent 13
  opportunities 17
  processes 16
  successes 17
  takeaways 17–18
  tools and resources 18–19
  turning vision into reality 16–17
William, Dylan 2
Williams, Lord 30, 32–3
Willow Brook Primary School Academy, curriculum of
  Digital Leadership programme 111
  impact 111–12
  implementation 110–11
  intent 109
  takeaways 114–15
  tools and resources 115
  turning vision into reality 112–14
workplace skills 226
world building 105
writing 118, 120